THE GREENING OF ARCHITECTURE

To the Western Black Rhino, declared extinct in 2011

The Greening of Architecture

A Critical History and Survey of
Contemporary Sustainable Architecture and Urban Design

Phillip James Tabb
Texas A&M University, USA

A. Senem Deviren
Istanbul Technical University, Turkey

ASHGATE

© Phillip James Tabb and A. Senem Deviren 2013

All rights reserved. No part of this publication may be reproduced, stored in a retrieval system or transmitted in any form or by any means, electronic, mechanical, photocopying, recording or otherwise without the prior permission of the publisher.

Phillip James Tabb and A. Senem Deviren have asserted their right under the Copyright, Designs and Patents Act, 1988, to be identified as the authors of this work.

Published by
Ashgate Publishing Limited
Wey Court East
Union Road
Farnham
Surrey, GU9 7PT
England

Ashgate Publishing Company
110 Cherry Street
Suite 3-1
Burlington, VT 05401-3818
USA

www.ashgate.com

British Library Cataloguing in Publication Data
A catalogue record for this book is available from the British Library.

Library of Congress Cataloging-in-Publication Data
Tabb, Phillip.
 The greening of architecture : a critical history and survey of contemporary sustainable architecture and urban design / by Phillip James Tabb and A. Senem Deviren.
   p. cm.
 Includes bibliographical references and index.
   ISBN 978-1-4094-4739-9 (hardback) -- ISBN 978-1-4094-4740-5 (ebook) -- ISBN 978-1-4724-0389-6 (epub) 1. Sustainable architecture. 2. Architecture--Environmental aspects. I. Deviren, A. Senem. II. Title.
   NA2542.36.T333 2013
   720'.47--dc23

2013021101

ISBN 9781409447399 (pbk)
ISBN 9781409447405 (ebk – PDF)
ISBN 9781472403896 (ebk – ePUB)

NA
2542.36
.T333
2013

Printed in the United Kingdom by Henry Ling Limited,
at the Dorset Press, Dorchester, DT1 1HD

Contents

List of Figures	*vii*
About the Authors	*xiii*
Acknowledgments	*xv*
Preface	*xvii*

1	**Origins of Green Architecture**	**1**
	Introduction	1
	Early Green Design Strategies	2
	Modern Green Antecedents	6
	Contradictions with Modernism and Sustainability	11
	Greening Architecture	13
	Greening Urbanism	14
	Temporal Landscape for Sustainability	18
	Endnotes	21
2	**1960s: An Environmental Awakening**	**25**
	The American Dream	26
	Early Warnings	28
	Social Sustainability	32
	Planning and Design Responses	34
	Visionary Beginnings	36
	Radical Architecture	40
	Mainstreaming Modernism	42
	Endnotes	47
3	**1970s: Solar Architecture**	**49**
	Impact of the 1973 Oil Embargo	50
	Active Solar Technologies	52
	Passive Solar Systems	55
	Architectural Integration	60

	Off-Grid and Unplugged	62
	Solar Communities	65
	Weaving Modernism	68
	Endnotes	73
4	**1980s: Postmodern Green**	**75**
	Postmodernism	76
	Conservation, Preservation and Historicism	79
	Contemporary Vernacular	81
	Postmodern Urbanism	85
	Critical Regionalism	89
	Postmodern Green Architecture	91
	Endnotes	97
5	**1990s: Eco-Technology**	**99**
	High-Tech Architecture	100
	Virtual Architecture	103
	Eco-Technology	105
	Low-Tech Hybrids	108
	Literal Greening of Architecture	111
	Health Concerns	114
	Green Certification Programs	117
	Endnotes	121
6	**2000s: Sustainable Pluralism**	**123**
	Poly-Scaler Sustainability	124
	Biometrics	128
	Infrastructure Architecture	131
	Sustainable Urbanism	134
	Agricultural Urbanism	137
	Ecological Footprint	141
	Next Generation Green	144
	Endnotes	152
7	**The Global Landscape of Green Architecture**	**155**
	Urban–Rural	155
	High-Tech–Low-Tech	158
	New–Existing	161
	Extreme–Mainstream	167
	X-Large–X-Small	170
	Proliferating Green Architecture	174
	Endnotes	176
8	**Conclusion**	**179**
	Endnotes	183

Index   *185*

List of Figures

Preface

P.1 View from Namba Tower, Osaka, Japan Namba Park

1 Origins of Green Architecture

1.1 Ancient Green Predecessors a) Priene Reconstruction Image (image courtesy of the German Archaeological Institute) b) Drawing for Early Roman Domus (image courtesy of the VRoma Project (www.vroma.org)) c) Oia, Santorini Today

1.2 Climate Responsive Examples a) Hyderabad, Pakistan Wind-catchers (Mangh) (1928) b) Mesa Verde, Colorado (image courtesy "Shutterstock") c) Yanqing Guyaju, China d) Oopungnewing Village (1865) e) Stilt House of Myanmar

1.3 Rural Village Cottage Designs a) Selborne Street Façade b) Rear Garden Façade c) Brittany Solar Vernacular

1.4 Le Corbusier and Hassan Fathy a) Chandigarth High Courts (1956) (image courtesy Eduardo Guiot) b) Ronchamp Chapel (1960) c) New Gourna Village (1948) (© Aga Khan Trust for Culture)

1.5 MIT's Baker House (1946) by Alvar Aalto a) Ground Level Plan b) Serpentine South Façade (courtesy Yan Da, novatrio3.com)

1.6 Frank Lloyd Wright and Constantinos Doxiadis a) The Robie House (1909) (Library of Congress, Prints & Photographs Division, ILL,16-CHIG, 33-1) b) Kaufman House (1939) (courtesy Jeffrey Howe) c) Ekistics Nodes and Networks (courtesy Random House)

1.7 Expressions of American Modernism a) Inland Steel Building (courtesy K. Devyn-Caldwell -24gotham.com b) Northland Shopping Center (courtesy Walter P. Reuther Library, Wayne State University) c) Levittown, New York (Special Collections/Long Island Studies Institute)

1.8 Differing Approaches to Sustainable Urbanism a) Mexcaltitan, Mexico (© Yann Arthus-Bertrand / Altitude) b) Renewable Technology Neighborhood Center (© Phillip Tabb)

1.9 Placemaking and Spaces Contained a) Castello di Gargonza b) Model of Piazza della Collegio c) Placemaking in the Siena Compo

2 1960s: An Environmental Awakening

2.1 The American Dream a) American Home b) The Neighborhood c) 1960 Cadillac d) Enabling Highways e) Agricultural Land. All images courtesy "Shutterstock"

2.2 Environmental Signs a) Spraying Pesticides b) Water Pollution c) Coal Plant Pollution d) Nuclear Plant. All images courtesy "Shutterstock"

2.3 Bio-climatic Planning and Design a) Arctic City (courtesy "Shutterstock") b) Comfort Zone c) Solar Window d) Lightning Storm (courtesy "Shutterstock")

2.4 Visionary Beginnings a) Archigram NYC (© 1964 By Ron Herron courtesy of the Ron Herron Archive) b) Arcosanti, Arizona (Consanti Foundation) c) Baer House (courtesy Jack Futon)

2.5 Sacred Places a) Findhorn Garden, Scotland (1963) (image courtesy of Findhorn Foundation) b) Pantheon, Rome c) Jarna Community, Sweden (1968) (courtesy Max Plunger)

2.6 Radical Developments a) Drop City, Colorado, Main Domes June, 1969 (© Roberta Price 2004, 2010 All Rights Reserved) b) Prickly Mountain, Vermont (courtesy of David Sellers) c) Cadillac Ranch (Amanda Kooser, courtesy of CNET) d) Endless Grid (courtesy of Superstudio, Florence)

2.7 Mainstream Architecture a) Habitat '67 (courtesy of "Shutterstock") b) Expo '67 Biosphere (courtesy of "Shutterstock") c) Trellick Tower 1966-72 (courtesy of "Shutterstock") d) Gateway Arch (1968) (courtesy of "Shutterstock") e) Lieb House (1969) (Used with permission of Philadelphia Inquirer Copyright © 2012. All rights reserved)

3   1970s: Solar Architecture

3.1 Oil Embargo Consequences (a) Gasoline Queues (courtesy of Walter P. Reuther Library, Wayne State University) b) Gasoline Shortage (US National Archives) c) 55 mph Speed Limit (courtesy of Walter P. Reuther Library, Wayne State University) d) Empty Gas Pump (courtesy of Phillip Tabb)

3.2 Active Solar Demonstrations a) Odeillo Solar Furnace b) Celestial Seasonings DOE Demonstration c) Boulder Student Housing HUD Demonstration

3.3 Passive Solar Demonstrations a) Terry House b) Balcomb House c) Bramwell Residence d) Loffredo Residence (courtesy DennisRHoliowayArchitect.com)

3.4 Architectural Integration Constraints a) Dominant Solar Section b) Optimal Tilt Angle and Spacing c) Shadow Masks and Solar Access d) Solar Envelope e) Development in Envelope f) Solar Envelope g) Development in Envelope (d–g taken from L. Knowles Ritual House, Island Press, 2006)

3.5 Off-Grid Architecture a) Earthship Tires (courtesy of Otis Bradley) b) Earthship Off-Grid Modules c) Earthship (b and c courtesy of Michael Reynolds) d) Advanced Green Builder Demonstration (image courtesy of the Center for Maximum Potential Building Systems, photograph by Paul Bardagjy) e) Beadwall Aspen Airport f) Strawbale Construction

3.6 Solar Communities a) Village Homes (courtesy Mike Corbett) b) Wonderland Hills Development c) Tinggarden Cohousing (courtesy William Sherlaw) d) Mainstreaming Solar Communities (courtesy DennisRHollowayArchitect.com)

3.7 Late Modernism a) Crystal Cathedral (courtesy "Shutterstock") b) Centre Georges Pompidou c) Thorncrown Chapel (courtesy of Ed Cooley) d) Citicorp Center (courtesy "Shutterstock")

4   1980s: Postmodern Green

4.1 Postmodern Architecture a) Venturi House (Photography © Vladimir Paperny) b) AT&T Building (courtesy David Shankbone) c) Portland Building (image courtesy City of Portland Archives, Oregon) d) Piazza d' Italia (courtesy of "Shutterstock")

4.2 Preservation, Re-creation and Recycling a) Wyoming, Ohio Historic Home (courtesy of Wyoming Historical Society) b) Rainwater Retrofit (courtesy of "Shutterstock") c) Portmeirion, Wales d) Universal Recycle Symbol

4.3 Contemporary Vernaculars a) Martin-Lancaster House (courtesy of Greg Richardson Photography) b) Martin-Lancaster Section (courtesy of Mackay-Lyons Sweetapple Architects) c) Alamo Cement House (courtesy of Hester + Hardaway Photographers) d) Downspout

LIST OF FIGURES ix

4.4 Regional Green Designs a) Magney House (Photo: Anthony Browell courtesy of the Architecture Foundation Australia) b) Masons Bend Community (courtesy Tim Hursley) c) Yestermorrow (courtesy Gary Hall) d) Parisian Postmodern

4.5 New Urbanism a) Poundbury, UK (Leon Krier) (© Duchy of Cornwall) b) Seaside, FL (Duany Plater-Zyberk) c) Laguna West, CA (Peter Calthorpe)

4.6 Critical Regionalism a) Brion Tomb b) Mississauga Civic Centre (permission Kirkland Partnership, Inc) c) MIT Rehan House (© Chant Avedissian / Aga Khan Award for Architecture) d) Sydney Opera House (courtesy "Shutterstock")

4.7 Postmodern Hybridity a) Breisach House (Photo: Friedrich Busam) b) Autonomous Artists' Housing (© Stephen Holl) c) Las Vegas Children's Museum (Photograph in the Carol M. Highsmith Archive, Library of Congress, Prints and Photographs Division)

4.8 Changing Syntax a) Rasin Building (Photo: Jordi Peralta) b) Boolean Matryoshka Doll (courtesy Jaime Pitarch)

5   1990s: Eco-Technology

5.1 High-Tech Architecture of the 1990s a) Alamillo Bridge (courtesy "Shutterstock") b) Petronas Towers (courtesy "Shutterstock") c) Caledonia Pavilions (Renzo Piano Office Workshop) d) London City Hall e) Stanford Center f) Stanford Center g) German Pavilion

5.2 Virtual Architecture a) Digital Architecture (LAVA Laboratory for Visionary Architecture) b) Guggenheim Museum, Bilbao (1997) (courtesy "Shutterstock") c) The Matrix (1999) (courtesy "Shutterstock")

5.3 Ecological Architecture a) Quadracci Pavilion (courtesy Douglas Krinke) b) British Pavilion (Photo: John Linden) c) Eden Project (courtesy "Shutterstock") d) IT Company Office Building

5.4 Low-Tech and Prefabricated Buildings a) Casey Jacal Retreat b) Jacal Floor Plan (courtesy Lake/Flato Architects c) Porch House (Photo: Frank Ooms) d) LivingHomes (courtesy Ray Kappe) e) Science Museum + Industry mkSolaire (permission Michelle Kaufmann Studio) f) Container Student Hostel (courtesy "Shutterstock")

5.5 Literal Greening of Architecture a) Hanging Gardens (© www.discoverparis.net) b) EDITT Tower (Copyright T.R. Hamzah and Yeang Sdn. Bhd. (2012)) c) IBM Tower (courtesy Kim Yeang) d) ACROS Fukuoka (courtesy Emilio Ambasz, Architect) e) Vertical Farm (courtesy "Shutterstock")

5.6 Healthy Buildings a) Vidar Clinic (courtesy Max Plunger) b) GAP Cherry Creek Offices (courtesy William McDonough + Partners)

5.7 LEED Platinum Buildings a) Cooper Union (courtesy "Shutterstock") b) Reid Heritage Home (courtesy Ashley Ferraro)

6   2000s: Sustainable Pluralism

6.1 Solar Decathlon a) National Mall (2002) (courtesy of US Department of Energy. Office of Energy Efficiency and Renewable Energy) b) CHIP SCI-Arc/CALTECH (2011) (© Southern California Institute of Architecture)

6.2 Scales of Greening a) Product Scale b) Single Building Scale (courtesy Himin Solar Co., Ltd) c) Urban Design Scale (SHAU Architects / Design by SHAU Architects for Green Campus Company, Delft) d) Ecological Scale (Aeter Architects)

6.3 Biometrics in Architecture a) Herb Greene Prairie House (courtesy Robert Alan Bowlby) b) JVC New Urban Entertainment Center (© Coop Himmelb(l)au / Armin Hess, Isochrom.com) c) Metropol Parasol Building (courtesy Fernando Alda)

6.4 Landform Architecture and Landscape Urbanism a) California Academy of Sciences b) Mineralogical Urbanism (permission Vicente Guallart) c) Vegetal City (permission Luc Schuiten Architecture) d) Olympic Sculpture Park (© 2007 Benjamin Benschneider / All Rights Reserved)

6.5 Infrastructure Architecture a) 2014 Asian Games Stadium (© Populous) b) Namba Parks (courtesy The Jerde Partnership. Photographer Hiroyuri Kawano) c) High Line Park (1934) d) High Line Park (2011) (photograph: Iwan Raan) e) Michael Sorkin Insertions (courtesy Michael Sorkin)

6.6 Sustainable Urbanism a) Kronsberg District (courtesy Karin Rumming) b) Kronsberg Street c) Paris Urban Landscape (Atelier Castro Denissaf Casi, international consultation for "Le grand pari de l'agglomeration parisienne") d) Masdar City Center (Day) (LAVA Laboratory for Visionary Architecture) e) Masdar City Center (Night) (LAVA Laboratory for Visionary Architecture) f) Crystal Island, Moscow (© Foster + Partners)

6.7 Agricultural Urbanism a) Guerrilla Farming in London (courtesy Geoff Pugh) b) Serenbe Farm to Table c) Serenbe Community Master Plan d) Selborne Hamlet e) Summit Village, Utah

6.8 Technological Farms a) Photovoltaic Farm in Italy (© Sig Solar) b) Wind Turbine Farm in USA (courtesy "Shutterstock") c) Hydro Electricity in Thailand (courtesy "Shutterstock")

6.9 Low Ecological Footprint a) Omega Center Rhinebeck, New York (courtesy of Omega Institute) b) BedZED Housing, London (courtesy Zedfactory) c) Flying Elephant Healthcare Centre (Architects—Flying Elephant Studio. Photography: Manoj Sudhakara) d) Findhorn Ecovillage, Scotland (courtesy Findhorn Community) e) Bosch Net Zero House, Serenbe f) Zero Energy House, Chicago (courtesy Zoka Zola)

6.10 The Nesting of Forms a) Nesting Platonic Solids (courtesy Robert Armon) b) Fractal (courtesy "Shutterstock") c) Matryoshka Dolls

6.11 A Future of Green Architecture a) Highrise Informal Settlement (Catherine Caldwell) b) Urban-Think Tank Metro Cable (eDesign Dynamics) c) NASA Space Colony (NASA Ames Research Center)

7 The Global Landscape of Green Architecture

7.1 Urban Projects a) Yusuhara Town Hall, Japan (Photograph: Takumi Ota Photography) b) Harmonia 57, Sao Paolo, Brazil (www.triptygue.com/Photograph Nelson Kon)

7.2 Rural Projects a) Mountain Crystal, Zermatt, Switzerland (© Siemens AG, Munich/Berlin) b) Energy Lab, Preparatory Academy, Hawaii (courtesy of Flansburgh Architects, Photo: Matthew Millman) c) Hanil Visitors Center, South Korea (courtesy of BCHO Architects Associates)

7.3 Low Tech Green Architecture a) A Yurt, Kyrgyzstan (courtesy stock.xchng) b) Quensel House, TR North Cyprus (© image courtesy A. Senem Deviren) c) Bali Green School, Indonesia (© Green School)

7.4 New Green Settlements (Communities) a) Eco City Montecorvo, Spain (courtesy of GRAS Architects) b) Solar City, Linz, Austria (© image courtesy A. Senem Deviren) c) Sonnnenschiff, Freiburg, Germany (© image courtesy A. Senem Deviren)

7.5 New Green Offices a) Vodafona Site Solution, Midrand, Africa (courtesy of GLH & Associate Architects) b) Solar Power Offices, Ljubliana, Slovenia (image courtesy OFIS Arhitekti)

7.6 Green Regeneration of Existing Building Complexes a) Setagaya-ku Fukasawa, Symbiotic Housing, Japan (courtesy of Prof. Kazuo Iwamura) b) Vauban, Freiburg, Germany (© image courtesy A. Senem Deviren)

7.7 Green Renovation of Existing Buildings a) Frontier Center for Environmental Symbiosis Technology, Japan (Photographed by Toshiharu Kitajima) b) Paineiras Hotel, Rio de Janeiro, Brazil (image courtesy Hiperstudio + Arkiz)

7.8 Extreme Green Projects From Macro to Micro Scales a) The Earthscraper, Mexico City (© image courtesy BNKR) b) Marine Research Center, Bali (courtesy of Architectural Design: solus4. Visualization: Tangram3DS)

7.9 Mainstream Green Buildings a) Pixel building, rendering of the west façade b) Pixel building, in real context, Australia (both images courtesy of Studio 505)

7.10 X-Large Green Buildings a) Aviva Stadium, Ireland (courtesy of Scott Tallon Walker Architects) b) Sun Moon Mansion, Dezhou, China (courtesy of Himin Solar Co. Ltd.)

7.11   X-Small Green Buildings a) Reisseck Terminal, Austria (courtesy of Zechner & Zechner ZT GmbH) b) Hardanger Retreat, Norway (courtesy of Saunders Architecture) c) The Sled House, New Zealand (courtesy of Crosson Clarke Carnachan Architects / photo by Jackie Meiring)

7.12   Locations of Selected Green Projects © courtesy of A. Senem Deviren

8   Conclusion

8.1   Contrast in Green Architectural Languages a) Amsterdam Avenue New York City b) BedZED PV and Wind Cowls c) Informal Settlement in Medellin, Colombia

About the Authors

Phillip James Tabb, PhD, is Professor of Architecture at Texas A&M University and is the Liz and Nelson Mitchell Professor of Residential Design. He served as Head of the Department from 2001 to 2005, and was Director of the School of Architecture and Construction Management at Washington State University from 1998 to 2001. He completed a PhD dissertation on The Solar Village Archetype: *A Study of English Village Form Applicable to Energy Integrated Planning Principles for Satellite Settlements in Temperate Climates* in 1990. Among his publications is *Solar Energy Planning* published by McGraw-Hill in 1984. In the late 1960s he worked for Walter Netsch at SOM in Chicago and was exposed to his Field Theory method of design. He worked with Keith Critchlow and taught sacred drawing in the Kairos School of Sacred Architecture (1986–1987), at Dar al Islam in Abiquiu, New Mexico (1988–1989), and at Naropa Institute, Boulder (1996). Since 2001, Tabb is the master plan architect for Serenbe Community—a sacred and sustainable community being realized near Atlanta, Georgia, and he was a planning consultant for Babcock Ranch Community in Florida, the Millican Reserve project in Texas, the Summit Series Community in Utah, and the Howell Mountain Conservation Community in Angwin, California. He has lectured internationally on the concept of placemaking as a viable sustainable strategy. He received six solar energy research and demonstrations awards from the AIA/RC, HUD, and DOE, and was a consultant to SERI. He is a founding fellow of the Sustainable Urbanism Certificate Program at Texas A&M University. He received his Bachelor of Science in Architecture from the University of Cincinnati, Master of Architecture from the University of Colorado, and PhD in the Energy and Environment Programme from the Architectural Association in London. Dr Tabb teaches studio design, the theory of placemaking, and he is a practicing urban designer and licensed architect. He has been a long time member of the American Institute of Architects, and holds a NCARB Certificate.

A. Senem Deviren, PhD, is an architect and Associate Professor at Istanbul Technical University, Faculty of Architecture. She attained her PhD degree in 2001 in the Architectural Design program from the Institute of Science and Technology at Istanbul Technical University, with her thesis titled *Place in Architecture: Conceptualization of the Relations between Site and Building*. She received her MSc in Architectural Design in 1996 and her Bachelor of

Architecture degree in 1994 from the Department of Architecture of Istanbul Technical University. She has taught as Senior Lecturer at Eastern Mediterranean University, Faculty of Architecture in North Cyprus between 1996 and 2006. As a Visiting Assistant Professor at Texas A&M University in the 2004–2005 academic year she coordinated four design studios and received a Blue Ribbon for her design studio teaching excellence. She has organized and attended international design events, workshops and design studio reviews in USA, Europe and Turkey. She has given lectures internationally on place, sustainability, interdisciplinary design strategies, design education and innovation. From March to September 2009 she was a Research Fellow at the Institute for Advanced Studies on Science, Technology and Society (IAS-STS) in Graz. Her research project on renewable energy use in architecture and urban landscape design was partly supported by Istanbul Technical University Rectorate Grant, Support Program for Long Term Research Abroad and as a Research Fellow at the IAS-STS (March to September 2009) her project was awarded with the Manfred Heindler Grant. She was advisor to the Rector of Istanbul Technical University for international relations, research, education and accreditation between 2009 and 2012. She is a member of the Chamber of Architects of Turkey, and holds Fulbright and ISES certificates. She is currently teaching in Interdisciplinary Urban Design graduate program and Landscape Architecture graduate and undergraduate programs. Her research and teaching focuses on interdisciplinary design research, education and strategies, place design and theory, urban design and landscape, energy efficient design and sustainability.

Acknowledgments

This book is an accumulation of nearly 50 years of study and a deep desire to better define sustainability and green architecture in order to contribute to further advancements in the field. This work goes beyond any single discipline and certainly is the result of many people who have contributed on so many levels. *The Greening of Architecture* is a moment in a larger process, which this book acknowledges and explains. Yet it is really a story about architecture, its changing role, the magic of its manifestation, and more miraculously, how it is truly becoming a living practice. In viewing the changes that have occurred over time, it is evident that the way in which we create architecture and cities are crucial to our survival. The works of many great projects and the people who created them supports a critical history of sustainable architecture and urban design, and this is evident with the explosion of examples worldwide.

Thanks goes to Valerie Rose, the Senior Commissioning Editor for Ashgate Publishing, who gave encouragement, enthusiasm and valuable feedback on the work throughout the process. My teachers gave the presence of mind, vision and ability to undertake a work such as this. I am grateful to Dr Simos Yannas at the Architectural Association for his guidance in village planning and bio-climatic design, which was an important foundation for the understanding of sustainable urbanism. Dr Keith Critchlow revealed the importance of significant geometry and the wonderful world of the sacred in architecture. Steve and Marie Nygren and Rawson and Nan Haverty were developers of Serenbe Community and provided a context for many green architecture and urban design measures discussed in this book. Thanks goes to architect Robert Armon who reviewed the manuscript at varying stages of development and gave valuable feedback. College of Architecture Dean Jorge Vanegas and Department Head Ward Wells were very supportive of this project from its inception. The Liz and Nelson Mitchell Professorship at Texas A&M University provided funding for many of the expenses in the preparation of the final manuscript. I am extremely indebted to all of the students at Texas A&M University, especially Miray Oktem and Erica Schneider, over the years who played a crucial role in the development of this work or helped directly with this publication. Very special thanks goes to my family, especially Michael, David, Kristin, Emrys and Caius Tabb, Shea Dunn, my sister Janice Nourse and brother-in-law Richard Nourse, and to all friends to whom this work is ultimately intended. And finally, very special thoughts go to the memory of my parents whom I am sure would be proud of this book.

Phillip Tabb
College Station

Thanks goes to my teachers at Istanbul Technical University Faculty of Architecture: Dr Atilla Yücel, who revealed the potential and passion of combining architecture and landscape cultures in this young architecture student's mind in the early 1990s and for his encouraging intellectual conversations on architecture and life; Dr Vedia Dökmeci who always supports and opens eyes for new horizons; to the memory of Dr Hülya Yürekli, together with Dr Ferhan Yürekli, who created encouraging design learning experiences and events, tolerated my freedom and independence to travel and work on my passion for understanding place, landscapes and architecture. They all opened the doors of their office, library and hearts for awakening critical design thinking. Thanks goes to Dr Günter Getzinger and the colleagues at the IFZ, Graz, who accepted me to the Institute of Advanced Studies on Science, Technology and Society (IAS-STS) and awarded me the Manfred Heindler Grant in 2009 that gave the chance for pursuing my research on the potential of in-between spaces for utilization of renewable energy resources in architecture and urban landscape design. Thanks to Dr Urs Hirschberg who welcomed me to participate in academic events at TU Graz in the same year and get to know the architectural culture. I am greatly honored and really appreciate all the support and care of the colleagues at Texas A&M University College of Architecture for sharing their world and giving me a life-changing academic career experience from 2004 to 2005, and still continue to do so. Thanks to all my students in different geographies for their enthusiasm and bright young spirits, to my friends, and to the heavenly landscapes of my country. And, always, my deepest thanks and gratitude goes from the depths of my heart to my mom Alev and brother Rifat and to the lovely memory of my father Asaf Deviren who was the best of all fathers; together they make my life unique, happy and beautiful.

A. Senem Deviren
Istanbul

Preface

The Brundtland Commission Report in 1987 defined sustainability in intergenerational terms: "Sustainable development is development that meets the needs of the present without compromising the ability of future generations to meet their own needs."[1] This was a useful and admirable approach to sustainability and was considered the most often-quoted definition. Integral to this definition was the overriding priority to be given to the world's poor according to the Report. The definition cited two fundamental dimensions to which sustainability is to be directed: to geographical space and differing global contexts, and to evolving systems over time. It did not establish a metrics to which present needs might be defined and achieved, nor did it give any indication as to what future needs might be, especially in the context of unknown population increases, undefined levels of equity and the enormous planetary scale. Present and future needs are moving targets and seem impossible to define. Therefore, sustainability is seen as a philosophical proposition within a context of uncertainty and supports a dynamic process with thoughtful incremental adjustments to the built environment in response to changing needs. In turn, green architecture is a sub-set of global cultural sustainability and, as a consequence, architecture is the process of designing, constructing and maintaining buildings in response to these principles of sustainability. Green architecture is, of course, subject to the inherent limitations of the discipline, which generally function at the aggregate building scale.

Within the term "architecture" certain green principles are coded and can be useful for sustainable design practice. The Oxford Dictionary defines architecture as being the "art and science of building." It is seen as an art because it has beauty of form, beauty of craft, and reflects contemporary ideas with important social, political and cultural content. It is a science because it must respond to important health, safety and welfare constraints and it needs to be technically competent, functional and affordable. Both art and science aspired to similar objectives, but employ different means. This suggests that architecture is the practice of the artful composition of design elements and scientifically responsible construction of buildings, and for green architecture, this means the inclusion of sustainable principles of design, introduction of renewable resource technologies and environmentally conscious use.

One view of the term "architecture," is derived from the Greek αρχιτεκτων, "a master builder" and from αρχι- "chief, leader." Rather than a focus on an object outcome, this meaning refers to the one who leads the design process: *archê*—chief authority (archbishop, archangel, arch-duke, or arch-enemy), *tektôn*—builder, any craftsman or worker, master in an art; and *ure*—simply a marker of function (prefecture, legislature, juncture).² "Architecture" then was the product of the one who leads the building work (Cicero). For green architecture this might suggest the heroic examples set by architects Frank Lloyd Wright, Le Corbusier, Ralph Erskine, Norman Foster, Richard Rogers, Renzo Piano, Zaha Hadid, as well as the influential works of Alvar Aalto, Hassan Fathy, Charles Rennie Mackintosh, and Glenn Murcutt, among others. This definition shifted its meaning from the product of the created building to the one who conducted this process. It focused on the position of superiority, authority, or simply, the powerful influence upon the discipline of architecture. These forward thinking architects were among the leaders of theoretical, aesthetic, formal and exemplar buildings that later gave impetus to the development of green architecture.

Another etymological exploration of the Greek roots of the term "architecture"³ provided a definition revealing something more noetic, completely different than the modern heroic notions of architecture, and containing more explicit green principles of design. The root terms function as noun, verb and suffix, and provide insights and keys to its operational meaning. The ancient view suggested a hierarchical approach to the term and gave an invigorated redefinition where the word itself became a sentence. Again referring to the three prime roots to the term; *archê*, *technê*, and *ure*.³

> ***archê***—noun, realm of archetypes, beginnings, first principles. This originates in the dwelling of the prime or essential potential of a beginning. It is the power-activity associated with creation and has the qualities of purity, clarity, perfection and initiation. The first term, archê, means both "beginning" and "principle" and therefore, relates to the realm of archetypes or the First Principles. The archê is a going back to the beginning where the prime or essential dwells and emanates. As "beginning," archê suggests focusing on essential human needs and the pure natural context within which we dwell. The function of creation suggests the dynamic interrelationship between nature and needs. As "principle," archê suggests a truth, which is powerful, essential and universally applicable.
>
> ***technê***—verb, process of bringing something into appearance, manifestation. It is the revealing of ideas, designs or principles into manifest form and material. It is the substantial and meaningful quality obtained in making. The middle term, technê, relates to the technique or technology of manifestation or simply "building." Yet it is building with a certain consciousness and presence of mind and tectonic realization between nature and need. To the early Greek, it referred not specifically to art or handcraft, but to making something appear—revealing or letting the physically constructed "thing" appear. It was the substantial expression of higher principles, and with respect to the greening of architecture it would refer to the tectonic expression of sustainable measures.
>
> ***ure***—from Latin (ura) a morpheme or suffix added to the end of a word performing a function, process or rank making a noun out of an adjective, such as picture, culture, gesture, measure, enclosure, structure, etc. In Greek, ure or ur means well fitted and is a weaving process that binds the other two terms into a unity of beauty and fitness. The third term, ure, relates to the crafting or weaving process as explained by Marcus Vitruvius: "And first, with upright forked props and twigs put between, they wove their walls." This third term also has associations with eurhythmy, which according to Vitruvius

was "beauty and fitness in the adjustments of the members." It relates to the integrative warp and weft of sustainable measures that occur with the natural flows of a place.

Then, in applying these root terms of the word architecture to green architecture, we have a very rich and useful three-fold meaning. Architecture is the revealing through the manifestation process the First Principles. Concisely stated, architecture is "the First Principles that are well-fitted to a context or woven into a dynamic place." Also embodied in this definition are the three prime functions in grammar: the noun, verb, and descriptive figure of speech (conjunction, adverb or adjective). The First Principles (noun) are dynamic and well-fitted (verb) into manifest tectonic form (suffix). So embodied into the very word of architecture is this three-fold essence of speech also found within the simplest sentence. The accumulative meaning derived by combining concepts of these terms becomes: "Architecture" is the weaving into manifestation of the First Principles. Which begs the question, what are the First Principles that architecture seeks to manifest, especially as encoded with the now relevant function of temporal and spatial sustainability?

First Principles, according to Plato, were manifestations of goodness (commodity), truth (firmness) and beauty (delight).[4] In architecture, they are realized through the unity, generative, formative, corporeal and re-generative processes.[5] Where these principles are applied to architecture in the most general sense, they do possess inherent green connotations. Unity implies a singularity of purpose, coherence and wholeness of form and continuity of detail. The generative principle suggests connections to the earth and responses to the diverse, proliferating and multifarious local contextual conditions. The formative principle implies an internal intelligence, integrity and logic to the spatial order, structural systems, and tectonic character of built form. The corporeal realm is grounded into pragmatic realities of materiality, constructability, cost, systems' performance, and project delivery. And finally, the regenerative principle brings the temporal, mutable, transformative and evolutionary dimensions into the work. The First Principles function as an accumulative and interactive set of directives that are intended to guide and inform the sustainable planning and design processes.

The temporal dimension to sustainability defines the potential changes for green architecture to become more familiar over time and to improve accumulatively and incrementally. It assumes innovation, technological refinements, and further invention, but more importantly it suggests that the greening process can become more pervasive connecting to all scales, locals and facets of contemporary life. This also assumes that small individual changes will grow and multiple influencing inter-scaler applications through a passive process of evolution. Incremental changes toward greater levels of sustainability are initially remedial and then progressed to more complex, dynamic and systemic measures with eventual reductions in embodied energy.[6] This is typical of any innovation or infusion of new technologies. They are additive and often awkward at first, and after time they become amalgamated and fuse into the function, mainstream of use and aesthetic of the host, which in the context of this work includes the entirety of the built environment.

The spatial dimension to sustainability emphasizes geographical differences in climate, ecology, culture, land-use patterns, density, technology, and architectural traditions. It also recognizes dynamic interactions as well. What is interesting are the ways in which the greening of architecture vary and express from East to West, where differences occur due to the geo-cultural influences of form. The urban to rural contexts generate drastically different demands upon the power, transportation and building sectors, and reflect differences in building typologies and tectonic characteristics. Industrial-world exemplifications tend to be more universal, utilizing higher technology, and project greater self-importance as compared to undeveloped regions where the architecture derives from mere survival and far less means. Low densities and high densities offer differing challenges and opportunities for addressing sustainable design strategies. New buildings afford fresh and innovative designs while the existing stock of buildings brings its own form of constraints and challenges. High technologies are prototyped, manufactured, mass-produced and exported, while low-tech sustainable technologies are often handmade utilizing local materials, labor and fabrication methods. Extreme examples of green architecture occurring with research stations in Antarctica or living sandstone wall dwellings in the Sahara Desert are compared to mainstream projects that could be found in any temperate climate zone where most people live. It is interesting to observe the degree to which these variations of approach manifest divergent architectural languages. And in the end, "green architecture" should simply be good "architecture."

The critical history of green architecture covers the past 50 years and provides a survey of recent works throughout the seven continents illustrating the growth in the field and breadth of development along with the diversity and character of the creative works. There has been a great deal of change from the visionary and technological explorations of the 1960s to the more biophilic and infrastructural green propositions of today. Much of this effort has been to undo the unsustainable mistakes of the past and to provide sustainable models that penetrate all facets of modern life. The challenge is to create a bridge from our current modes of consumption, waste, use of resources, inventory of existing cities, infrastructures and stock of buildings, and styles of living to an evolutionary green architecture that serves as a link that truly can help ensure the ability of future generations to meet their own needs—leaving an inheritance of bountiful renewable resources, energy, intellectual capital and the inventory of a healthy living environment.

This work represents research, travel, practice and analysis of an accumulation of material on the subject of sustainability over a 50-year period. Dr Tabb began architectural practice in the late 1960s and focused on solar applications throughout the decade of the 1970s. His research on English villages during his studies at the Architectural Association in the mid-1980s contributed to informing characteristics associated with multiple buildings and community placemaking. In the 1990s his commissioned work was directed toward off-grid architectural demonstrations and sustainable site development projects, and after the millennium 12 years of design work for Serenbe Community brought together the integration of both sustainable architecture and planning agendas. This accession of familiarity led to a personal history informed by actual lived experiences in these critical phases of the development of sustainable architecture and urban design, and gave valuable insights in the writing of the first six chapters on the historic development of the greening of architecture. Dr Deviren's research into placemaking, regional context and especially the relationship between site and building, give a background for the understanding of global effects of sustainable design and a unique perspective from both the European and Asian continents. Her more recent interests in emergent green technology and her teaching and current research at Istanbul Technical University provide a common thread for her contribution to this work and the proliferation of the greening of architecture into the global landscape in distinct and diverse ways. The blend of these two dimensions of *time* (historic development) and *space* (geographic exemplifications) present a full account of an extremely complex and often contentious subject.

P.1 View from Namba Tower, Osaka, Japan Namba Park

ENDNOTES

1   World Commission on Environment and Development (WCED). *Our Common Future*. Oxford, UK: Oxford University Press, 1987: 43.

2   Oxford American Dictionary. Oxford, UK: Oxford University Press, 2010.

3   Source: http://www.perseus.tufts.edu, accessed May 2000.

4   Robert Lawlor, *Sacred Geometry—Philosophy and Practice*. London: Thames and Hudson, 1982.

5   Plato, *Timaeus*, translated by Peter Kalkavage. Newburyport, MA: Focus Publishing/R. Pullins Co., 2001.

6   Melissa Leach, Ian Scoones and Andy Stirling, *Dynamic Sustainabilities: Technology, Environment Social Justice*. London, UK: Earthscan Publications, 2010.

Chapter 1
Origins of Green Architecture

Phillip Tabb

> **As from a seed the tree grows, so from a seed idea a pattern issues forth from the Center, passed on by ranks of silent angels—silent and still because that idea is too unformed and unfixed to endure any but the most exacting care.**[1]

INTRODUCTION

Modern architecture, and the contemporary culture it reflected, contributed to the cause and necessity of a burgeoning *green process* that has emerged over the past half-century. Modern architecture broke from the eclectic traditions of the 18th century and focused on abstraction, standardization and serial production seeking a homogeneous international identity. As the world evolved with greater complexity and increased reliance upon technology, it was exhilarating and bewildering—and to a large extent was energy inefficient. As a result, it added unintended adverse consequences to the environment and exposed our dependence on fossil fuels. Beginning in the 1960s, works of Rachel Carson, E.F. Schumacher, Buckminster Fuller, Ian McHarg, and Stewart Brand, focused on the harmful effects to the environment and the awareness of holistic environmental thinking. Fortunately, earlier climate responsive architectural works by Le Corbusier, Frank Lloyd Wright, Ralph Erskine, Constantinos Doxiadis, Louis I. Kahn and Alvar Aalto, emerged as early modernist green precedents. The ever-closing circle of a single set of modernist universal principles was reconsidered by place-oriented intentions that initiated a diversity of environmentally conscious designs.

The Greening of architecture became an emerging process that attempted to transform modern architecture into more benign, environmentally oriented buildings. Green architecture evolved into a practice that advanced initially from rationalist, performance-based and remediating measures in response to particular unsustainable concerns, to far more encompassing ecological and systemic processes cutting deep across contemporary culture. So pervasive was the greening of architecture that, according to Julien de Smedt (JDS Architects), there was a definition problem. "'Green' and 'Sustainability,' the terms used to name the answer to the most pressing problem of our time, have become dangerously afloat in ambiguity and indeterminacy. Sustainable architecture is everywhere and nowhere."[2] Nevertheless, the green movement grew as a global phenomenon seeking an accumulative reduction in the negative environmental effects caused by buildings, urban designs, settlements and other public works. Simultaneously, it served to explore environmentally oriented canons with new tectonic and emergent architectural languages.

The need for sustainable planning and design was not a new design consideration or determinant. Certain constructions for shelter, protection, and the need to create tolerable levels of comfort were considered in ancient designs and not surprisingly, still remain important today. The very term "shelter," meaning to provide cover, derives from the need for physical safety, to mitigate the negative effects of weather and adverse conditions of the environment, and to provide a place of dwelling. Over the centuries, various cultures developed specific architecture and planning responses to differing climatic conditions. These responses were refined progressively over time, usually from the development of single vernacular dwellings to larger urban settings. The English village, for example, grew from the rural cottage to the agglomeration of cottages into more compact settlement forms, especially during Celtic and Anglo-Saxon times (500 BC–1066 AD).[3] There were many lessons to be learned from the past's coping with climate and growing societal complexities that together with new green architectural technologies, could provide appropriate and intelligent approaches for future current and use.

The reaction to the harmful consequences of the Modern Movement—wasteful use of land and resources, inefficient and unhealthy construction practices, over-dependence upon fossil fuel-driven technologies, and reliance on the automobile for transportation to name a few—is warranted, but not entirely without a truly acceptable alternative. Yet, there seems to be an inextricable bond that still remains between modernism and the greening of architecture, which is amplified with the newest of examples in green building. This contradiction in philosophy, principles and perception of need has led to confusing and ambiguous results, which this chapter addresses. It is important to see the greening of architecture as an evolutionary process and cyclical ecology rather than simply a fixed set of strategies for a fixed period of time. A more dynamic and iterative view allows for the natural shifting of cultural values and needs to ever-increasing levels of sustainability, which in turn fosters a maturing architectural and urban response. It is a process that can affect every facet of contemporary culture toward attaining a more sustainable future. Sustainability goes far beyond the buildings and cities to include nations, continents and the planet as a whole.

EARLY GREEN DESIGN STRATEGIES

Early examples of green architecture were by necessity climate responsive, providing shelter from inclement weather, and they also responded to other environmental concerns, such as on-site water collection, sewage removal and fuel for heating. Butti and Perlin suggested that the ancient Greeks had no artificial means of heating or cooling their homes. In winter they used mostly portable charcoal-burning braziers along with warmth they could glean from the sun during the day. However, as populated areas began to expand, surrounding forests were ravaged for wood for heating and cooking. By the 5th century BC many parts of Greece were almost totally denuded of trees.[4] Knowledge of seasonal changing of sun angles precipitated more aggressive vernacular designs that allowed the lower winter sun within the dwelling for warmth and the higher summer sun excluded to help mitigate overheating. The northern façades, with few or no windows at all, were constructed of thick masonry walls to keep out the cold winds in winter. These ingenious design measures crossed class lines from temple or palace to commoner's dwelling, which resulted in a cultural proliferating effect.

The Olynthian house, for example, was typically organized around a south-facing exterior portico and court that served as a private outdoor room and provided light and solar heat to the adjacent indoor spaces. The portico and roof eaves served to shade the sun in summer. The house designed with an integrated courtyard was the general scheme. The entrance to the dwelling was from the street and led directly to the courtyard. Surrounding the courtyard were all the other rooms, which opened into it. A portico with colonnade was built on the north side of the courtyard, which faced south for maximum sunlight. At ground level was a living room with a central hearth surrounded by a kitchen and bathroom. A men's room was fitted with typically seven couches around the perimeter for dining. The remaining rooms on the ground floor were for storage. The women's quarters and bedrooms were built above the northern half of the house. Slaves and family lived together as one big family. The significance of this work was in both the development of single building sustainable strategies in conjunction with urban design schemes, which provided the context for a compact sun-oriented settlement plan. Figures 1.1a and b illustrate the predominant cardinal grid pattern for Priene and a reconstructive drawing of a typical early Roman urban residence with interior court.

Modern excavations of many Classical Greek cities reveal the principles that generated these effective vernacular designs, which carried over into urban planning where street widths and orientations considered this solar phenomenon giving equal access to the sun for all structures. The Ionian city of Priene (1000 BC), located on the southwestern coast of Turkey, was a good example of urban design for challenging topography and excellent solar access. The region of between 4,000 and 5,000 residents was relocated because its original site was plagued with constant flooding, and therefore Priene was planned on higher ground beneath the escarpment of Mount Mycale. The six main avenues were placed on terraces paralleling contours and running east and west including the central avenue that was fed by the main west gate entrance. The avenues were wider providing solar access to south-facing building façades. Secondary streets ran up the north–south slopes and tended to be narrower. The agora occupied the center of the plan was situated on a widened contour to accommodate the larger open space.

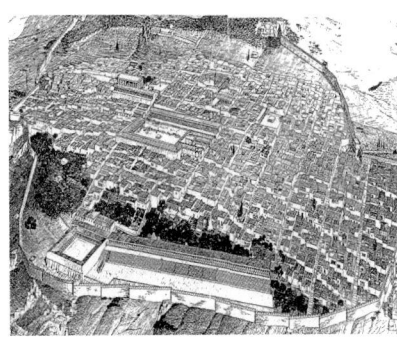

1.1 Ancient Green Predecessors a) Priene Reconstruction Image (image courtesy of the German Archaeological Institute) b) Drawing for Early Roman Domus (image courtesy of the VRoma Project (www.vroma.org)) c) Oia, Santorini Today

1.2 Climate Responsive Examples a) Hyderabad, Pakistan Wind-catchers (Mangh) (1928) b) Mesa Verde, Colorado (image courtesy "Shutterstock") c) Yanqing Guyaju, China d) Oopungnewing Village (1865) e) Stilt House of Myanmar

The city was divided into four districts—political (Bouleterion), cultural (Theater), commercial (Agora), and religious (Temple of Athena). According to city planner Edmund Bacon, "the most remarkable thing about Priene is the total harmony of architecture and planning, extending from the over-all form of the city down to the last detail."[5] The photograph of Oia, Santorini in Figure 1.1c shows the earth sheltered solar-oriented residential forms cascading along the island's interior. These same principles were practiced in ancient China with important streets aligned along cardinal directions and the design for solar-oriented houses. In other climate zones and geographic locations, architectural and planning measures have responded to climatic conditions. For example, the powerful image of the city of Hyderabad, Pakistan demonstrates the pervasive use of hundreds of wind catchers used in many Persian cities as seen in Figure 1.2a. These examples are a good illustration of multiplicity of form, land-based design, and the Generative Principle.

Certainly, climate-responsive architecture and planning were not only confined to Ancient Greece and Asia Minor. Other locations worldwide indicated architectural designs for varying climate zones, extreme weather and natural hazards, and according to architectural historian Paul Oliver, these buildings did not "control" climate, but rather "modified" climate by affecting internal conditions toward greater levels of acceptable comfort.[6] Oliver suggested that, "arguments have been powerfully made for a physical and environmental determinism that considers that advantageous climates and temperatures, soils and seasons give shape to man's culture." These examples cross both time and geography representing varied design responses to differing environmental conditions. For example, the Swiss alpine house, the English cottage, the igloo of the Inuit, raised platform dwellings of the Amazon Basin, the adobe dwellings in southwest North America, the underground dwellings in China, and the wind towers of Pakistan, all have formal characteristics unique to the environments within which they respond.

The Long House at Mesa Verde, Colorado, shown in Figure 1.2b, utilized the concave rock formation for the advantage of solar energy exposure in winter and solar shading in summer. Typical, among the climatic design strategies were direct form and material responses to the prevailing climatic and environmental conditions, such as, the use of insulating and heat retaining materials and solar energy in colder climates or use of stilts, raised platforms for flood-prone tropical areas, and extended roofs for capturing breezes and for solar shading.

Roman architect, Marcus Vitruvius, in the 1st century BC, developed a set of architectural principles, known today as *The Ten Books on Architecture*,[7] which included planning and design guides and patterns on different aspects of building. In Book VI, Vitruvius described the importance of climate in siting and design, recognizing that different climates required different design approaches. He also addressed the proper exposure of different rooms to qualities of light and exposure to the sun for warmth. In Book VIII he described the finding of water, its differing qualities, collecting and exporting it and uses for it—showering, drinking and cooking. He felt that rainwater was wholesome and that the vaporous properties of different waters should be considered. He describes the many innovations made in building design to improve the living conditions of the inhabitants. Foremost among them was the development of the hypocaust; a type of central heating where hot air generated by a fire was channeled under the floor and inside the walls of public baths and villas. Vitruvius also recommended that in hot climates the north facades should be open away from the sun. In *A Green Vitruvius,* J. Owen Lewis suggested that the sustainable principles put forward by Vitruvius could be distilled into relevant design patterns, which are applicable today.[8]

The shelter with protective roof, thick walls and openings became the archetype for refuge and early climatic designs. The roof provided protection directly above from rain, sleet, snow, winds and the high hot sun in summer, and was also a symbolic element mediating between heaven and earth. Heat naturally rises, so roofs in cold climates tended to be lighter with higher insulation values for containing it. Thatch, straw and mud were used in early roof construction, and later clay tiles were used for greater fire protection and the protective outer layer exposed to the elements. Walls emerged from the ground and support the roof. Generally made from local materials of a site, they tended to be load-bearing masonry or earthen and quite thick, dividing domains of inside and outside. Mass walls served the function for defensive protection, heat retention as well as protection from climate. Stonewalling, for example, used a wet process of bonding stones with mortar made from lime and cement as early as 300 BC. These ancient walls had two thermal characteristics—the thicker the wall, the greater the insulative value, and the increase of thermal lag or flywheel effect.

Primitive windows were merely small holes placed in walls, and later were covered with animal hides, cloths, or wood. Shutters, that could be opened and closed, evolved next and enabled inhabitants to respond to diurnal (day–night) cycles. Over time, windows were made from natural translucent materials, such as mica and alabaster that gave protection from the elements while simultaneously letting in light. The Romans were the first to use glass for windows as they discovered the transparent optical qualities of amorphous materials. In Alexandria around 100 AD, cast glass windows, with poor optical properties, began to appear. Mullioned glass windows were the windows of choice among European elite, whereas paper windows were economical and widely used in ancient China, Korea and Japan. Double-glazing, with a resistance value of around R-2 ($ft^2 \cdot °F \cdot h/Btu$), was introduced in the 1930s and was designed to increase the insulative value of glass especially in colder climates.

1.3 Rural Village Cottage Designs a) Selborne Street Façade b) Rear Garden Façade c) Brittany Solar Vernacular

Using a "float glass" process developed in the early 1950s, larger continuous sheets of glass were produced and used in greenhouses and other larger-scaled applications. Heat Mirror glazing (R-4) and Low-E glass (R-3) were developed in the 1980s to further increase transmission of light and resistance to heat flow. Critical to the function of passive solar technologies was the use of improved glazing systems necessary to enhance the greenhouse effect and increase the efficiency of the system. Figures 1.3a and b illustrate vernacular cottages located in Selborne, Hampshire with more formal "eyes to the street," front façades and manicured landscapes, thatch roofs and informal rear garden in the back. Primary ridgelines run parallel to the street for good solar access into the streets, and hip and half-hip roof forms provide sunshine to rear gardens. Figure 1.3c is a typical rural house in Brittany, France, constructed using a simple gable roof form, masonry walls with integral fireplaces, and both south-facing windows and dormers that employed operable shutters.

Many of the conditions for planning and design that existed thousands of years ago still remain today, particularly the needs for shelter, climatic design and environmental modulation. However, the magnitude of the contemporary global culture has created a more complicated and far reaching set of sustainable problems. The initiating sustainable principles practiced before have tremendous obstacles to overcome in order to re-emerge as effective measures for today's labyrinthian complexity. If modernism was considered the cause of the present environmental problems, then it too was responsible for many of the solutions. Most of the green designs maintained close connections to modernism, especially using modernist structural, HVAC and material systems, and the tendencies of economy and functionality. Modernism's pervasive nature was a welcome consequence of the greening process. Key leaders in the Modern Movement provided valuable architectural works that embodied sustainable principles and design measures, which inspired a generation of greening of architecture.

MODERN GREEN ANTECEDENTS

While the effects of the Modern Movement became a worldwide phenomenon, it produced a relatively unified architectural language. A few architects and their works provided welcome examples of more environmentally oriented approaches to design that later had significant effects on the development of green architecture. These works tended to integrate climatic design principles with modernist forms, technologies and materials. Critical to this process was the matching of the more extreme climatic conditions, such as overheating or underheating, with appropriate building forms that became sculpted through intentional climatic determinants. Historian William Curtis explained that nature was a growing source of inspiration, and that "several major 20th-century architects, notably Frank Lloyd Wright, Le Corbusier, and Alvar Aalto who, far from being just 'materialists,' had a lofty vision of 'nature' as a counterforce to banal mechanization."[9] Philip Johnson's Geier House (1968) located in Indian Hills, Ohio, was one of the first modern underground buildings. Daylight spilled through reflectors in the cycloid geometric vaults in Louis Kahn's Kimbell Art Museum (1972) in Fort Worth, Texas. In some instances the International Style had undergone a process of naturalization with rural vernaculars as continuing references and sources of inspiration.

Le Corbusier, who was considered to be one of the most influential architects of the 20th century, invigorated the modern movement with new shape grammars with universal implications. Although he had regionalist beginnings, most of his works had traces of salient and discriminating extractions from traditional and eclectic examples of the 19th century, but mainly forged new geometries, spatial orders and materials that were transformed for contemporary purposes. His search for a set of ideal principles led to a process of prototyping, which in turn advised his proposition of architecture as machine and his interest in mass-production. According to architectural historian Charles Jencks, Le Corbusier did not see the machine as a fetish, but rather it was being celebrated as an expression of evolution toward "higher states of organization."[10] He developed a means by which he could apply several levels of significance to single configurations. He was fascinated with light that created bold fenestration and light producing schemes, such as the monumental works in Chandigarh, the courtyard scheme at Sante Marie de La Tourette and the renown Virgo constellation window-wall at Notre Dame du Haut Chapel at Ronchamp, to name a few. Climate became an important consideration as his commissions had taken him to difficult climatic regions—the Mediterranean, Africa, Argentina, Brazil, Chili, Iraq, India and Russia.

Le Corbusier's plan for the Chandigarth capital (1953) was organized with shifted axis, asymmetrical symmetry, divisions of urban functions and institutional hierarchies, grand boulevards and focal points, and monumental buildings. The High Court of Punjab and Haryana in Chandigarh (1956) exemplified the bold phototropic form with large upturned parasol for sun and rain protection and the functional separation and articulation of the four principal operations of the window, and according to Jencks, was accomplished with "the various *brises-soleil* shade the glass wall from the sun; vertical, pivoting ventilators of sheet metal allow fresh air in—otherwise ventilation is achieved by fans; finally, the fixed glass wall, obscured at points for indirect light and open at other points for view." These formal characteristics were suffused in elemental sunlight, breezes, and rain and in many ways derived from the earlier Mogul traditions of Muslim India in the 16th century. Le Corbusier's architecture had far reaching impact because it communicated something profound and had a seemingly transferable language. It was not surprising that his works and ideas influenced both modern and green architecture alike.

The more modest works of Egyptian architect Hassan Fathy were quite different than the heroic works of Le Corbusier. Fathy was disillusioned with the modern movement and with the environments created by it. Rather, he felt missing was the need for socially-oriented architecture and planning. New technology was supposed to change the quality of life, but for Fathy this was a failing of modern architecture. Nevertheless, his work aimed to be a part of the modern movement with focus on improving human living conditions, especially the poor.[11]

1.4 Le Corbusier and Hassan Fathy a) Chandigarth High Courts (1956) (image courtesy Eduardo Guiot) b) Ronchamp Chapel (1960) c) New Gourna Village (1948) (© Aga Khan Trust for Culture)

Key to his belief system was the idea that cultural authenticity was an essential non-interchangeability of cultures and that climate played an important role in this. New Gourna Village, located in West Luxor, was constructed in 1948 and was one of the most renowned and successful examples of Egyptian public projects. Construction began with the most public buildings—the mosque, market, village hall, theater, crafts exhibition hall and boy's school. Both the master plan and individual buildings within it responded to climate-oriented considerations with the close packing of buildings, narrow streets, thick adobe walls and courtyard dwelling designs. Two important observations can be made. First is that modern architecture and urban planning are inextricably wed. Second, is that climatic design determinants of form, rather than high technology, can produce effective green designs. Figures 1.4 a, b and c show photographs of the boldly formed sun-shaded façade for the Chandigarth High Courts Building, the daylit Chapel Notre Dame du Haut at Ronchamp, France by Le Corbusier, and the close-packing city blocks composed of courtyard dwellings in Fathy's New Gourna Village.

The works of Alvar Aalto expressed the mood of a new regionalism where the principles of vernacular architecture were crossbred with the languages of modern design. This suggested the adoption of local traditions, climate and construction methods and materials that were more place-adapted. While teaching at MIT in the late 1940s, Aalto acquired the commission to design new student dormitories for a site located to the south of the campus that overlooked Memorial Drive and the Charles River. The program was broken down into two different space types: first was the served or more livable functions, such as the sleeping quarters and dining hall, and second was the service functions, such as circulation, bathrooms, stairs, storage and laundry facilities. A serpentine double-loaded spine and spatial organization was employed with the service functions to the north and the dorm room functions to the south, which maximized the views and solar orientation from the more livable areas of the building. The architectural language of the north and south façades differ with planer walls and the cantilevered stair on the north in contrast to the undulating wall with regularly punctuated fenestrations on the south, which were only interrupted by the public functions of the program including the lounge and dining hall on the ground level. Figures 1.5a and b indicates the Baker House ground floor plan with the double-loaded serpentine shape and separation of the space types, and a photograph of the south façade.

This eccentric functional and serpentine plan organization was used in other projects as well, most notably the Neue Vahr housing project in Bremen, Germany (1959) that also employed the expressive fanning of the livable activities. It also echoed his New York World's Fair design of 1938–9.

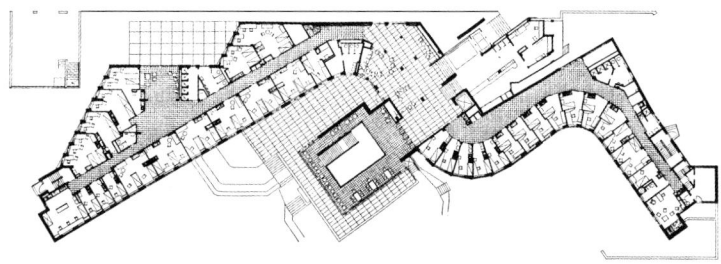

1.5   MIT's Baker House (1946) by Alvar Aalto a) Ground Level Plan b) Serpentine South Façade (courtesy Yan Da, novatrio3.com)

Aalto's works certainly were inspired by metaphors of nature and served as a basis for regional abstractions for design and principles for architecture and urbanism. Architectural historian Malcolm Quantrill observed, "To many the Baker Dormitory remains as an American anomaly in Aalto's *oeuvre*; but in its bold use of apparently conflicting geometries and an equally confident handling of the fenestrations, both towards the river and Memorial Drive, it clearly outlines the programme for Aalto's direction in the next two decades."[12] The differentiated front and back façade treatment was reminiscent of earlier Greek architecture and later played an important role in the development of modern-day phototropic solar architecture common in the 1970s.

The early works of Frank Lloyd Wright generally focused on domestic architecture, in particular the Prairie houses, Usonian houses and a myriad of private commissions, but also included a range of other building typologies that included the Larkin Building, Unity Church and the Guggenheim Museum. Wright's early domestic works demonstrated sensitivity to nature, site, climate and context. Wright's works were considered to have green elements, which included a sensitive and often evocative relationship to the land, topography and surrounding site. His organic architecture possessed new spatial ordering systems, adaptable forms and innovative building materials, and were inclusive of the careful and integrated design and geometric control of all buildings elements from overall form to door handle creating an aesthetic continuity and unity. His Prairie Style works, with open living areas, low horizontal roofs, the use of natural materials, and the central hearth, were responsive to local climatic conditions. The Kaufmann Residence (1939) in Bear Run, Pennsylvania was certainly an expression of intense engagement between architecture and its immediate site, especially with the topography and adjacent waterfalls. It was given the "best all-time work of American architecture" by the American Institute of Architects in 1991.

The Robie house built in 1908 in Hyde Park, Illinois was probably the most celebrated example of his Prairie house typology, which was masterfully crafted into striations and asymmetrical unity within the urban setting. Figure 1.6a shows the strong horizontal roof planes that are cantilevered to cover integrated outdoor patios and circulation. Some of the principles derived from the Prairie house designs contributed to the concept of an organic architecture, and included extending the building form into the site for more participation, placing living spaces on raised foundations or platforms, organizing spaces with axial control and horizontality, creating open spatial connections for increased light, natural ventilation and view, mono-materiality where possible to contribute to a more harmonious whole, and incorporation of environmental control systems (heating, lighting and plumbing) into the constituent parts of the architecture. These principles were certainly important in generating a green agenda for architectural design a half-century later.

And of course, his Usonian houses were created to moderate cost single-family homes in response to the Depression in the 1930s. Concurrently, the designs resulted in reductions in energy loads because of their smaller size and the utilization of their sun tempering and passive solar heating schemes. They were extremely practical and were constructed from a kit of parts that included modular floor plans, standardized natural materials, unit wall systems, service cores, built-in components, zoned living areas with open living, dining and kitchen, and a central hearth. The insulated flat roofs extended beyond the walls to provide sun shading and throw water clear of the house. With these design principles there was an emphasis on "spaciousness" rather than "space," and simplicity above all. Simplicity was not merely reduction without complexity, especially in regards to organic elaboration. Rather, it dissolved its diversity of parts into an integrated whole.

The Jacobs' house was the first of the Usonian houses to be built and was located near Madison, Wisconsin. This project was organized by an orthogonal grid and an "L-shaped" plan, which accommodated 1,340 square feet (180 square meters), and in 1936 had a construction cost of $5,500. The plan shape served to separate public and private zones of the house with entrance at the right angle. These design strategies were later re-iterated in E.F. Schumacher's *Small is Beautiful* (1973).[13] Nature-embodied principles served as inspiration for Wright's organic architecture, which provided similar cannons for Biometrics and to some degree Landscape Urbanism nearly a century later. In Wright's own words, "Nature is my manifestation of God. I go to nature every day for inspiration in the day's work. I follow in building the principles which nature has used in its domain."[14] The contrasting climatic design approaches to Taliesin East in Spring Green, Wisconsin (1911) and Taliesin West in Scottsdale, Arizona (1937) clearly demonstrated Wright's knowledge and mastery of seasonal and climate-oriented architecture. Fallingwater or the Kaufmann House, completed in 1939, was designed for 2885 finished square feet (268 square meters), and was an extraordinary expression of the intense cantilevered patios interacting between dwelling and the 30-foot (nine meters) waterfall (Figure 1.6b).

Constantinos Doxiadis proposed the concept and intellectual framework for Ekistics, which was defined as the science of human settlements. By encompassing all scales of human habitation along with archeological, historical and morphological patterns of growth, Ekistics models were organized by five distinct and hierarchical elements—nature, anthropos (human beings), society, shells and networks. The coordination of scales inherent to settlement structure was a major objective of the Ekistics model as container (form) and content (function) formed a dynamic unity, as pictured in Figure 1.6c with the plan of Paris.

1.6   Frank Lloyd Wright and Constantinos Doxiadis a) The Robie House (1909) (Library of Congress, Prints & Photographs Division, ILL,16-CHIG, 33-1) b) Kaufman House (1939) (courtesy Jeffrey Howe) c) Ekistics Nodes and Networks (courtesy Random House)

Ekistics approached the problem through the interactions among these various elements. Importance was gained in the inclusive and relational functions of these elements, which later became influential in the development of emergent green urban philosophies and ecological design strategies. After his death in 1975, the Ekistics movement fell into obscurity. Yet, important concepts were exposed that today are integral to sustainable urban thinking. Doxiadis boldly stated that: "Human settlements are no longer satisfactory for their inhabitants. This is true everywhere in the world, in under-developed as well as developed countries."[15]

CONTRADICTIONS WITH MODERNISM AND SUSTAINABILITY

Modernism was a general set of cultural tendencies considered to have begun in the late 19th and early 20th centuries. In its initial reaction to the tradition and the ambiguity of enlightenment, modernism grew as a simplifying agent that later provided sympathetic resonance for advancing and changing technology and form. According to William Curtis, "modern architecture" was an invention conceived to oppose earlier chaotic, eclectic and historic forms, and sought to generate its own authenticity for an emerging modern industrial society.[16] He argued that modernism was a break to rediscover the true and genuine path of architecture, which was led by the Modern Movement of the Congres Internationaux d'Architecture Moderne (CIAM), the Bauhaus and Le Corbusier's *Vers une Architecture*. The modernist polemic of aesthetic reduction and abstraction and the secularization of development as a tool of everyday economic practice were aspects that critics have attacked. Architectural theorist Kate Nesbitt suggested that, "Abstraction, atonality, and atemporality, however, are merely stylistic manifestations of modernism, not its essential nature."[17] It was, therefore, important to see the framework of the motivations as well as the formulations to which the greening of architecture needed to relate and against which it was charged to rebel.

Current environmental problems can be traced to several general phenomena—rapid increase in world population, dependence upon fossil fuels for nearly every aspect of contemporary life, and the increasing addiction of use of the automobile for transportation. Confronting these phenomena according to Carl Stein, "Renewable resources are limited by the rate at which they are received and by the environmental disruption caused by their capture and use."[18] This includes fossil fuels, timber, arable land, and fresh water. Stein further went on to say that the waste from this process was another untenable consequence. The shifting of wealth and emergent modernity in large-population, developing countries has posed further environmental concern. The blame cannot be entirely laid on modernism as the evolution of our immense global culture, with its insatiable appetite for consumption, dominates the current placemaking process. Much of green architecture, while designed with renewable technologies, utilized the same construction methods, conventional building equipment, and materials, as was commonplace in modern architecture it sought to improve. A massive large-scale shift in city and building making could only occur with ubiquitous change in engineering, energy production, manufacturing, transportation, and construction methods.

Where modernism reacted to history and the traditions of the Enlightenment, it created a culture of consumerism and a vocabulary of a reductionist architectural language. New technologies and the use of modern materials, components and construction methods gave new expression to design. The curtain wall, first used by Skidmore Owings and Merrill (SOM) in the Lever House in New York City (1952), featured a 24-story, blue-green heat-resistant fixed glazing system with a stainless steel frame curtain wall. Later, the Inland Steel Building (Figure 1.7a) in Chicago (1956) featured a totally open plan with separate service core and curtain wall of brushed stainless steel. The Seagram Building (1958) by Ludwig Mies van der Rohe was another example of the curtain-wall technology. The elevator, central HVAC systems and innovations in structure, glazing materials and telecommunication systems helped enable an expanding modern urban architecture. Also pictured in Figures 1.7b and c are the Northland Shopping Center in Detroit, Michigan and Levittown, New York. Taken together, the proliferation of steel and glass buildings, suburban shopping centers and low-density suburban housing developments contributed to a rapidly expanding and automobile-dependent post World War Two settlement pattern.

Modernism did not only inform building design, but influenced land use planning as well, especially within the suburban landscape, which in large part was a manifestation of it. Access to abundant and seemingly endless supplies of petroleum and mass production of automobiles opened a floodgate for a low density, single use settlement form. Numerous single-family housing developments followed with development of large shopping malls expanded into bordering agriculture land. Northland Shopping Center (1954) in Southland, Michigan was designed by Victor Gruen and was one of the first suburban malls. Schools and office parks followed in turn. This new suburban phenomenon was replete with all the modern facilities and services as long as there were inexhaustible supplies of gasoline nearby. Necessary life-support functions were separated by use, or what Leon Krier called "functional zoning," and required and elaborate automobile systems to connect all the disparate parts. Levittown, New York (1947–51), for example, spawned a generation of postwar suburban growth tied to this model. Interestingly, Levittown began with 2,000 small rental houses, and in time the development expanded to include larger homes with populuxe aesthetic that Levitt called "ranch houses," which spawned a total of 17,747 homes by 1951. Regional planner Marcial Echenique (1976) observed the inextricable relationship among the type and abundance of the source of energy, the kind of transport system and settlement form. If energy was cheap and the prevailing transport method was the automobile, then according to Echenique's formula, that naturally translated into a dispersed, low-density settlement form.

1.7   Expressions of American Modernism a) Inland Steel Building (courtesy K. Devyn-Caldwell -24gotham.com b) Northland Shopping Center (courtesy Walter P. Reuther Library, Wayne State University) c) Levittown, New York (Special Collections/Long Island Studies Institute)

It is important to present a discussion on modernism as it was not only the precursor to the contemporary architecture that followed, but embodied the ideals and constructions that exist at the core of many of the environmental problems in which green architecture attempts to correct. This included both the architectural and planning manifestations of it. The reaction to modernism fell into two overarching greening theories offering covalent alternatives, either future-oriented strategies promoting neo-avant-garde forms and innovative technologies, or backward-looking solutions with revivals of traditional pre-modern forms, vernaculars and methods. To summarize, modernism in cultural terms enabled a global society to evolve, expand and consume vast resources. As long as the predominant means of growth maintained the use of fossil fuels in energy production, manufacturing, transport and construction of buildings and cities, green architecture would have difficulty truly distancing from its co-dependent relationship to modernism and thus, effecting an independent developmental approach in large measure. An inherent contradiction remains—the greening of architecture requires the use of modernist construction and manufacturing, by which to realize the sustainable design measures and systems.

GREENING ARCHITECTURE

"Greening" is a *verb*, not a noun or adjective. Coincidently, the greening of architecture is not a finite set of conditions or simple application of design measures, but rather it is a dynamic process. Definitions for sustainability, fixing unsustainability, self-sufficiency, renewability, green building, bio-climatic and environmental design vary, and generally are interchangeable references to a greening process applicable to architecture and urban design. Some definitions, such as the Brundtland Report, referred to meeting the needs of the present without compromising the ability of future generations to meet their own needs. Green architecture, or green design, was also seen as an approach to building that minimized harmful effects on human health and the environment. Other definitions focused more on conservation and preservation of resources, especially non-renewable ones, and the enormous inventory of existing buildings worldwide. Generally, sustainable architecture intended to minimize the negative environmental impact of buildings by enhancing efficiency and moderation in the use of materials, energy, and development space. There were also concerns about diminishing the toxicity caused by the built environment. At the urban scale, sustainable communities were places planned, built, or modified to promote sustainable living. This included sustainability aspects relating to reproduction, water, transportation, energy, and waste and materials.

Issues of technology, scale, health, embodied resources, existing inventory, and energy conscious-behavior have also been considered and add to the difficulty of any single comprehensive and useful definition. Disagreement exists about the precise meaning of "*sustainability*." The term was used in many contexts, including development, cities, agriculture, economy, technology, environment, and buildings. Confusion existed about the meaning of the term, since it was used in so many different connotations and often was defined differently. Julien de Smedt's observation has growing relevance, that "*sustainability*" has become an ineffective term to explain either the complexity of the problem or an appropriate course of action. To better understand an effective working definition for the greening of architecture, it might be useful to discuss the problems to which it seeks to address. Vivienne Brophy and J. Owen Lewis observed that, "since the industrial revolution, but particularly in the past

100 years, the twin phenomena of more widely-diffused wealth and relatively cheaper energy have resulted in widespread increases in energy use."[8] Carl Stein argued for a focus on two areas: the use of sustainable principles applied to all new buildings and the need to upgrade the environmental performance of most of the existing stock of buildings worldwide. And finally, Abdel-Hadi, Tolda and Soliman saw the relationships between the environment and human health, in addition to well-being and behavior as a necessity for sustainable design.[19]

Sustainability and green architecture must address design, building-making and consumer use patterns looking at issues of efficiency, health and longevity for both new and existing buildings. At the architectural scale it was both the construction and maintenance of buildings that green architecture broadly needed to improve. This implied the need to address the embodied energy of building materials, products and construction methods, thermal comfort, along with the maintenance and use of the building over time. Modernism produced buildings with shorter lives, built with lighter mass, and heavy reliance on HVAC systems that required large amounts of fossil fuel energy, approaching one-third of the useful energy produced. Thermal efficiency meant equal attention to building skin losses and gains, and the effects of climate, as well as internally generated heat gains from equipment, artificial lighting and people. James Marston Fitch published *American Building* (1966) where he discussed what he called the environmental impacts of the wall, both inside and out.[20] These environmental conditions were organized into four categories: atmospheric, luminous, sonic and biological impacts, in which the wall must ideally respond in multi-functional ways. These studies were important because they directed attention to the wall as a mediating system responding to dynamic internal and external influences.

Unlike the Modern Movement in architecture, green architecture did not express a single set of formal principles, manifest through an explicit pallet of materials or technologies, and did not have a strict and identifiable architectural form language. In the long run this was most likely a blessing in disguise, as sustainability issues were not going to disappear, but rather increase in importance and magnitude as competition for non-renewable resources increases. Dating sustainability with a particular language of form would confine it to a determinant period of time and would not allow for a natural evolution in design, function, technology and use. A new paradigm seemed necessary that has embedded in its DNA an evolutionary sustainable function and continuing reinterpretation of contemporary needs and corresponding forms.

GREENING URBANISM

Two planning forms organized by a central place have two drastically different architectural languages and approaches to sustainability. The first example, Mexcaltitan, was presumed to be a birthplace of the Aztecs and is today a living fishing community of 818 inhabitants (2010 census) that specializes in dried shrimp. It was a sustaining cruciform and circular island-city more than a thousand years old and less than a mile (1.6 kilometers) in diameter located in an estuary along the Pacific coast of Mexico. Its sustainability takes the form of a living place inextricably connected to its place for shelter, commerce, religion and community (Figure 1.8a). The second example was the proposal for a sustainable neighborhood in the Babcock Ranch Development in southwest Florida by Texas A&M University students (Figure 1.8b).[21] The orthogonal grids supported a density gradient and mix of neighborhood-scale commercial and residential uses.

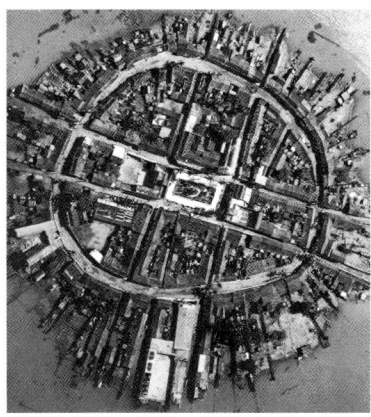

1.8 Differing Approaches to Sustainable Urbanism a) Mexcaltitan, Mexico (© Yann Arthus-Bertrand / Altitude) b) Renewable Technology Neighborhood Center (© Phillip Tabb)

A central plaza was designed as a pedestrian-gathering place and was structured with saw-tooth photovoltaic collector arrays, which provided electricity for community uses, sun-shading and daylight behind the arrays. Both places relied on the spatial order, characteristics of centrality and Unity Principle. Mexcaltitan was a sustainable island plan that evolved organically over time using circumferential geometry, while the Babcock neighborhood was a new proposal featuring renewable systems and an orthogonal grid—design versus technology.

The issues of scale and context for sustainable measures enter the discussion when larger ecological principles are related to the complexity of the urban environment and the myriad of interrelated systems that are required to maintain it. Geographer Susan Owens argued that different sustainable measures or structural variables are applicable to different scales of development from single plots, buildings and neighborhoods to individual settlements and regions.[22] This is to imply, for example, that dealing with regional movement of energy and resources required different sustainable interventions than reducing thermal loads to separate dwellings. Patrick Condon argued for a set of rules or what he calls "simple steps to recovery" for sustainable communities.[23] His measures were fairly specific and covered the needs to restore the streetcar, re-establish the interconnected street system, create pedestrian zones with integral commercial, schools and transit stops, locate jobs close to homes, provide a diversity of housing types, create linked greenway systems, and invest in more sustainable infrastructure. Splintering Urbanism has promoted an infrastructurally mediated network as an emerging pattern.

Planner Nan Ellin echoed these steps with a more abstract manifesto of urban design that she called *"qualities of an integral urbanism."* They included hybridity and connectivity, porosity, authenticity and vulnerability.[24] What was interesting with these urban measures for sustainability was the shift from isolated technological or specific design solutions to broader issues addressing integration and inter-connectedness. Analysis of Ellin's manifesto reveals relational rather than fixed qualities. Architectural historian David Grahame Shane's *Recombinant Urbanism* put forward the idea of a mutable process of self-correction through recombination of urban attributes that in the case of a fossil fuel based settings could in fact be sustainability altered and re-formed genetically.[25] This suggests a heterotopic urban environment of fragments and patches grafted together, such as theme parks, mega shopping malls, automobile dealership campuses, and entertainment districts that especially occur in larger multicultural cities. A common thread to these emergent theories was the more complex systemic nature of the issues that exist at the urban scale and the necessity for transformable and tractable sustainable measures.

These correspond to Ken Yeang's notions of the dynamic qualities of a region's ecosystems and their changing interactions with the built environment.[26] He suggested that with "the ecological approach, there is no single '*technological fix*' or universal design approach that will solve all the environmental problems or eliminate all the negative effects." Furthermore, Yeang promoted the idea of an ecological context within which to reinvent the built environment as a greater part of the organic system that formed a dynamic and interactive involvement with the environment and the changes it undergoes. The artificial environment, according to Yeang, was like a set of circuits that should systematically process incoming natural resource inputs (energy and materials), utilize them efficiently, and discharge the outputs cleanly. This view was about relating the diversity of contemporary human activity to ecological flows. This ecological model, while ambitious in concept, was in direct conflict with the indiscriminate piecemeal urban growth that typically continues worldwide.

By the nature of their scale, sustainable planning measures require larger systems of consideration, including reforms with land use, density, infrastructure and transportation planning along with urban architecture. Expanding human populations, especially in developing countries, continues to increase the inventory of buildings and urban environments, which brings remediation rather than innovation to the forefront of sustainable planning and design agendas. Timothy Beatley states that variety and extent of greening initiatives and activities were impressive, and ranged from promotion of compact urban forms, commitment to public transit and pedestrian design, to efforts to operationalize more circular or ecological approaches to existing cities.[27] The *New Urbanism*, with examples like Seaside, Florida and Pounbury, England, attempted to develop a more compact, pedestrian friendly environment, but has drawn criticism because of the rigid and formal nature of the prescriptive work. Additionally, the apparent lack of serious sustainable planning and architecture measures were apparent especially in the early examples. With the emergence and appropriation of *Agricultural Urbanism*, the gap between the New Urbanism and sustainability has decreased. The notion of, "*placemaking as a sustainable strategy*," had promise, as it could become an integrative adhesive for both the planning and architectural scales with focused attention to the quality of dwelling and stewardship instead of technology.[28] The Generative Principle seemed to be a driving force in the beginning with strong reactive tendencies and a direct focus on developing architecture and urbanism. The Re-generative Principle emerged later with a more integrative, dynamic and holistic focus.

Meanwhile, the prevailing tendencies remain toward "business-as-usual," albeit some stiffening of energy and environmental standards and certification programs, and the development of heroic and monumental versions of green architecture. A sustainable future is faced with overcoming the context of an incredibly complex existing built environment that was generally developed unsustainably. The life expectancy of buildings varies with age, quality of materials, use, location, weather, degree of maintenance, and quality of architectural design. Factors that determine durability include moisture, UV radiation, temperature, chemicals, decay and corrosion, insects, fungi, natural hazards and wear and tear. For example, the lifespan of an office building is around 70 years. Therefore, office buildings constructed in the mid-1960s are due to be replaced in 2025.

1.9 Placemaking and Spaces Contained a) Castello di Gargonza b) Model of Piazza della Collegio c) Placemaking in the Siena Compo

The explosion of building worldwide over the past half-century has created a confusing context within which there have been places of relief and a few moments of sanity. Figure 1.9a illustrated an aerial photograph of Castello di Gargonza located in the hills overlooking the Val di Chiana with its clear boundary, internal grid system and place-marking tower. Figure 1.9b was a model of the Piazza della Collegio that formed a portal entry into the medieval center of Castiglion Fiorentino, Italy. And Figure 1.9c illustrated several social pockets or intimate places formed within the context of the Piazza del Compo in the center of Siena, Italy. Placemaking was a sustainable strategy that could also be found with Central Park in New York City, Golden Gate Park in San Francisco, Hyde Park in London, Tiergarten in Berlin and Jardin de Luxembourg in Paris all offer connections back to nature with incredible health and economic benefits. Placemaking offered tremendous opportunities in addressing sustainability on multiple levels including both building energy and transportation energy needs.

The Greening of Architecture, including urbanism, becomes a progressive and accumulative process for remediation and repurposing within the context of the tremendous inventory of the existing built environment, and innovation directed at the relationship between evolving cultural needs and new models of green architectural and urban design responses to them. Rather than merely adding sustainable measures externally, green architecture emerges through its authentic and internally generative nature and original purpose. Critical to the development of a sustainable future is the creation of inclusive intellectual capital applicable to all scales of development, existing and new. The greening architecture has many dimensions and scales of consideration, much like the earlier pioneering Ekistics' elements developed by Doxiadis—nature, anthropos, society, shells, and networks, and the qualities of Ellin's Integral Urbanism and Shane's Recombinant Urbanism. The greening of architecture is posited by the following 12 objectives and defining characteristics:

1. The greening of architecture must address resource and energy use *conservation*, *preservation* and *efficiency*, reducing loads and demands. This also includes saving energy and resources through efficient consumption and re-use.
2. The greening of architecture must address both *skin-dominated* energy flows (gains and losses) and *load-dominated* energy sources (solar gain, lights, equipment, people and outside make-up air) and employ efficient control systems.

3. The greening of architecture is *climate responsive* and seeks to utilize the beneficial qualities of local and *natural resources*, especially sun, light, wind, and water, and it needs to protect from negative environmental extremes and damaging effects.
4. The greening of architecture incorporates *low-embodied* building materials, equipment, products and construction methods. Measures should be *obtainable* and *affordable*.
5. The greening of architecture must address the *health issues* associated with site geology and outgassing from building materials, finishes, products, equipment and construction methods.
6. The greening of architecture acknowledges the need for *preservation* and the need to *recycle*, continuously *repurpose* and *up-grade* the existing building stock.
7. The greening of architecture must address the differences in single and multiple building contexts and variable *building typologies*, that have different needs, functions, and environmental conditions.
8. The greening of architecture responds interactively to *natural ecological flows* of a particular site, microclimate, region and eco-system.
9. The greening of architecture is a nested part of a larger *planning and design* process and context within which it exists, participates and contributes. Appropriate sustainable strategies need to be targeted the specific scales of application.
10. The greening of architecture seeks advanced, clean, hybrid and efficient *sources of energy* for buildings, transportation and power production.
11. The greening of architecture is a *mutable* and *iterative process* that occurs, changes, builds intelligence, and evolves over time. In the context of this work is defined by generalized measures, technologies and planning schemes found within increments of decades.
12. The greening of architecture is a *global phenomenon* that expresses both regionally and transnationally, in urban and rural contexts, with new and existing structures, and in industrialized and developing countries.

TEMPORAL LANDSCAPE FOR SUSTAINABILITY

The development of a particular movement in architecture matriculates through cycles—reaction, development, refinement, innovation, re-invention and re-generation. The greening of architecture has moved from simple process of remediation to holistic models of design. In the 1960s the term for sustainability would address bio-climatic design features of single buildings and would promote the diversity of formal design approaches in response to varying climatic conditions. Issues of form complexity, orientation, plan aspect ratios and degrees of transparency were considered. The conditions surrounding comfort were examined and the architectural means to achieve appropriate comfort levels were explored. The broader term *"environmentalism"* was used to describe the larger effects of our modern world on the environment, especially the elemental and biological systems. Beginning in the 1960s, works of Rachel Carson, E.F. Schumacher, Buckminster Fuller, and Stewart Brand, focused on the harmful effects to the environment and the awareness of holistic and environmental thinking. The work of the Metabolists in Japan and the emergence of the megastructure provided alternative paradigms of urban design with the bio-technical notion of the city as an organic process. Team Ten, beginning in the early 1950s, provided continuity with CIAM, but broke away to promote further ideas of an urbanism and socially transformative architecture and planning. Their theoretical framework had a profound influence on the development of architectural thinking in the second half of the 20th century, especially in Europe.

In the 1970s the focus was more on emergent solar technologies that were coupled with more aggressive energy conservation measures. Sustainability was directed to reducing energy demand and utilization of on-site resources, especially solar energy. The profound effect of the 1973 Oil Embargo spawned a change from a "form-function" architectural preoccupation to one of "form-performance." At this time a building's value was measured in its ability to save energy. As a consequence, many scientific ideas and energy technologies were developed, including solar optics, thermal storage and control systems. Passive solar designs emerged that transformed single buildings into highly insulated solar collectors. Architects Michael Reynolds, James Lambeth, Malcolm Wells, and Ralph Knowles, were influential with radical, playful and dramatic designs. The optical and thermal dynamic characteristics of energy collection and storage were explored and folded into an expanding definition of green architecture. The more rigid orientation constraints of these solar systems began to impinge upon and create the need for the necessity of more flexible and varied site responses, and the collector tilt angle requirements affected south façade designs.

In the 1980s green architecture looked to more historic-driven and vernacular forms and to de-emphasized the tectonic characteristic of the decade before. Issues of preservation, conservation and historic formalism were in part driven by postmodern theory. Postmodernism in the 1980s had an interesting gentrifying effect over these works that over-emphasized the energy function of a building. The contextual and vernacular-sensitive works of Sam Mockbee, Brian MacKay-Lyons, Glenn Murcutt and Lake Flato exemplify this re-direction with local socially conscious designs. The New Urbanism was a form of postmodern planning aimed at providing an alternative to functionally zoned, single use residential developments that proliferated suburban planning practices. It promoted place-oriented development that was inspired by traditional town planning methods and forms replete with city blocks, boulevards, more densely packed and varying housing typologies, mixes of use and formal public buildings and spaces. In his essay, *Towards a Critical Regionalism* (1983), architectural historian Kenneth Frampton called for an architecture that would strive to overcome placelessness and lack of identity by utilizing a building's geographical context.[29]

The 1990s brought Green Architecture fully into the mainstream with larger and differentiated building typologies and eco-technologies, as evidenced in the works of Arup, Calatrava, Grimshaw, Piano and Rogers. The structural and environmental control system technologies were carefully integrated into the architecture and boldly expressed. Minimalist building skins were being replaced with more complex and functional layers, and eco-technologies. Many of these new technologies were not merely fixed responses to environmental forces, but rather were dynamic and moved with them. Additionally, this time spawned the literal greening of buildings with the vegetated architectural examples of Yeang and Ambasz. These works ostensibly represented a host of similar projects that took on the literal greening of a building including green roofs, green walls, greenhouses, and sky gardens. *Cradle to Cradle* by William McDonough brought attention to the negative health effects of building materials, products and construction practices.[30] There was also a growing concern to address the embodied energy associated with imports of foreign materials and products, many of which were in themselves deemed "sustainable," but required vast amounts of energy to transport them to local sites.

This past decade beginning at the millennium has seen the ever-expanding diversity of sustainable thinking in architecture, which evolved beyond the greening of single buildings to focus on larger urban, suburban and exurban contexts. Village Homes in the 1970s, New Urbanism in the 1980s, Kronsberg in the late 1990s, Serenbe Community in the 2000s, and Masdar City projected to be completed in 2015, featured climate responsiveness, land preservation, renewable technologies, densification, active living, aging in place, mixes of use, and integral agriculture at the urban scale. Green urbanism has emerged with less to do with building technology and greater focus on shifting cultural values toward reforms in land use, density, modes of transport, and the development of community-scale clean energy systems. There was increasing recognition that the worldwide building stock was an important focus for green design interventions as they represent such a large value of embodied energy. Environmental entrepreneur Paul Hawken stated, "Modern buildings are temporal in every sense."[31] This means they have a life cycle and increasingly they are not made to last. Especially in housing, where durability of building components and materials has been reduced with increased economic demands for lower initial capital costs for construction and reduced time in project delivery. In contrast, sustainable solutions need greater attention to quality and detail. The Greening of Architecture evolved to a global phenomenon incrementally moving toward a climax planetary environmentalism. James Wines began his book, *Green Architecture* (2000), by writing; "Architecture in the 20th century began as a celebration of the Age of Industry and Technology; but today this is rapidly changing in response to a new Age of Information and Ecology."[32] The combination of these tendencies has moved the greening process to greater depth, feedback and connectedness.

Global themes in green architecture occur within a diverse international geographic landscape. The themes identify important trends and realizations of contemporary and postcolonial seminal architecture and urbanism with accompanying sustainable measures. The geographic dispositions give a more complete picture of the pervasiveness of the greening process and the diversity of design approaches worldwide. Earlier green development reveals contrast between critically derived indigenous practices that rely strongly on local building cultures, materials and methods and low technology, and the more refined and bold works characterized by high technology, hybrid systems and varying building typologies. Approaches to higher densities and urban design are a logical developmental synthesis that can be seen throughout the world.

The *Greening of Architecture* from a global perspective presents a diversity of place and geo-centered exemplifications driven by cultural, ideological, climatic, economic and tectonic determinants creating a varied landscape of geographic, oppositional divisions (Industrialized–Developing, East–West, Urban–Rural, High Tech–Low Tech, Large–Small, New–Existing, and Extreme–Conventional). Regional diversity, global congruity, and hybridization characterize green architectural approaches worldwide and tend to be distributed by building typology and urban location. The phrase "think global, act local" was attributed to Scottish town planner Patrick Geddes (1915) and captured a common sentiment connecting global issues and concerns with local sensitivity and action. The regional "modifiers" gave emerging global green architecture particular authenticity, relevance and sustainable utility, while universal tendencies presented continuity and contemporaneous global parity.

This landscape of time represented the development of an incremental response to the need for higher levels of sustainable design. Abraham Maslow's "*hierarchy of needs*" was an echo that articulated the psychology of the whole and its constituent parts in the form of a cascading order of importance.[33] In the field of sustainability, it gave a sorted account of the critical needs and evolving circumstances that had corresponding design responses to them. Yet, the *Greening of Architecture* was not a fixed prescription, as it tended to be more transient, contingent, resilient and nonlinear. Therefore, it was the principal objective of this work to delineate the complexity of approaches and the underlying nature of developments in green architecture over time and to describe the diverse approaches to it. This work has been divided into three parts: this chapter, which is a brief overview of the environmental issues and the nature of earlier green architecture in response to them. Second is a historic perspective of the pioneering evolution of green technology and architectural integration over the past 50 years. Third is a survey that is intended to show the intransigent and culturally pervasive exemplifications *au courant* by a wide range of geographic territories and cultural contexts.

The Greening of Architecture is seen as an evolutionary process that is informed by significant world affairs, a response to climate change, intelligent management of available natural resources, emerging environmental theories, movements in architecture, technological innovations, and seminal works in architecture and planning throughout each decade over the past 50 years. The developmental effects of influential works are not always obvious as change is often a result of many parallel and seemingly unrelated events. A benefit of looking back in time is the ability to see the patterns and connections that may not have been originally visible. Nevertheless, both intended and unintended efforts have contributed to the positive change. Similar to the objectives of the Brundtand Commission Report, this understanding of sustainability, and likewise the greening of architecture, is a phenomenal process of improving, over time, the quality of human life while simultaneously living responsively within the carrying capacity of supporting ecosystems.

ENDNOTES

1 Findhorn Community, *The Findhorn Garden: Pioneering a New Vision of Man and Nature in Cooperation*. New York: Harper and Row, 1975.

2 JDS Architects, "From 'Sustain' to 'Ability,'" *Ecological Urbanism*, edited by Mohsen Mostafavi and Gareth Doherty. London: Lars Muller Publishers, 2010: 122.

3 Phillip Tabb, "The Solar Village Archetype: A Study of English Village Form Applicable to Energy-integrated Planning Principles for Satellite Settlements in Temperate Climates," PhD dissertation. London: The AA Graduate School, 1990.

4 Ken Butti and John Perlin, *A Golden Thread: 2500 Years of Solar Architecture and Technology*. Palo Alto: Cheshire Books, 1980.

5 Edmund N. Bacon, *Design of Cities*. New York: The Viking Press, 1967.

6 Paul Oliver, *Dwellings: The House Across the World*. Austin, TX: University of Texas Press, 1987.

7 Marcus Vitruvius Pollio, *The Ten Books on Architecture*, edited by Herbert Langford Warren and Morris Hicky Morgan. Whitefish, MT: Kessinger Publishing, 2010.

8 J. Owen Lewis, *A Green Vitruvius: Principles and Practice of Sustainable Architectural Design*. London: Routledge Publishing, 2011.

9 William J. Curtis, *Contemporary Architecture Since 1900*, Third Edition. London: Phaidon Press Ltd., 1996.

10 Charles Jencks, *Le Corbusier and the Continual Revolution in Architecture*. New York: The Monacelli Press, 2000.

11 J.M. Richards, Ismail Serageldin and Darl Rastorfer, *Hassan Fathy*. London: A Mimar Book, 1985.

12 Malcolm Quantrill, *Alvar Aalto: A Critical Study*. Amsterdam: New Amsterdam Books, 1990.

13 E.F. Schumacher, *Small is Beautiful: Economics As If People Mattered*. London: Blond & Briggs Publishers, 1973.

14 Henry-Russell Hitchcock, *In the Nature of Materials: 1887–1941 The Buildings of Frank Lloyd Wright*. New York: Duell, Sloan and Pearce, 1942.

15 Constantinos Doxiadis, *Ekistics: An Introduction to the Science of Human Settlements*. London: Hutchinson & Co., 1968.

16 William Curtis, *Contemporary Architecture Since 1900*, Third Edition. London: Phaidon Press Ltd., 1996.

17 Kate Nesbitt, *Theorizing A New Agenda for Architecture: An Anthology of Architectural Theory*. Princeton: Princeton Architectural Press, 1996.

18 Carl Stein, *Greening Modernism*. New York: W.W. Norton and Company, 2010.

19 Aleya Abdel-Hadi, Mostaft K. Tolba and Salah Soliman, *Environment, Health, and Sustainable Development*. Boston, MA: Hogrefe Publishing, 2010.

20 James Marston Fitch, *American Building: The Historical Forces that Shaped it*, Revised Edition. New York: Oxford University Press USA, 1999.

21 The Prototype Neighborhood was designed to provide neighborhood-appropriate non-residential functions including a small grocery store, bank, Internet café, daycare center and central gathering space. Housing typologies varied with higher density housing closer to the neighborhood center, which included flats, townhomes, semi-detached and single-family detached housing types.

22 Susan Owens put forward the idea that certain structural variables existing at various scales, such as settlement shape, interspersion of activities, density of built form, clustering of trip ends, building siting, orientation and landscape, would affect travel requirements and building loads. Susan Owens, *Energy Planning and Urban Design*. London: Pion Press, 1985.

23 Patrick M. Condon, *Seven Rules for Sustainable Communities: Design Strategies for the Post-Carbon World*. Washington DC: Island Press, 2010.

24 Nan Ellin, *Integral Urbanism*. London: Routledge, 2006.

25 David Grahame Shane, *Recombinant Urbanism: Conceptual Modeling in Architecture, Urban Design, and City Theory*. London: John Wiley & Sons, 2005.

26 Ken Yeang, *Designing with Nature, the Ecological Basis for Architectural Design*. New York: McGraw-Hill Book Company, 1995.

27 Timothy Beatley, *Green Urbanism: Learning from European Cities*. Washington DC: Island Press, 2000.

28 Phillip Tabb, "Placemaking as a Sustainable Planning Strategy: Serenbe Community," The 8th International Housing Symposium on The Urban Regeneration and Sustainability. Seoul, Korea, February 2009.

29 Kenneth Frampton, "Toward a Critical Regionalism: Six Points for an Architecture of Resistance," *The Anti-Aesthetic: Essays on Postmodern Culture*, edited by Hal Foster. Port Townsend, Washington: Bay Press, 1983: 26–7.

30 William McDonough and Michael Braungart, *Cradle to Cradle: Remaking the Way We Make Things*. New York: North Point Press, 2002.

31 Paul Hawken, "Preface" to *Sustainable Architecture White Papers*. New York: Earth Pledge Foundation Series on Sustainable Development, 2000.

32 James Wines, *Green Architecture*. Köln, Germany: Taschen, 2000.
33 Abraham Maslow, "A Theory of Human Motivation," *Psychological Review*, 50: 70–96. Washington DC, 1943.

Chapter 2
1960s: An Environmental Awakening

Phillip Tabb

The failure of our society to recognize the severity or, in many cases, even the legitimacy of the environmental crisis allowed architects to conduct their work with minimal attention to the potentially catastrophic effects resulting from this work.[1]

The earliest beginnings in the greening of architecture were created out of necessity for survival for water, food, fuel, defense and shelter with direct and pragmatic architectural responses to regional climatic conditions. Survival and architecture were simultaneously considered. In the 20th century, design responses to the environment were explored by a few of the influential architects, Frank Lloyd Wright, Le Corbusier, Alvar Aalto, Louis Kahn, Charles Rennie Mackintosh, and Hassan Fathy to name a few, as they inspired and established an important linage for the formative phases of the Green Movement in architecture. In the 1960s the powerful desire for attainment of the *American Dream* served to accommodate the housing of a growing middle class and provided modern environments for expanding commerce and industrial manufacturing. While the majority of building occurred in pursuit of this dream, a number of visionary and countercultural architectural and planning projects emerged while mainstream modernist architecture evolved without concern for environmental issues. However, the main thrust of the greening process did not emerge until after the negative impacts of modern life upon the environment were initially exposed and made public.

There were only scattered architectural responses to an increasing awareness of sustainable design. The publications of Rachel Carson, E.F. Schumacher, Howard T. Odum, Victor Olgyay and Ian McHarg strengthened the bridge between a growing awareness of the importance of bioclimatic design, the natural environment, and ecological zones with architectural design and planning. The architectural responses that surfaced at this time, tended toward dramatic and often idealistic visions of a new kind of environmentalism, such as examples by Ralph Erskine, R. Buckminster Fuller, and Paolo Soleri, with propositions of new urban forms and technologies. Other propositions of design, such as the works of Archigram, Ant Farm, SITE, and Superstudio, surfaced as well, but for the mainstream, they were considered far too radical. The greening of architecture was a slow evolving process that was distanced from the mainstream consumptive impetus toward "progress" and the powerful modern movement in architecture that enabled it.

A spiritual dimension to the greening of architecture surfaced with sensitivity to indigenous cultures' ideas of a living Earth, especially with Hopi Native American sacred concepts of stewardship of the land, reverence, connectedness to nature and wholeness. The term *Hopi* means "The Peaceful People," where there was no separation of the religious life from all other activities of the Hopi. Other sacred and philosophical teachings were also influential in expanding the environmental movement, including those of Plato, Vitruvius, Henry David Thoreau, Georges Ivanovic Gurdjieff and Rudolf Steiner, and practices related to Western geomancy, Vastu Shastra, and Feng Shui. Meanwhile, the primary thrust of mainstream architecture followed along more profane modernist lines of functionalism and inducements to consume. They developed in myopic and unconscionable ways that ignored the early warning signs, which later would fuel a contagious greening process in architecture. What evolved was an opportunistic architecture of convenience and expedience with little regard for the environment or the emergent sacred sensitivities. However, some important seeds had been planted in the 1960s that would eventually attach to the American Dream and help contribute to an expanding greening process.

THE AMERICAN DREAM

The *American Dream* was a national ethos of the United States in which freedom included the opportunity for prosperity and success. In the definition of the American Dream by James Truslow Adams in 1931, "life should be better and richer and fuller for everyone, with opportunity for each according to ability or achievement regardless of social class or circumstances of birth."[2] After World War Two in the 1950s and 1960s there was a remarkable period of growth, prosperity and development that contributed to a cohesive American experience and expression of this American Dream. During the 1960s the United States experienced its longest uninterrupted period of economic expansion in history. Credited as being "*a consumer culture,*" this floodgate of prosperity included the sense of a positive future, increased home ownership, equal access to goods and services, the freedom of choice, and the creation of an automobile culture that allowed for greater individual mobility and self-expression. Low-density and single-use development, separation of uses through functional zoning, single-family detached housing typology, automobile dependent spatial structures, and predominate use of fossil fuels for electricity production and transportation characterized the organization for this post war suburban landscape.

The dream was in part a function of who was defining it. The early founders of America saw the dream as everyone's "unalienable rights" to possessing a certain quality of life, with guaranteed liberties and opportunities for success and happiness. The feminist movement of the 19th and 20th centuries focused on overcoming suffrage and cultural and political inequalities. For many associated with the post-WWII middle class, the American Dream included the opportunity for one's children to grow up and receive a good education and career opportunities without artificial barriers. In the 1960s, Dr. Martin Luther King, Jr. dreamed of a racial equality. As America expanded, there was the propensity for a consumer's dream of material plenty, quickly getting rich, and where "more was seen to be better." Consequently, there was a marked difference between the original ethos and intentions of the equality of opportunity according to one's abilities or achievement versus the contemporary sense of a presumed entitlement with deserving guarantee of access to the benefits and prosperity of previous generations.

The home was a central image and component of the American Dream. A decent house was a symbol and measure of a successful middle class. It was considered a safe store for increasing value and a secure haven for family life. The average American home has doubled in size since the middle of the 20th century. In 1950 the average house size was 950 square feet (88 square meters), by 1970 it grew to 1,500 square feet (139 square meters), in 1990 it was a little over 2,000 square feet (186 square meters) and in the 2000s it is around 2,350 square feet (218 square meters). This phenomenon was explained by the increase of family sizes, the need for up-sizing domestic spaces, including living and dining, bedrooms and bathrooms, and the rise in family income. The home became more than a simple place of shelter and was adorned with new technologies and equipment, including central heating and air conditioning, automatic washing machines and dryers, larger refrigerators and freezers, television and the telephone, which connected each home to one another and the outside world. Today, of course, the smart home is a computer, home theater and the housing of multiple automobiles.

2.1   The American Dream a) American Home b) The Neighborhood c) 1960 Cadillac d) Enabling Highways e) Agricultural Land. All images courtesy "Shutterstock"

Along similar lines was the evolution of the American automobile, which eventually found a prominent place "inside the home." Attached storage of automobiles had grown from outside parking to carports, to one-car garages and eventually to more than three internal parking places. Throughout the 1960s, the size of the American automobile also increased in size replete with its V-8 engine, four doors, large storage truck, expansive rear "tail-lights," and insatiable thirst for gasoline. This was a time dominated by family station wagons and muscle cars. Individual land ownership was equally important to the American Dream. Suburban housing plots correspondingly increased in size where the single-family "detached" house sat in the middle of a residential land plot between a quarter acre and 35 acres (0.1 to 14 hectares). The accumulation of these expressions of progress contributed to a growing increase in consumption, occupation of land, energy usage and creation of waste.

The American Dream was followed in similar ways in Western Europe, Russian Federation, Middle East, and now in the Far East. It became a process of entitlement and a bourgeois model of ownership gained through prosperity and economic success. While the dream was an affirmation of progress, it took on different nationalistic forms, in which the common denominator appeared to be accelerated modernity, an increase in wealth and consumerism, proliferation new technologies and industrialization, shiny new architecture, and the need for vast amounts of energy, often producing devastating effects on the environment. At this scale the dream transformed and shifted to national and cultural survival objectives with access to vast amounts global resources in order to build and sustain a future world; and it triggered what Fareed Zakaria called: "the rise of the rest."

EARLY WARNINGS

In the 1960s a growing awareness of the deleterious effects that contemporary life had on the environment became more present. Rachel Carson's *Silent Spring* (1962) was a startling wake-up call.[3] This work was credited with helping launch the environmental movement. Carson, a marine biologist, documented damage caused on the environment by the aerial spraying of pesticides to kill mosquitoes. She focused on the example of birds, whose populations had dwindled as a result of damage caused to their eggshells by exposure to DDT. Unlike most pesticides, whose effectiveness was limited to destroying one or two species of insects, DDT, developed in 1939, was capable of killing hundreds of different kinds at once. Widespread use, she argued, harmed many other animals as well as humans. She also attacked the chemical industry for the spreading of disinformation about the negative effects of pesticides. The title of the book was a call to bring back the singing of birds in springtime.

Ralph Nader came to prominence where he claimed that many American automobiles were unsafe. In 1965 with the publication of his book, *Unsafe at Any Speed*, it was a critique of the safety record of American automobile manufacturers in general, and most famously the Chevrolet Corvair.[4] He pointed out the resistance by automobile manufacturers to provide safety features, such as seat belts, and other measures that would protect public safety. Nader's advocacy of automobile safety and the publicity generated by his book, along with concern over escalating nationwide traffic fatalities (47,089 US fatalities in 1965), contributed to the unanimous passage of the 1966 National Traffic and Motor Vehicle Safety Act. The federal government set and regulated new standards including mandatory provision of headrests, energy-absorbing steering wheels, shatter-resistant windshields, and seat belts. Road environments were also improved with better curve delineation, centerline strips and reflectors, improved illumination and the addition of guardrails.

Limits to Growth (1972) was another poignant warning that the growing world population was reaching the limits to its carrying capacity of finite planetary resource supplies.[5] It was a pioneering report modeling the interactions and consequences between the natural and human-made systems. The pattern of exponential growth was analyzed using five variables: world population, industrialization, pollution, food production and resource depletion. While generally dismissed by critics as a doomsday prophecy, it did reaffirm the dynamic interactions among important finite environmental factors and brought awareness to the behavior of societal growth. The concept of a "carrying capacity" suggested that there was a maximum population and pattern of resource use of food, water, energy and other necessities available in the environment. This included the managing of wastes and consideration of sanitation and health. Eugene Odum performed pioneering work in ecosystem ecology, and together with his brother Howard Odum, wrote *Fundamentals of Ecology* (1953), considered the first textbook on ecology. Howard Odum saw a living Earth as interlaced ecosystems, and performed work on the General Systems Theory developed by Ludwig von Bertalanffy in 1928, and related it to ecology. This work had a profound effect upon environmental, non-linear thinking that later was to become an informing dimension to green architecture.

The obsession for larger buildings in cities and lower densities in suburbs in the United States after World War Two exacerbated the problem with increasing demands on land, infrastructure, transportation networks, building construction resources, and energy. The average American home more than doubled in size since the 1950s. The preference for the single-family detached residence type also contributed to sprawl. E.F. Schumacher's *Small is Beautiful* (1973) challenged this version of the American Dream of a larger home and suggested, "less can be more."[6] Schumacher believed in human scale, and that self-imposed limitations and small, appropriate technologies would be empowering choice for people. For the emerging green approaches to architecture, it was clear that *size* mattered—the larger the building, the greater the energy requirement. Writer Jane Jacobs's *The Death and Life of Great American Cities* (1961), was a powerful critique of urban renewal policies, expressways, and suburbs that were destroying existing communities, neighborhoods and street life.[7] She promoted grass-roots, organic neighborhood processes, mixes of use, short walkable blocks, density and a diversity of building types and ages.

According to economist Daniel Yergin in his book, *The Quest* (2011), electricity underpinned modern culture, where one only needed to flip a switch for instant energy.[8] Electricity was not a primary source of energy, but one that was generated from other sources, like coal, river or wind power. Yergin went on to ask what would not work without electricity? The answer would include refrigerators, air-conditioning, interior lighting, televisions, hospital operating theaters, and elevators to name a few. It was in the 1950s and 1960s that America became an electric society with rising marriages, birth rates and the G.I. Bill that enabled veterans to purchase homes. The 1950 all-electric home, now located in the Johnson County Museum of History, Kansas, included heating systems, ranges and ovens, kitchen appliances, artificial lighting, built-in television and other electrical devices. The emergence of the electric home conveniently disconnected it from the resources that enabled it.

The OPEC Oil Embargo of 1973 added another complication that prompted an increase in awareness of the United States' dependence upon foreign energy. In 2006, former Vice President Al Gore brought these issues to public attention more vividly through his impressive documentary *An Inconvenient Truth*,⁹ consequently, raising public awareness of environmental degradation, climate change, depletion of renewable resources, increasing global population, and the critical relationship between the natural and built environments. According to the US National Climate Data Center, the summer of 2010 recorded the highest global temperatures on record. Scientists agreed that these increased temperatures were created by trapped solar radiation due to rising anthropogenic greenhouse gasses, especially carbon dioxide, which was generated mainly through the burning of fossil fuels within the building, power and transportation sectors. This became to be known as the "global greenhouse effect." By the 1973 Oil Embargo, it was not only the artificial petroleum shortages that initiated the energy crisis, but also the over increasing urban growth that exceeded utility districts' ability to meet the increasing demands.

The common definition for pollution is the introduction of contaminants into the environment, both natural and human-made, that cause disease, harm, instability and destruction. Pollutants usually affect the elemental substances that include the earth, water and air, and can manifest in the very places we live—our homes, schools and places of work. The very materials used to construct buildings can also be highly toxic. Friable asbestos-containing materials, for example, were used as an insulating material extensively prior to the 1970s. When disturbed asbestos crumbled into a dust of microscopic fibers, it could remain in the air for long periods of time. If inhaled, they posed a serious health threat as asbestos fibers could become permanently lodged in body tissues and could eventually lead to cancer. Many other construction materials have subsequently been found to be harmful, and are no longer used.

The classical elements, and the phases of matter they express, became an important part of environmental conservation. In ancient Greece there were four elements, Fire, Water, Earth and Air, and sometimes included a fifth element Ether, and they possessed qualities that were considered either healthy, or they were detrimental to life. On both local levels and on a planetary scale, these elements are being polluted as illustrated in Figures 2.2a–d. Emissions from fossil fuel plants have a serious impact on the environment. Not only are the combustion gases toxic at the site of the fire, but during a fire, very large quantities of particulates are also released into the environment. The particles consist, among others, of soot, tar, unburned materials, and inorganic debris. Burning coal was a leading cause of smog, acid rain, global warming, and air toxics. Nuclear power plants generated waste heat energy, which was a form of energy pollution, and radioactive wastes. While radiation leaks were rare, there have been some small leaks and even a few larger ones, most notably the Three Mile Island core Reactor Two meltdown in 1979 in the United States and the Chernobyl disaster of 1986 in the former Soviet Union. The Laguna Beach, Michigan Fermi fast breeder nuclear power plant was closed in 1966 because of a near catastrophic loss of coolant. Plutonium was one of the waste by-products of nuclear fission and has a half-life of 24,000 years. Questions of where this waste is finally deposited and the effects upon the storage sites still remain. Because uranium and plutonium were weapons-grade materials, there have been proliferation concerns for their use for terrorist attacks. There was more than 350,000 cubic feet of high-level nuclear waste generated each year worldwide. In 1963 the Nuclear Test Ban Treaty between US and the former Soviet Union stopped above ground, water and outer space tests of nuclear weapons. However, underground testing was permitted. The most recent nuclear test was conducted by North Korea, which occurred in 2009.

2.2 Environmental Signs a) Spraying Pesticides b) Water Pollution c) Coal Plant Pollution d) Nuclear Plant. All images courtesy "Shutterstock"

Water pollution derives from two general sources: direct and indirect contaminants. Direct sources included effluent outfalls from factories, refineries, waste treatment and power plants that emit fluids of varying quality directly into urban water supplies. Indirect sources included contaminants that enter the water supply from soils/groundwater systems and from the atmosphere via rainwater. Soils and groundwater contained the residue of agricultural practices, including fertilizers, pesticides, and improperly disposed of industrial wastes. The effects of water pollution were varied and included poisonous drinking water and poisonous food animals due to these organisms having bio-accumulated toxins from the environment over their life spans as revealed by Rachel Carson in *Silent Spring*. Unbalanced river and lake ecosystems were often no longer able to support full biological diversity. Deforestation from acid rain and many other effects occurred. Water tables were slowly shrinking as consumption was surpassing normal renewable hydrologic cycles. In 1965 the US Congress passed the Water Quality Act, Noise Control Act and the Solid Waste Disposal Act setting standards for all states. And in 1968 Congress passed the Wild and Scenic Rivers Act and National Trails System Act.

A primary source of air pollution was the combustion of gasoline and other hydrocarbon fuels in automobiles, trucks, and jet airplanes, which all produced several primary pollutants: nitrogen oxides, gaseous hydrocarbons, carbon dioxide, and carbon monoxide, as well as large quantities of particulates, chiefly lead. Smog hanging over cities was the most familiar and obvious form of air pollution. Indoor air quality and urban air pollution were listed as two of the world's worst pollution problems. Key contaminants were sulfur oxides (SO_x), nitrogen oxides (NO_x), carbon monoxide (CO), volatile organic compounds (VOC's), carbon dioxide (CO_2), and fine particles. Ozone (O_3) was also problematic in trapping atmospheric heat. The primary cause of human-made external air pollution was the burning of fossil fuels. And the principle causes of indoor air pollution and sick building syndrome were chemical toxins from common household products, out-gassing from building materials, combustion gasses from heating and kitchen appliances, smoking, and radon gas from the surrounding ground. As a consequence, in 1960 that the First Clean Air Act was passed in the US Congress.

In the United States millions of tons of household and other municipal solid waste were placed in disposal sites annually. Soil contamination was caused by the presence of xenobiotic (human-made) chemicals or other alteration in the natural soil environment. The types of contamination or earth pollution typically arose from failure due to corrosion of underground storage tanks or of the piping associated with them, historical disposal of coal ash, application of pesticides, percolation of contaminated surface water to subsurface strata, oil and fuel dumping, leaching of wastes from landfills or direct discharge of industrial wastes to the soil. Large-scale agriculture and industrial incursions began to reduce the soil's restorative function, and the clearing of tropical rainforests, due primarily to cattle ranching, contributed to loss of species' habitat and global warming caused by disruption of the natural hydrology cycle. In the late 1960s, then President Richard Nixon established the US Environmental Protection Agency to lead in the war on pollution, following a decade of awareness and reflection of the environmental effects of modernity.

SOCIAL SUSTAINABILITY

Social sustainability focused on individual and group behaviors, attitudes and actions, and developed from seeds of the social upheaval of the 1960s. The rising tide of political frustration culminated in the 1968 student riots in Chicago, Paris and copycat protests in London, Tokyo and Prague. There were growing concerns about the validity of the Vietnam War. Women formed fledgling feminist movements such as the Women's Liberation Front in the US and Mouvement de Libération des Femmes in France. Between 1955 and 1968, acts of nonviolent protest and civil disobedience produced crisis situations between activists and government authorities. Federal, state, and local governments, businesses, and communities often had to respond to the inequities faced by African Americans. Decades of oppression against gay men and women erupted in a pitched battle in New York, when the police tried to close the Stonewall, a gay bar in the West Village and a politicized gay rights movement exploded.

A socially sustainable way of living was not necessarily providing luxury and wealth as defined by contemporary versions of the American Dream, but rather, it supported the development of reverse-consumerism and a behavioral dimension to environmentalism. This was not to say that consumption was wrong, but rather that consumption should be practiced responsibly.

In common with environmental sustainability, social sustainability was the intra-generational idea that future generations should have the same or even greater access to social resources as the current generation, while there should also be equal access to social resources within the current generation. Issues related to social sustainability included equity, diversity, access to resources, interconnectedness, quality of life, stewardship and accountability. Social sustainability also supported more inclusive community participation of planning and design and governance processes. Any discussion of social sustainability must include the physical design of the place, the culture for which it is intended and the economic system that supports it. President Lyndon B. Johnson promoted the Great Society social reforms whose two main goals were the elimination of poverty and racial injustice.

Key to the function of a socially sustainable environment was that the physical and cultural context responded to meeting basic needs for shelter, food, education, and work, and that the benefits of development were equably distributed. It ensured that historic, cultural and the ecological heritages were preserved and strengthened. It was the "soft" infrastructure that was integral to a community's health, safety and ability to achieve and maintain sustainable living. Pro-environmental behavior was instrumental in realizing sustainable actions; according to Christopher Clark, Matthew and Michael Moore, there were two overarching motivations for changes. The first was external socio-economic theory that suggested that external influences, such as income, price and socio-economic characteristics influenced behavior. The second was more psychological where beliefs, values and attitudes directed certain actions in which individual behavior generated collective benefits.[10]

The physical environment (hardware) and the social behavioral systems (software) were inextricably linked and mutually informed one another. This tandem functioned where sustainable intentions and shifts in behavior influenced the development of green architectural forms and associated technologies and vice versa. Conversely, new spatial structures and technologies suggested specific behavioral responses. For example, in 1966, there were 168 reported deaths in New York City by pollution aggravated by an inversion. Some of the more environmentally informed public rejected the muscle, large passenger and luxury cars; instead they were interested in smaller automobiles with much higher gas mileage. The American automobile industry responded with the Nash Metropolitan, Corvair Monza, Pontiac Tempest, Ford Falcon and Buick Special to name a few. The influx of smaller foreign cars, most notably the Volkswagen Beetle and Morris Mini-Minor, provided the American public with an alternative to the predominantly larger gas-guzzling vehicles. However, the prevailing choice still remained with the larger pony cars and family automobiles. During this time, the most popular cars were the 1965 Chevrolet Impala and 1964 Ford Mustang.

Food security, production and consumption were a dimension of social sustainability. This included the need for sufficient supplies of food, ecosystem resilience, availability to resident populations and the quality of agriculture itself. Mono-crop agricultural production, pollution from local industries, and the use of pesticides resulted in reduction of diversity and nutritional quality. Post-WWII United States food production and consumption patterns changed from previous generations. Household freezers allowed for greater volumes of frozen foods, and there was a proliferation of canned and packaged goods made for convenient use and rapid preparation. Space exploration also influenced food products, exemplified by Tang. Larger grocery and convenience stores chains were slowly replacing traditional corner grocery stores. These food consumptive patterns were echoed by an evolving lifestyle that was more responsive to a faster pace and instant gratification.

Other similar sustainable couplings included the relationship between changing consumer behavior and recycling, which occurred during World War One and World War Two. The war efforts demanded much of the resources, leaving little for the home front. Some items (e.g. metal, rubber and even certain food items) had to be rationed, as they were needed overseas at the warfront. It became necessary for most homes to recycle their waste, as recycling offered an extra source of materials. Gary Anderson designed the universal recycling symbol in the form of a Mobius strip in the late 1960s, after a Chicago-based recycled-container company sponsored an art contest to raise environmental awareness. Examples of other forms of sustainable behavior in the 1960s included recycling milk bottles, Lady Bird Johnson's beautification campaign for reviving recycling initiatives, Earth Day on April 22, 1970 pioneered by John McConnell at a UNESCO Conference in San Francisco, the increasing use of storm windows for houses, Target's early recycling of cardboard, and a political awareness that grew from anti-war sentiment by the decade's end.

PLANNING AND DESIGN RESPONSES

The scholarly publications of Victor Olgyay and Ian McHarg brought attention to the importance of environmental considerations to planning and design. Together with the work of James Marston Fitch, the relationship between human comfort and the changing climatic conditions were emphasized. Victor Olgyay was one of the early theoreticians to propose a bioclimatic approach to architecture. His book, *Design with Climate* (1963) was influential in architectural education throughout the 1960s and 1970s.[11] His suggestions, that climatic factors, such as solar radiation, variations in temperature, precipitation, wind and humidity, and on-site resources could be related to comfort and utilized through appropriate regional designs, were important green principles. Four generalized climate zones, which included the cold, temperate, hot-humid and hot-arid zones, were identified with specific characteristics and recommended conceptualized design approaches. The physical form responses involved building siting and orientation, utilization of natural ventilation, plan aspect ratios relative to the predominant southern sun, degrees of simplicity and complexity, and material selections. For example, in colder climates the recommended plan aspect and overall form was square and cubical respectively in order to reduce surface area and resulting heat loss. As the climate zones moved to warmer and hotter regions, the building plan aspects were elongated and fragmented to take advantage of cooling breezes-the dogtrot effect. Olgyay also focused on solar geometry, the annual and diurnal sunpaths and analytical methods of providing shading and solar control, especially for roofs, south, east and west facades. These principles were applied to both building and settlement scales. Amos Rapoport's book, *House Form and Culture* (1969), also expressed the idea of climate as a form-generating force in design and methods for modulating climatic effects.[12]

Ian McHarg's philosophies and works became renowned for their relationship between regional planning and natural ecological systems through integral and regenerative ecological layers coexisting with morphological land use patterns and cluster developments. His book, *Design with Nature* (1969), was an influential work that promoted the intertwined worlds of local natural and human-made environments.[13] He promoted the idea that human development should be derived from the ecological framework within which it exists.

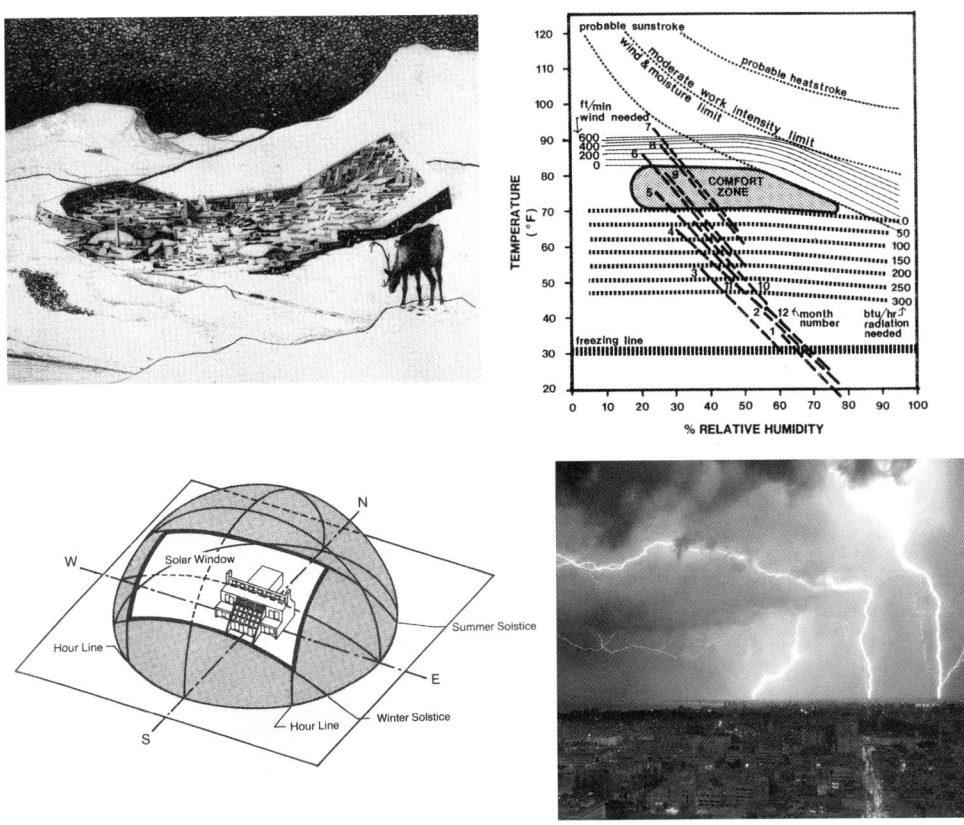

2.3 Bio-climatic Planning and Design a) Arctic City (courtesy "Shutterstock") b) Comfort Zone c) Solar Window d) Lightning Storm (courtesy "Shutterstock")

McHarg studied ecological transects and developed a typological layering system that identified distinct natural preservation zones and acceptable development areas. He was interested in the design issues that spanned from garden to regional planning. Given the context of the 1960s, he viewed the automobile as a permanent fixture, and discussed how highways could be better situated in the landscape, not eliminated or scaled back. This was an acceptable proposition given the propensity for automobile use in the United States.

The elemental and ambient environmental forces became potential form-givers as illustrated in Ralph Erskine's boreal climate image of *Arctic City* with its compact urban form, southern aspect with response to the low winter's sun and protective boundary and wind-excluding devices responding to the severe Sub Arctic climate. In the design of his Svappavaara Housing Block in northern Sweden (1961), Erskine first realized the idea of a deflecting roof and block of flats as a windbreak. Equally dramatic examples exist in extreme hot climates as well, such as the work of Hassan Fathy, who demonstrated appropriate technologies and local materials for building in Egypt. Response to climatic conditions, public health considerations, affordability, maintaining cultural values, and ancient craft skills also affected his design decisions. He utilized ancient design methods and traditional materials, and integrated a wide knowledge of ancient architectural and town design techniques. Figures 2.3b and c illustrate Olgyay's comfort zone and the solar window, a temporal space formed by the solstice movements, top and bottom, and the hour curves of 9am and 3pm.

The effectiveness of green architecture depended upon the balance of on-site energy sources with building energy conservation. The more "conservative" the building, which included the envelope, insulation levels and the tightness of construction, the easier it was to match essential energy loads to the availability of on-site resources. The design mantra was "conservation first!" In colder climates, construction was focused on solar energy gain, heat retention using higher insulation values and double-glazing, and even movable insulation. In warmer climates attention was given to the solar control of the envelope, especially roofs and western facades, as well as to natural ventilation and daylighting. In hot-dry climates evaporative cooling was employed. Conservation conscious design was in sharp contrast to previous modernist tendencies of spatial generosity, complexity of form, expansive glazing areas, and reliance on abundant fossil fuels and mechanical systems for heating, cooling, dehumidification and ventilation.

Aldo van Eyck, who was a member of C.I.A.M. and a cofounder of Team Ten, evolved ideas, projects and works of architecture that were critical of the post-war prevailing preoccupation with functionalism and reductionist architecture.[14] He focused on authenticity, humanism and a meaningful architectural language. His ideas, such as, identity, reciprocity, twin-phenomena and the realm of the "in-between," place and occasion, opened new insight and later became appropriate corollaries to green architectural agendas.[15] Twin-phenomena, for example, suggested that a single architectural gesture or formal action could in fact serve to perform multiple functions simultaneously. This is important to green architecture as this concept of duality of function was most likely efficient and resource conserving. For example, a brize-soleil could serve to function as a definition for circulation, for solar protection and as a structural system. He considered the correspondence of the leaf and tree as similar to that of the house and city. This was to imply the simultaneous presence of part and whole, which was another important canon of green architecture. While part and whole are related and co-exist, the sustainable measures they require can be quite different.

Susan Owens in her book, *Energy, Planning and Urban Design* (1985), posited that different sustainable measures operated at differing scales of development.[16] Owens went on to say that it was the combination of spatial factors and sustainable mechanisms that produced the greatest savings. These included measures important to a region, settlement, neighborhood and building site. The researches of McHarg, Fitch, Olgyay and Rapoport connected planning and design to objective considerations of the environment and comfort, and especially to the importance of the response to solar control. Van Eyck's observation was important in developing a more comprehensive approach to sustainability that crossed architecture, planning and the natural environment.

VISIONARY BEGINNINGS

Architectural responses to the early warnings of the environmental problems tended to occur in isolated places at the fringe of cities, out of sight, often on cheap land or in undesirable places. Also, there was a great deal of work performed through conceptual propositions designed to challenge current architectural practice. Experimentations were better explored outside of normal contexts because they represented rather unusual and sometimes contextually inappropriate designs, or they were theoretical constructs oriented toward publications to provoke changes in architectural thinking. However, the works that emerged found ways in which to influence the status quo, such as the on-going constructions of Arcosanti in Arizona and the designs of Archigram in Britain and the conceptions of Superstudio in Florence. Often these works derived from multiple agendas that included social reforms, conservation and preservation, environmentalism, and new technologies.

The utopian vision of Paolo Soleri contributed to his life-long commitment at Arcosanti in the high desert of central Arizona. Planned for 5,000 residents, Arcosanti began construction in 1970 and embodied Soleri's philosophy blending architecture and ecology, or the portmanteau he called "arcology." Soleri's vision was for the design of an urban environment within a rural setting promoting social interaction, density, accessibility, use of on-site resources and heavy mass construction, reduction of waste, and access to the surrounding natural environment. The designs promoted large-scale responses to the harsh desert climate and were constructed with tilt-up concrete panels colored and textured to blend with the surrounding landscape. Steve Baer, inspired by Fuller and Drop City, formed Zomeworks and began building polyhedral structures, which incorporated both active and passive solar energy utilization techniques as pictured in Figure 2.4c.

In contrast, the architectural visions of Archigram, initially formed at the Architectural Association in London by Peter Cook, Warren Chalk, Ron Herron, Dennis Crompton, Michael Webb and David Greene, were not essentially ecological in nature, but championed the high-tech, "survival technology," and lightweight approach towards a modular technology within the urban setting. Their urban projects created in 1964, including Plug-in-City, Instant City, Walking City, and Tuned City, were bold propositions intended to inspire and provoke, and in some ways these early designs represented creative, innovative, and impermanent works. Archigram influenced high-tech works, such as the Pompidou Centre in Paris (1971) by Rogers and Piano, the Spacelab in Graz, Austria (2000) designed by Peter Cook and Colin Fournier, and later the eco-technology of the 1990s, and was an impetus for the megastructure movement. Their works offered a seductive conceptual vision of a glamorous future machine age; however, social and sustainable issues were left largely unaddressed.

Superstudio was founded in Florence, Italy, by Adolfo Natalini and Cristiano Toraldo di Francia, in the mid-1960s and produced powerful conceptions of what they called a: "tecnomorphic" architecture and a technocratic optimism. They were concerned with the disillusionment of the modernist ideals that had dominated architectural and design thinking since the early 1900s. Their attack on the preoccupation with luxurious objects and rampant consumerism led to a different kind of architecture, hidden and characterized with their endless continuous grid environments and minimalist furniture.

2.4 Visionary Beginnings a) Archigram NYC (© 1964 By Ron Herron courtesy of the Ron Herron Archive) b) Arcosanti, Arizona (Consanti Foundation) c) Baer House (courtesy Jack Futon)

For them this image illustrated a kind of democratic human experience where every point on the grid was identical and therefore accessible by all. Their connection to sustainability was subtle. According to William Minking, "a lot of the work, because they weren't in a position to build, was created for magazines."[17] However, the work was visually compelling and thought provoking.

The utopian impetus extended beyond secular and monumental visions of green architecture to include concepts of sacred architecture and placemaking, which had complementary objectives with it. The term "sacred" was as difficult to define as sustainability in that it had so many connotations and connections to the myriad of religious institutions, interpretations and meanings. More secular definitions of the sacred referred to concepts of unity, reverence, respect and importance of the land, and could be applied to any place or building type. The associations with sustainability were obvious. It was not a coincidence that with the dawning of a new solar movement in the early 1970s, that the sun and solar energy became an inspiration for a renewed form of sacredness. As an energy source, it was a clean, safe and accessible to everyone. The research of David Sailes revealed concepts related to sacredness, such as location, siting and construction of dwellings and sacred ceremonial spaces. Sailes spoke of three common cosmic levels within which house and village dwell—an upper or spiritual level (realm of sun, sky, clouds and eagles), the lower underworld level (lakes, springs and spirits of the dead), and an earthly level (living place) that exists in-between. These correlate architecturally with a building's roof, foundations and spaces respectively (termination, base, and shaft).

> "The world has an upper spirit level, with super-natural beings or power associated with the sun, sky, clouds, eagles and other birds. There is a lower spirit level, the underworld, home of the spirits of ancestors, and with supernatural being associated with lakes, springs, caves and some burrowing animals. The earth lies between these two levels and is where people live."[18]

The Chinese use of Feng Shui, literally meaning, "wind-water" was a system of auspicious placement of buildings relative to a site's physical and energetic features, such as, bodies of water, hills or mountains, slope of the land, orientation to compass points or geomagnetic currents in the ground called "dragon lines." Feng Shui was certainly not a new concept as it had been practiced as early as 4000 BC. The principal goal of Feng Shui was to enhance the Ch'i, or life force of a place, thereby improving the health and safety of its inhabitants. In the West it was similarly referred to as geomancy, *genius loci* or the spirit of place. There were generally two schools of Feng Shui—the Compass School (celestial divination), the Form School (terrestrial divination), often used with the Bagua – an eight symbols used in Taoist cosmology to represent the fundamental principles of reality. Each was based on celestial orientation and the natural features of a specific site. Wind, water, rain, fog, sun, and clouds were believed to be the energy of heaven and earth. Gentle winds meant good harvest, and harsh winds destroyed crops, and stagnant waters caused disease, where wild waters were a poor source of food. Gentle waters and lakes were seen as healthy and beneficial. These auspicious or detrimental energies of a site became the basis for planning and design. The concept of *yin* (receptive) and *yang* (creative) formed the basis of the binary system that was central to the formation and practice of Feng Shui.

The Form School, in particular, placed significance upon concepts of wholeness and symbolic programs related with the four cardinal directions that had direct validity for sustainable design. For example, buildings designed with complete whole forms, with symmetry and balance, were seen to be healthier than those with complex, disjunctive fragmentations.

This corresponds with the green agenda for thermally efficient exterior building volumes and forms. Significant numbers, colors, materials and elements were carefully considered in architectural design. Further, associations with the four directions related to sacred sites, were made with animal guardians—the east was associated with the green dragon, the south with the red phoenix, the west with the white tiger, and the north with the black tortoise.[19] Each was symbolic of the nature of the time of day, quality of the season of the year and compass directions. These iconic programs correspond with green planning and design especially in temperate and cold climate regions where there are vast differences in winter and summer weather, and diurnal temperature swings. For example, the Black Turtle has the black, absorptive shell to protect and shed off inclement weather of the north while the Red Phoenix symbolizes skyward flight and the intense heat from the sun.

Western philosophical and esoteric concepts established by Pythagoras, Plato, Vitruvius, Gurdjieff, Steiner, Critchlow, among others, developed archetypal principles that directly related to ideas of wholeness, harmony, health and wellbeing, which resulted in authentic and integral architectural responses. Keith Critchlow observed that "Architecture, as sacred expression, is concerned with the power of levity in the physical, emotional, intellectual, inspirational and ontological realms, always dedicated to raising experience to a more inclusive and comprehensive unity and integrity."[20] French philosopher Gastonia Bachelard argued that there still was a hidden presence of the sacred and that there was not just empty space. Secular sacred architecture, sacred buildings and places that were not purposed specifically for religious functions, were designed for a higher and more integral and inclusive everyday experiences. Examples of these principles can be seen at Findhorn Garden in northern Scotland, and the Jarna community near Stockholm, Sweden. Findhorn was established in the early 1960s by Peter and Eileen Caddy, and grew into a community because of a remarkable garden that was created there. They prepared the ground upon the sandy barren soil of coastal Scotland, planted with care and phenomenal success, and became wonderful stewards of the place that evolved from a garden to a community. The Pantheon in Rome (126 AD) was an extraordinary expression of sacred architecture with its open oculus and dramatic connections to the elemental forces. Today over a million visitors each year are awe-inspired by its intact presence, sheer beauty of form and inspiring quality of light as seen in Figure 2.5b.

2.5 Sacred Places a) Findhorn Garden, Scotland (1963) (image courtesy of Findhorn Foundation) b) Pantheon, Rome c) Jarna Community, Sweden (1968) (courtesy Max Plunger)

Buildings and even settlements were sited with favorable orientation to the southern sun and night zodiac. Jarna was described as a constellation of businesses and social activities, which were all connected to concepts developed by philosopher and architect Rudolf Steiner. At the beginning of the 20th century, Steiner founded a spiritual movement, *Anthroposophy*, as an esoteric philosophy growing out of European transcendentalism and with links to Theosophy.[21] Buildings within the community, shown in Figure 2.5c, were designed by Erik Asmussen using Steiner's principles. The community also employed biodynamic agriculture, composting and created a network of farms using this practice. The roofs, foundations and livable spaces used similar formal patterns and those suggested by Sailes, Critchlow and Steiner. The significance to sustainability occurred in the sensitivity of the masterplan and careful building designs relative to the land. This environment engendered a sense of stewardship and genuine love of the place. Auroville, located in Tamil Nadu, India with more than 2,000 residents and designed by Roger Anger in 1968, was another example of sacred urbanism. The original spiral nebula plan with megastructural forms emanated from the center and the Matrimandir—a sacred mandallic sphere honoring the spiritual leader Mirra Alfassa.[22] The Arts and Craft movement was also a good fit for the emerging green design and projects like Findhorn and Jarna with focus on appropriate natural and healthy materials, regional building techniques, and authentic vernacular architecture with a secular form of sacredness. These works combined with the dramatic examples of Arcosanti, Archigram, and Superstudio made interesting visionary beginnings.

RADICAL ARCHITECTURE

Many of the first green architectural explorations were quite radical. Author Alastair Gordon explained in his essay *True Green: Lessons from 1960s'–70s' Counterculture Architecture* (2008), that a corporate, mechanistic and monumental architecture was being replaced by young architects in search of more popular sources of inspiration—cocoons, anthills, honeycombs, seashells, nests, earth mounds, spaceships, and seedpods.[23] Buildings were constructed out of earth, recycled and scavenged materials and common off-the-shelf building products. Gordon went on to ask, "Are we still waiting for the green version of the Villa Savoie or the Farnsworth House? There is no unity or single direction apparent."

Validating Gordon's observation, the work of R. Buckminster Fuller was innovative and inventive, especially for his shelter designs.[24] Fuller's experiments with the Dymaxion House (1929), geodesic structures, and concepts of structural and material efficiencies led to the development of another important tenet for green architecture—"synergy," which emphasized systems' components relational behavior. Plato saw the spherical form as an ideal representation of the universe; so it was no surprise that the dome became a symbol of perfection and change in the 1960s. The theoretical foundations of Deep Ecology, advocated by Arne Naess (1973), saw an ecological community of inclusive memberships where "everything was connected to everything." This systemic view of part and whole was critical in understanding the scaler complexity of structural design and sustainability as the need for systems that could transcend scales in self-similar and efficient ways.

The 425-acre (171-hectare) Prickly Mountain in Vermont, the vision of David Sellers, proposed design-built experiments that were "improvised into existence," including sustainable constructions. They were anti-establishment inventions of single-family architectural forms:

Euclidian wedges sticking this way and that, cantilevered bridges with nowhere to go, balconies and decks that took maximum advantage of spectacular views, sloping floors, and oddly positioned windows, skylights, and portals. With one residence you walked along a bridge high off the ground and passed a submarine-like hatch to enter the house. A significance of the work was the construction in plywood and other common, off-the-shelf or locally available materials. Most projects were small in scale and took advantage of local site conditions. The design-build pedagogy afforded constant experience of the site and creative and immediate adjustments to the design.

The New York City-based firm SITE, established in 1970, known for its "environmental thinking" as well as, innovative projects, brought forward a philosophy informed by communication systems, the natural sciences and energy technologies. Their work was motivated by the social and political melee of the 1960s and was critical of the stylistic dominance of modernism. They were probably most well known for their work with Best Products Company where portions for the "big-box" façade were precariously peeled away and in their words created "a state of tentativeness and instability," which served as commentary on the shopping center strip and its significance within the suburban environment. The historical significance of these works was clear as they challenged architectural discourse to consider new and more environmentally oriented architectural forms and technologies.

In 1965, a group of art students founded Drop City, a domed commune in southeastern Colorado, on a seven and a half acre (3 hectares) tract of land, which they called a "dropped-in work of art." It was not able to sustain itself, however, and ultimately abandoned in 1977, yet its spontaneous spirit did carry over to other emerging green utopias. Inspired by the work of R. Buckminster Fuller, the community was a collection of eight geodesic domes scattered over a rather desolate land. Drop City had been built using trial and error over a three-year period and by 1966 there were 20 full-time residents. Its random siting was inspired by the impromptu happenings of John Cage and paintings of Robert Rauschenberg. The architecture featured the design efficiency of the dome forms and construction made from panels of recycled automobiles and other scrounged or inexpensive materials. Drop City influenced Steve Baer of Santa Fe, New Mexico and his designs with the zonagon and other polyhedral domes with Zomeworks. Baer mixed the new paradigm of domes with an interest in rudimentary passive solar systems that later dominated the solar architecture of the 1970s. The dome form was self-supporting, nonhierarchical, and embodied a new communal spatial order, and it was the most recognizable symbol of rebellion.[25]

Ant Farm formed by Chip Lord and Doug Michels in 1968 considered their work as being underground architecture with cultural introspection. They promoted pneumatic structures and performed guerilla moments across the United States. Cadillac Ranch (1974), for example seen in Figure 2.6c, was a public installation with a row of 10 used Cadillacs representing a number of iterations of the car's design dating from 1949 to 1963, most notably the birth and death of the defining feature of early Cadillac; the tail fin. The cars were placed in a wheat field nose down into the ground along the famous Route 66. The work was clearly a statement about stimulating alternative thinking and was a critique on the American consumer society and infatuation with the automobile. Works such as Drop City, the installations of Ant Farm and SITE, and the Prickly Mountain creative homes were improvised into existence and often were impermanent and unable to stand the sands of time. Yet they provided a vision and impetus for a free spirit and independence that later prompted interest in alternative energy, organic cuisine, alternative healing, electric cars, and sustainable design, which have become more commonplace and mainstream now.

2.6 Radical Developments a) Drop City, Colorado, Main Domes June, 1969 (© Roberta Price 2004, 2010 All Rights Reserved) b) Prickly Mountain, Vermont (courtesy of David Sellers) c) Cadillac Ranch (Amanda Kooser, courtesy of CNET) d) Endless Grid (courtesy of Superstudio, Florence)

The relationship between the environmental movement and architecture grew as public awareness of the environmental issues and the emergence of new green technologies increased. In 1968, using the most basic of typesetting and page-layout tools, Stewart Brand created the first issue of *The Whole Earth Catalog*.[26] The Catalog's publication coincided with the great wave of experimentalism, convention-breaking, and "do it yourself" attitude associated with the "counterculture." Apple, Inc. co-founder Steve Jobs described it as a conceptual forerunner of the World Wide Web. Despite this early interest in green architecture, Michael Sorkin in an article written for a special issue of *Architectural Record* on the Young Architects in 1972, was critical of what he called Fuller's "fellow adherents," and claimed that the "totem happy dome dwellers, staked out under their geodesic icons in backwoods utopias," would not solve social problems.[27] During the green beginnings, concepts of environmental health, building size, efficiency, conservation, on-site resource utilization, and emerging sustainable technologies did, however, began to influence architectural thinking. The significance of projects like Drop City, Arcosanti, Prickly Mountain and Archigram's imaginary cities, in addition to the environmental literature, were instrumental for the development of the emergent architectural forms in the 1970s that followed, including the widespread and inceptual application of solar technologies.

MAINSTREAMING MODERNISM

Meanwhile, the majority of architectural projects were not designed with sustainable agendas, but rather were created to promote an expanding middle class and the function of a powerful industrial nation. Despite the early successes in the greening of architecture, the prevailing impetus was towards a "business-as-usual" and "entropic" modernism. Domestic populations were expanding, land was cheap and available to develop, and there was a seemingly endless supply of energy. What resulted was what James Kunstler called the development of a "geography of nowhere."[28] Modernist high-rise buildings had become in most instances monolithic, rejecting the concept of a hierarchal varied design vocabulary in favor of a single extrusion from ground level to the top, with no wit or ornament, and they were skinned in opaque glass that no longer revealed the functions and activities inside. The infamous Pruitt-Igoe public housing project in St Louis was designed by Minoru Yamasaki and was first occupied in 1956 and later because of poverty, despair, crime and segregation, it was torn down in 1972. It became a symbol of failure of urban housing and the high-rise housing typology. Nevertheless, the 1960s became an architectural battleground for the canons of "the bigger the better" and "less is more."

Hugh Hardy recalled, that what he called the modern archetypal architectural box or space, evolved through iterative stages during the 1960s. First was this initiating modernist and reductionist box of Mies van der Rohe and Walter Gropius that focused on purity and the mantra "less is more." Second was the repetitious, more complex and articulated box exemplified by Paul Rudolf and Peter Eisenman. Third came the ambiguous box of Robert Venturi and Charles Moore. And fourth was the collision of boxes and smashing of forms into one another, such as the early work of Hardy, Holzman and Pfeiffer, illustrated by the Hadley House in Martha's Vineyard (1967). Each evolution progressed to a greater level of complexity, and visual interest. Unfortunately for the environmental movement, this conceptual design development generally produced greater levels of energy and resource inefficiency—the complexity created an increase in thermal bridging, infiltration and exterior surface areas that meant more building materials and waste, and higher levels of heat gain and/or loss, and consequently the need for more energy that was required in order to compensate.

Robert Venturi's *Complexity and Contradiction in Architecture* (1966) was a seminal work, which criticized corporate modernism and the precious picturesque in architecture. Venturi admonished the legacy of orthodox and derivative Modernist's vocabularies. He characterized modern sculptural and self-absorbed architecture as "ducks," while praising the complex, random billboard-like character of the buildings along the American commercial street as "decorated sheds." Venturi was in favor of architecture steeped in ambiguity, perversity and discontinuity.[29] According to Venturi, "a valid architecture evokes many levels of meaning and combinations of focus; its space and its elements become readable and workable in several ways at once." While this sentiment was not specifically directed to sustainable architecture, it did speak to the duality of meaning and multiple levels of expression, and was reminiscent of Aldo van Eyck's notion of "twin-phenomena." This brought up the question, was there a possible over-responsibility, over-simplification and over-reduction of sustainable design while simultaneously having an expectation of a progressive architectural form with richness and interest? Using Venturi's term, this could be a "both-and," affirming his theories of ambiguity and contradiction.

Venturi's Lieb House was constructed in 1969 in New Jersey and was a good example of what Hugh Hardy would have called the ambiguous box. The modest form with flat roof was articulated with negative voids cut into the form, simple, but ironic, unadorned surface treatments, and it was made with conventional elements that were used in unexpected ways.

2.7 Mainstream Architecture a) Habitat '67 (courtesy of "Shutterstock") b) Expo '67 Biosphere (courtesy of "Shutterstock") c) Trellick Tower 1966–72) (courtesy of "Shutterstock") d) Gateway Arch (1968) (courtesy of "Shutterstock") e) Lieb House (1969) (Used with permission of Philadelphia Inquirer Copyright © 2012. All rights reserved)

The street number was expressed with a large number "9." It was a little house with a large scale and interesting presence. This work challenged its context of the vernacular beech houses of the day with peaked roofs and cedar shingles. The 1,500-square feet (139-square meters) iconic structure was eventually moved from its original address to a site on Glen Cove, Long Island in 2009. While Venturi's ideas and works were seen as early beginnings to Postmodernism, they were a nexus of thoughts that open the door to a challenge of the modernist status quo of the 1960s—a doorway that green design was happy to enter in the next decade that followed. Certainly, the relocation and reuse of this structure would be considered a positive sustainable measure today.

The Lieb House also served to confront stark modernist works of overly resolved and highly reduced designs, corporate highrise buildings and the monumental megastructures that were propagated at this same time. In concept the megastructures would aggregate multiple building programs until they were assumed into a single structure, such as Montreal's Place Bonaventure in 1967. Additionally, many of buildings in the World's Fair held in Montreal, Canada in 1967 exhibited megastructure features, most notably the Netherlands, US and other Theme pavilions, and the highly acclaimed Habitat 67 by Moshe Sofdie. Brutalist architecture in Great Britain grew from C.I.A.M. and Team Ten and was articulated in Reyner Banham's book, *The New Brutalism: Ethic or Aesthetic,* where he saw the megastructure as a way to combine the vision of city planning and architecture.[30] The megastructure by John Andrews at Scarborough College, now the University of Toronto Scarborough, was designed for the cold Canadian climate and was reminiscent of the spatial organization and site considerations of Erskine's Arctic City and the much smaller Baker House by Aalto. However, the language of Scarborough College was Brutalist with monumental, zigzagging linear spatial structure, raw concrete and bold forms that stair-stepped along the irregular escarpment. Trellick Tower by Erno Goldfinger represented many of the Brutalist housing tower blocks of this time as seen in the facade in Figure 2.7c.

The Gateway Arch designed by Eero Saarinen, was a vivid place marker giving regional identity to the city of St Louis marking it not only a symbol for the city, but as the gateway to the West towering to 630 feet (192 meters). It was among a number of conceptually unique, functionally derived and culturally responsive projects. In contrast to the contextually significant work of Saarinen, the highrise building form had long been a symbol of immense and universal power. San Gimignano, Italy was a walled in medieval hilltown built along the Via Francigena trading and pilgrimage route (Canterbury to Rome) and dominated the Elsa Valley. There were originally 72 towers, built by aristocratic families. Perhaps Italy's best-known medieval tower was Torre degli Asinelli in Bologna, which stretched to more than 320 feet (98 meters) into the sky. The race for the world's highest building was a preoccupation in the 1960s, and still is an obsession for many developing countries. The Willis Tower in Chicago, formally the Sears Tower designed by Skidmore, Owings and Merrill in the late 1960s and completed in 1973 (1,729 feet), was the tallest building in the United States. It was followed by the World Trade Center in New York City at 1,368 feet (417 meters) before they were tragically destroyed in 2011. Minoru Yamasaki and Associates designed the World Trade Center, and the north and south towers were completed in 1970 and 1971 respectively. The slender, crystalline forms represented the power of American commercial activity and international trade. To Yamasaki the towers had a larger purpose and represented a living symbol of world peace through cooperation, commerce and trade. Today, the tallest building in the world, the Burj Khalifa (2009) in Dubai United Arab Emirates, was designed by Skidmore, Owings and Merrill with Adrian Smith, and it stands at an astounding 2,717 feet high (828 meters). Validity of the highrise, as a sustainable building type and its proper place in today's urban environment strategy, has not been settled and remains an important subject for future consideration and debate. It should be noted that in many cities, especially in the Far East (Hong Kong, Tokyo, Manila, Seoul, Shanghai, and Singapore), greater density and the high-rise typology were far more commonplace.

The tremendous difference between the early examples of utopian green architecture and mainstream modernism in the 1960s was irreconcilable. On the one hand were the backwoods technological utopias (funky domes in the woods) and on the other were the mainstream modernists (mega-corporate machines high in the sky). The difficulty for most young architects was in the bridging of the gap between their personal inclinations and social concerns and the inflexible and monumental infatuations of professional architecture at that time. The root social and political circumstances were defined by conditions that existed outside the scope and competence of normal architectural practice. What appeared to be missing was the evolution of a responsible architectural language that embodied green principles, which would pervasively affect mainstream architecture. Mainstream architecture reflected culture of this time, but was highly selective in its interpretation of the populous contemporary values and social needs. Experimental architecture found life on the fringe, and according to Michael Sorkin, "The search for radical architecture is not for a way of designing but for a place to begin to design." And Alastair Gordon concluded, "In the funky, self-built revolution, making shelter was seen as an act of personal transformation and revelation."

Two urban territories seemed to have generally emerged. First was the "urban jungle," which was characterized by overgrowth and an uncontrollable nature—law of the jungle, survival of the fittest, and unlimited egoism. Second was with the creation of "non-places," vapid land uses sprinkled in and between coherent neighborhood that contained no redeeming features and complete loss of humanity.[31] Yet in spite of a decade of upheaval and questionable growth, the 1960s established important green architectural seeds that illuminated considerations of climate, ecology, conservation, on-site resources, new technologies, health, stewardship, sacred placemaking, and the need for non-toxic building construction. They tended to not be defined so much by alternative environmental technologies, but rather presented new forms, building methods and conceptual ideas. It was not until the early 1970s that the environmental consciousness combined with the pursuit of a new range of energy options, known at first as "alternative energy" and then later as "renewables," each based on neither fossil fuels nor nuclear energy. Green architecture was certainly accumulating a design intent and rudimentary vocabulary informed by past and present.

The green seeds were cast in a context that was separated by a pervasive modernism, the expanding and ambivalent middle class, arresting social change and the growing awareness of the effects of contemporary life on the environment. What resulted were a few dramatic and provocative examples of architecture constructed generally at the edge of mainstream development, that expressed a wide range of alternatives—visionary, experimental and down-to-earth. It was certainly a time of contrasts from the slowly evolving, monumental and controlled work of Soleri in contrast to the improvised and scruffy work at Drop City, or from the monumental megastructures and skyscrapers versus the sensitive and anthropomorphic designs found at Findhorn and Jarna. In spite the impassive nature of the status quo, there was an environmental awakening that in subsequent decades gave form and new meaning to the greening of architecture.

ENDNOTES

1. Carl Stein, *Greening Modernism: Preservation, Sustainability, and the Modern Movement*. New York: W.W. Norton & Company, Inc., 2010.

2. James Truslow Adams, *The Epic of America*, First Edition. Bethesda, Simon Publications, MD, 2001.

3. Rachel Carson, *Silent Spring*, Anniversary edition. New York, NY: Houghton Mifflin Company, 2002.

4. Ralph Nader, *Unsafe at Any Speed*. MA: Knightsbridge Publishing Company, 1991.

5. Donella H. Meadows, Jorgen Randers and William W. Behrens III, *Limits to Growth*. New York, NY: Signet Publishers, 1972.

6. E.F. Schumacher, *Small is Beautiful: Economics As If People Mattered*. London: Blond & Briggs Publishers, 1973.

7. Jane Jacobs, *The Death and Life of Great American Cities*. New York: Random House, 1961.

8. Daniel Yergin, *The Quest: Energy, Security, and the Remaking of the Modern World*. New York: The Penguin Press, 2011.

9. The origins of *An Inconvenient Truth* began as a slide presentation that later was made into a documentary film that was first presented at the 2006 Sundance Film Festival. Al Gore, *An Inconvenient Truth*. Emmaus, PA: Rodale Books, 2006.

10. Christopher F. Clark, Matthew J. Kotchen and Michael R. Moore, "Internal and External Influences on Pro-Environmental Behavior: Participation in a Green Electricity Program," *Journal of Environmental Psychology*, 23, 2003.

11. This was an extensively used textbook for architectural courses in environmental systems classes and delineated the varying bio-climatic impacts to four differing regions of the United States. The National Climatic Data Center identifies nine regions: Northwest, West, Southwest, Northern Rockies and Plains, Upper Midwest, Ohio Valley, Northeast, South and Southeast. Victor Olgyay, *Design with Climate: Bioclimatic Approach to Architectural Regionalism*. Princeton, PA: Princeton University Press, 1963.

12. Amos Rapoport, *House, Form and Culture*. Englewood Cliffs, NJ: Prentice-Hall, 1969.

13. Ian L. McHarg, *Design with Nature*. Philadelphia: Doubleday/Natural History Press, 1969.

14. Francis Strauven, "Aldo van Eyck: The Shape of Relativity," *Architectura and Natura*. Amsterdam, 1998.

15. Dr Owens presents the concept of energy planning strategies appropriate to varying scales of the built environment from a dwelling site to entire regions. Susan Owens, *Energy Planning and Urban Design*. London: Pion, 1985.

16. Team Ten was group of architects who had broken away from C.I.A.M. in the early 1960s. Their core members included: Alison and Peter Smithson, Shadrach Woods, Aldo van Eyck, Jacob Bakema, Giancarlo De Carlo, Jersey Soltan, Charles Pologni, Jose Coderch, Stefan Wewerka and Georges Candilis. Alison Smithson, *Team Ten Primer*. Cambridge, MA: MIT Press, 1968. Susan Owens, *Energy Planning and Urban Design*. London: Pion, 1985.

17. Jonathan Ringen, "Superstudio: Pioneers of Conceptual Architecture," *Metropolis Magazine*, April 2004.

18. David G. Saile, "Making a House: Building Rituals and Spatial Concepts in the Pueblo Indian World," *Architectural Association Quarterly*, 9 (2, 3). London, 1977.

19. Evelyn Lip, *Feng Shui: Environments of Power*. London: Academy Editions, 1995.

20 Sacred architecture and sustainable designs share similar objectives, especially in considering issues of health, on-site resources, and experience with and respect for nature. Keith Critchlow, "Geometry and Architecture," *Lindisfarne Letter 10*. West Stockbridge, MA: The Lindisfarne Press, 1980.

21 Gary J. Coates, *Erik Asmussen, Architect*. Stockholm: Byggforlaget Publishers, 1997.

22 Auroville was considered a transnational city and experimental township founded in 1968 by Mirra Alfassa as a project of the Sri Aurobindo Society. According to a report by Bharat Nivas, Auroville belongs to nobody in particular, but belongs to humanity as a whole (1971).

23 Alastair Gordon, "True Green: Lessons from 1960s'–70s' Counterculture Architecture." *Architectural Record*, April 2008: 1–2.

24 Alastair Gordon, *Spaced Out: Radical Environments of the Psychedelic Sixties*. New York: Rizzoli International, 2008.

25 R. Buckminster Fuller, *Operating Manual for Spaceship Earth*. New York: E.P. Dutton, 1978.

26 Stewart Brand, *Whole Earth Catalog: Access to Tools*. Whole Earth Catalog Publisher, 1968.

27 Michael Sorkin, "A Radical Alternative," *Architectural Record*. New York: McGraw-Hill Publication, December 1972.

28 James Howard Kunstler, *The Geography of Nowhere: The Rise and Decline of America's Man-Made Landscape*. Free Press, 1994.

29 Robert Venturi, *Complexity and Contradiction in Architecture*. New York: Museum of Modern Art Press, 1966.

30 Rayner Banham, *The New Brutalism: Ethic or Aesthetic?* New York: Reinhold Publishing, 1966.

31 Liliana Gomez and Walter Van Herck, *The Sacred in the City*. London, UK: Continuum International Publishing Group, 2012: 24–5.

Chapter 3
1970s: Solar Architecture

Phillip Tabb

> Solar energy is present in sufficient abundance on the earth to supply all energy needs, but like fossil fuels its practical availability is limited to specific localities.[1]

The first several years of the 1970s were a continuation of the marginal greening efforts experienced in the late 1960s. Following the social upheavals, including the civil-rights movement, peace marches, hippie movement, women's movement, political assassinations, and continuation of the war with Vietnam, the 1970s opened in a tense but somewhat exhausted mood. With the fall of Saigon in 1973 the United States withdrew from Vietnam, and a year later president Nixon was forced to resign after the Watergate scandal. The Volkswagen's "Beetle" became the most produced car of all time, a living symbol of Germany's economic might. Ironically, the two countries that the Allied Powers had defeated in World War Two, Germany and Japan had become America's main competitors. Catalytic converters were developed in the 1970s as a way to convert pollutants into safer emissions.

To Charles Jencks, modern architecture died in St Louis, Missouri on July 15, 1972 when Pruit-Igoe was dynamited.[2] To the early critics of modernism, not yet dubbed "postmodernists," the unaddressed issues of social responsibility and urbanism were not being mainstreamed into American life and culture. The debate echoed between those believing in the instrumentality of technology, yet condemning consumer culture, and those rejecting the determinacy of technology, but finding in popular culture the impulses of a new order. It was the Oil Embargo of 1973, which resulted in long queues at gasoline stations and acute shortages that prompted the pursuit of alternative energy sources and a growth spurt in the green movement.

New organizations were formed and environmental legislation was created. Greenpeace, a non-governmental environmental organization, grew from the peace movement and anti-nuclear protests in Vancouver, British Columbia in 1971. Greenpeace stated its goal was to "ensure the ability of the Earth to nurture life in all its diversity" and focused its campaigning on worldwide issues such as global warming, deforestation, over-fishing, commercial whaling and anti-nuclear issues. The Sierra Club, which was one of the oldest environmental organizations established in 1892 by preservationist John Muir, had three main purposes: to explore, enjoy, and protect the wild places of the earth, to practice and promote the responsible use of the earth's ecosystems and resources, to educate and enlist humanity to protect and restore the quality of the natural and human environment, and to use all lawful means to carry out these objectives. In the 1970s they guided conservation campaigns and supported the Toxic Substances Control Act of 1976, the Clean Air Act Amendments, the Water Pollution Control Act Amendments of 1972, and the Surface Mining Control and Reclamation Act of 1977.

The 1970s brought a new era in the development of energy independence with direct application to the architectural and engineering disciplines. After the Oil Embargo there was an explosion of creative activity from multiple sources. Research throughout the United States in national labs focused on solar optics, thermal dynamics and high technology solutions. Simultaneously, back-yard inventors forged interesting and innovative designs that were often simple and cost effective. The Solar Energy Society meeting in Los Angeles in 1975 was a smorgasbord of solar components exhibiting from parabolic concentrating collectors, new selective surfaces for absorber plates and evacuated tubes to various thermal storage, phase-change materials and control systems. In the latter half of the decade passive solar systems came to the forefront as more and more architects became involved in the development of solar architecture. According to Wilson Clark in his book *Energy for Survival*, "The wealth of today's technology is based on fossil fuels and cheap resources; and as these decline, the wealth of the future may be based on the technologies looked down upon by today's standards."[2]

IMPACT OF THE 1973 OIL EMBARGO

The 1973 oil crisis started in October 1973, when the members of Organization of Arab Petroleum Exporting Countries or the OAPEC, consisting of the Arab members of OPEC, plus Egypt, Syria and Tunisia, proclaimed an oil embargo. This occurred as a response to the US decision to re-supply the Israeli military during the Yom Kippur war where Syria and Egypt launched a surprise attack on Israel. President Richard Nixon authorized Operation Nickel Grass, an overt strategic airlift to deliver weapons and supplies to Israel, after the former Soviet Union began sending arms to Syria and Egypt. OPEC responded with a fourfold increase in the price of oil. Before the embargo the oil price averaged $3 a barrel and at the end, it was at $12 a barrel. Concurrently, the retail price of gasoline more than doubled.

Daniel Yergin explained, "the embargo—and the massive disruption that it engendered—created a surprise, panic, chaos, shortages, and economic disarray around the world."[3] The embargo created inconveniences with price increases, long waits, and in many instances shortages that left many gasoline stations empty; confidence fell to an all-time low. The American Automobile Association recorded that up to 20 percent of the country's gas stations had no fuel one week during the crisis. In some places drivers were forced to wait in line for two to three hours to get gas. Lines as long as 50 cars or more were commonplace throughout the United States. By January of 1974, Secretary of State Henry Kissinger had negotiated an Israeli troop withdrawal from parts of the Sinai Peninsula. The promise of a negotiated settlement between Israel and Syria was sufficient to convince Arab oil producers to lift the embargo in March 1974.

The Oil embargo certainly created public awareness of the dependence upon Middle Eastern oil, and stimulated reforms and research agendas. Homeowners were encouraged to turn their thermostats down in winter to 65°F (18°C) and to refrain from putting up holiday lights. In Detroit, production of giant, gas-guzzling cars was halted. Cars with big engines and heavy bodies were no longer made in order to reduce gasoline and oil consumption.

1970s: SOLAR ARCHITECTURE 51

3.1 Oil Embargo Consequences (a) Gasoline Queues (courtesy of Walter P. Reuther Library, Wayne State University) b) Gasoline Shortage (US National Archives) c) 55 mph Speed Limit (courtesy of Walter P. Reuther Library, Wayne State University) d) Empty Gas Pump (courtesy of Phillip Tabb)

The National Maximum Speed Law in the United States was a provision of the 1974 Emergency Highway Energy Conservation Act that prohibited speed limits higher than 55 miles per hour. In 1974 the 24 Hours of Daytona was canceled. Though the embargo was not enforced uniformly in Europe, countries such as Great Britain, Germany, Switzerland, Norway and Denmark placed limitations on driving, boating and flying, while in Britain homeowners were urged to heat one room in their homes during winter.

Environmentalism reached new heights during the crisis, and became a motivating force behind policymaking in Washington. In 1974 the first of several solar energy bills went into law, and federal research jumped substantially. Congress responded by enacting the Solar Energy

Research, Development and Demonstration Act of 1974. The act stated that it was henceforth the policy of the federal government to "pursue a vigorous and viable program of research and resource assessment of solar energy as a major source of energy for our national needs." The act's scope embraced all energy sources, which were renewable by the sun—including solar thermal energy, photovoltaic energy, and energy derived from wind, sea thermal gradients, and photosynthesis. The Solar Heating and Cooling Demonstration Act of 1974 followed. The AIA Research Corporation, directed by John Eberhard at the time, participated in solar energy research to help fulfill the charge of the solar demonstration programs. They were given the task of identifying the history of the renewable technology development, available types of solar energy systems and components, and the ways in which they integrated into varying housing typologies in different climatic contexts as part of the Department of Housing and Urban Development Solar Demonstration projects. This resulted in a handbook of solar design guides, *Solar Dwelling Design Concepts* (1976), written by Michael Holtz through his involvement with the AIA/RC.[4]

ACTIVE SOLAR TECHNOLOGIES

Solar technologies have been around for several centuries; for example, in the 18th century Horace de Saussure successfully constructed a rectangular box out of half-inch pine, lined with black cork and having three panes of glass. It was reported to have generated 228°F (109°C) temperatures at the bottom of the box. Sir John Herschel and Samuel Langley carried out similar experiments in the 19th century. Focus on solar hot water, accelerated in the turn of the 20th century, directed attention to development of black water tanks that were directly heated by the sun. It wasn't until William Bailley's "Day and Night" system separated collector and storage tank and connected them with a circulating fluid. This was the forerunner of the flat-plate solar hot water system that flourished in California and Florida in the 1920s. According to Butti and Perlin (1980), more than half of Miami, Florida used solar-heated water by 1941.[5] Modern-day active solar technologies were developed with a number of interrelated components that normally required both mechanical means and electrical energy for their operation. The primary components of an active solar system were the solar collector, storage and distribution systems. Since the early solar technologies were solar thermal systems, it was the purpose of the systems to capture solar radiation as heat, transfer it to a working fluid (water, air or water mixed with propylene glycol), and distribute the working fluid to an insulated storage tank, which then could be used for distribution for service hot water.

The solar collector grew out of hotbox technology and was essentially a sandwich of layered materials selected to enhance the transfer solar radiation into thermal energy. The layers consisted, from outside-to-inside respectively, of a layer of glass (double glazing in cold climates), an air space, a dark-colored metal absorber plate, working fluid tubes, insulation and mounting structure. Panels were typically two or three feet wide by six to eight feet in length. Several panels linked together formed an array. The working fluid passed through pipes attached to the absorber plate and then to a heat exchanger to the storage tank. Some systems used thermosiphoning between collector and storage tank and this was considered a passive method utilizing natural convection. In his book, *The Solar Heating Design Process* (1982), solar engineer Jan Kreider explained that there were only two components to an active solar system that were unfamiliar to the architecture and engineering professionals. They were the collector and control system.[6] The collector was the component with the greatest need for solar access, optimal orientation and tilt in order to maximize efficiency. As a consequence, it was the most visible component, and the lack of aesthetic considerations and understanding of the area intensiveness of solar collector installations remains problematic today.

The first examples of active solar architecture simply applied the emergent technologies unceremoniously onto buildings, usually rooftops. Solar collector arrays faced south for optimal efficiency and often did not match building orientations and structural geometry, resulting in an awkward massing. Eventually, building forms assimilated the blossoming technologies and their constraints, where solar collector orientation, tilt angle, and area intensiveness became more integrative to the formal characteristics of a building. The solar furnace, "heliocaminus" shown in Figure 3.2a, was designed at the Centre National de la Rescherche Scientifique (CNRS) in Odeillo, France and opened in 1970, and was an early example of integrated design. The 10-story curtain-wall structure housed research labs and offices on the south side of the building while the north side was made of a large parabolic array of mirrors. From a field of 10,000 movable mirrors, sunlight was reflected to the parabolic dish or heliostat and then focused in a concentrated form to a small-boxed furnace. It produced 1,000 kilowatts of electricity and temperatures as high as 5,430°F (3,000°C).

Several early active solar projects were influential in the development of solar architecture. First was a series of experimental solar houses at the Massachusetts Institute of Technology constructed in the 1940s. The last one built in 1958 was designed with a south-facing roof, which housed a large solar collector array. The George Löf House in Denver, Colorado was completed in 1958 and served as a laboratory and residence. This was a solar heated, forced air system where thermal storage occurred in unique storage bins filled with smooth 1½-inch (3.8 cm) diameter river rocks, which contained the heat. The system was fully automated with control systems and a forced-air auxiliary heating system. Solar engineer Karl Böer conducted test houses that experimented with photoelectric solar-cell systems at the University of Delaware in the early 1970s. The first solar air-conditioned house was designed by Richard Crowther and George Löf and constructed on the campus of Colorado State University. These early demonstrations were mainly concerned with the operation of the solar systems and interface with conventional systems while there was less concern with the quality of architectural integration, especially from formal and aesthetic points of view.

The early demonstrations of active solar architecture, especially in temperate and cold climates, revealed competition for sunlight between the area requirements of the opaque solar collector arrays and daylight needs of the users inside. South façades were either dominated or completely covered with solar collector devices in order to meet the buildings' space heating and hot water demands. Consequently, there was little-to-no area left for normal windows for daylight, view and natural ventilation. Designed in 1975 by Joint Venture Architects and solar engineer Jan Kreider, the Student Housing project in Boulder, Colorado, Figure 3.2c, was part of the Cycle Two HUD Solar Demonstration Program. The building was designed with 70 percent of the space-heating and domestic water heating requirements provided by the active solar system.[7] The building responded to the systems' orientation constraints, collector area of 700 square-feet (65 square meters) and optimal tilt angle (58°) with sloping south façades. A 1,700-gallon insulated tank was used for solar energy storage. The opacity issue was addressed by breaking up the south façade with a "pushing and pulling" of secondary forms. As the forms moved in north-south directions, they simultaneously shifted apart in the east-west direction, thereby allowing for solar access to in-between spaces for stairs and balconies, and they created space for conventional windows for daylight to penetrate deep into the livable spaces. This was a good solution to the problem of collector integration of active solar collectors, but brought to focus the issue of the dominant solar south façade, which later would be criticized as being too inflexible and dated.

Located in Golden Colorado, the Colorado School of Mines student dormitories, designed by Anderson, Mason and Dale Architects, housed 230 students and utilized an impressive single monolithic solar collector array that spanned across a residential street joining two five-story dormitory structures. Celestial Seasonings Headquarters Building (1977), designed by Joint Venture Architects and pictured in Figure 3.2b, was an early Department of Energy Commercial Passive Solar Demonstration Award that featured an active solar heating system over the manufacturing areas of the building along with passive solar pre-heating greenhouses positioned on the south-facing façades. Many of the active solar projects in the later 1970s tended toward commercial and institutional building types. While most passive technologies were being embraced in the residential sector; it was not uncommon to see larger buildings with increased roof areas and large collector arrays.

Active solar technology progressed throughout the 1970s with primary focus on innovations in solar collector designs through improvements in optical and thermal efficiencies. Flat-plate technology was commercialized relatively inexpensively with lower temperature conversions.

3.2 Active Solar Demonstrations a) Odeillo Solar Furnace b) Celestial Seasonings DOE Demonstration c) Boulder Student Housing HUD Demonstration

The Compound Parabolic Collector (CPC) concentrated solar radiation with linear reflective parabolic mirrors, usually made with mylar or stainless steel, focusing radiation to the working fluid and thereby was able to generate higher temperatures. The Stationary Reflector Tracking Absorber (SRTA), designed by engineer W. Gene Steward, was a fixed spherical mirror with optical principles that concentrated solar radiation to a single cylindrical absorber that tracked the movement of the sun. This collector was able to generate low temperature steam, but presented difficulties with architectural integration of the large and cumbersome spherical form. In some collector designs, the absorber pipe was placed inside an evacuated tube of glass, thereby reducing heat loss through emissivity.

While the technology of photosynthesis had evolved in the 19th century with the photovoltaic effect in solid selenium by W.G. Adams and R.E. Day (1877), the public became aware of the technology with the launching of NASA's Skylab in 1973. Skylab was the first US unmanned orbital space station, which operated for six years. Light from diffused, direct and reflected solar radiation generally freed electrons in photovoltaic cells that in turn initiated an electrical voltage. Solar powered calculators were introduced on the market in the late 1970s. The challenge for architectural assimilation of photovoltaic technology was twofold—the need to increase of solar cell efficiency and reduce cost. Several factors affected the performance of a solar electric system, which included the cell chemistry, operating temperature, solar intensity, and incident sun angles. Both the tilt angle and orientation of the photovoltaic cells affected the electrical production. Solar power density was greatest when incident angles were normal to the collector surface. According to Othmar Humm and Peter Toggweiler (1993), between 4 and 28 percent of the available solar radiation was converted to electrical energy. Monocrystal silicon modules produced between 13 to 16 percent efficiency.[8] The first all-solar residence to utilize photovoltaics was in Carlisle, Massachusetts. It was a 7Wp photovoltaic system that was supported by the US Department of Energy. The 3,200 square feet (297 square meters) house demonstrated a utility interface system that fed excess electricity back into the public utility grid.

PASSIVE SOLAR SYSTEMS

While solar techniques have been used for millennia, the term *passive*, meaning not relying on mechanical or electrical components, was popularized during the 1970s by Richard Crowther of Denver, Colorado.[9] Amory Lovins later promoted the term *soft energy* as a way of defining more benign and environmentally friendly sources of energy where production was matched in scale and quality to end use requirements.[10] The opaque systems' components of active solar technologies were replaced with transparent building elements that provided heat over a 24-hour period, such as windows, doors, skylights, clerestories, and the mass of building materials, such as floors and walls, were used for thermal storage: the building became an energy collector. The first passive solar home designed in 1940 by George Keck in the United States was built for Howard Sloan in Glenview, Illinois. The design took advantage of a long east–west aspect that allowed for large south-facing clearstories and sunroom.[11] Named "the solar house" by the Chicago Tribune, it was the first modern use of that term.

The greenhouse effect works when an aperture can collect more solar heat during daylight than it loses throughout the 24 hours of the day. Short-wave radiation passes into a space and is trapped as long-wave radiation, and therefore is useful as a heat source. Solar tempering was the first technique to be used before more effective passive systems were developed.

Sun tempered design took advantage of window area allocations with reductions to the north side and increases on the south side (in the northern hemisphere). The process occurred with increased fenestration areas on southern façades, but sun tempering tended to overheat because of inadequate thermal storage. In America, the light-mass construction, wood studs, drywall and thin exterior sheathing, did not provide adequate thermal mass in the building structure itself. Consequently, solar energy was stored in the interior raising air temperatures substantially above comfort levels. At mid-day in winter, often windows were opened to reduce the overheating and thereby nullifying the solar heating benefit. For solar tempering to function effectively, increases in south glazing needed a corresponding increase of thermal mass—generally one cubic foot of mass is required for each square foot a south glazing.

Full passive solar systems were defined by their ability to provide solar energy heating with no mechanical or electrical means for the duration of a full 24 hours. There were generally three major types of passive solar systems commonly used. They were the direct-gain distributed-mass system, the concentrated mass system, and the sunspace system. Direct gain systems were flexible and adaptable to most building types and architectural conditions. There were two types of concentrated mass systems, which used either water or masonry as a storage medium. And there were two types of sunspaces, isolated gain and integrated sunrooms. The effectiveness of a passive solar system depended upon ways in which the architecture responded to the entire range of solar systems' functions, including accommodating the area intensiveness of collection, adequate matching of solar glazing to internal thermal mass for overnight storage, efficient coupling of solar-charged spaces with other less irradiated internal spaces, and response to potential overheating conditions, especially in summer and at mid-day in winter. The integrated solar guides in Edward Mazria's book *The Passive Solar Energy Book* (1979) also provided passive design strategies and details for architects and designers worldwide.[12] Organized through a series of patterns, the book illustrated passive solar techniques, rules of thumb and quick design guides. Following are descriptions of the three passive solar systems:

- Direct Gain Distributed Mass Systems—Primarily vertical collector glazing with thermal mass distributed throughout the conditioned interior. This was the most common and flexible of the passive solar heating methods that was more conventionally integrated into the architecture. The collector could occupy single or distributed glazing areas, atriums, clerestories, dormers, and commonly was south-facing windows or glazed doors.
- Concentrated Mass Systems—Vertical glazing was directly coupled to a thermal mass, usually concrete or solid concrete masonry unit walls, commonly referred to as the "Trombe Wall System." Some systems employed water tubes because of the high heat capacity of water, but they often proved to be impractical and unaesthetic. The thermal mass was solar charged during the day and discharged as heat into adjacent spaces at night.
- Sunspace Systems—Vertical and sloped glazing that formed actual south-oriented walk-in rooms. There were two primary types, the isolate gain where the sunspace could be thermally separated from the adjacent living area (parent space), or the integrated sunspace that combined the sunspace heating function with the actual living or occupied space. Sunspace systems also required either concentrated or distributed mass for thermal storage, and for sloped glazing schemes required night insulation and mid-day shading in summer.

The solar collector or collection system was the most critical component of a passive solar system and was generally area intensive making it an important design consideration. In colder climates, larger internal heating loads were generated requiring larger solar collection areas. In order to maximize efficiency of the collection cycle, it was important to employ as true a south orientation as possible and optimal collector tilt angles, which depended upon the latitude of the site. In direct gain systems the glazing had the most flexibility and could adapt to most architectural form languages. The coupling to the distributed mass and to adjacent un-radiated spaces was the greatest challenge, especially with basements or rooms filled with furniture and carpets. The thermal wall system was generally opaque because of the vertical placement of thermal mass. This was cause for both aesthetic and visual conflicts. The sunspace was the most efficient and clearly had a language of its own. Shading the sloped components of the sunspace in summer was sometimes difficult and costly, and without proper shading, overheating became problematic. Many designs combined these various passive systems depending on the function inside and desired degree of privacy required. Hybrid systems also incorporated active components, such as, solar thermal systems for water heating, photovoltaic arrays, and heat-recovery sub-systems capturing stratified layers of internal heat.

Thermal storage methods were tied to the efficient function of a passive solar system and critical in reducing overheating, especially during the summer season and midday. Overnight heat storage was critical for the function of a passive solar system and therefore, had to be large and effective enough to supply a constant flow of heat until the next morning when the mass could be recharged. The rule of thumb was one cubic foot (0.03 cubic meters) of mass for each square foot (0.09 square meters) of solar glazing. Solar tempered, light mass buildings did not have sufficient thermal storage capacity to keep from overheating or to supply heat throughout the night. There were two full-passive storage methods that were integral to a building form—distributed mass and concentrated mass. The mass to glass relationship was often blocked and shaded with furniture and other solid architectural elements of the building form. Buildings constructed in Europe, by contrast, were typically concrete masonry units or poured concrete, which was of much higher mass especially for the interior walls. A unique system was developed by Harold Hay in which the water storage was positioned on the roof of experimental houses in southern California. These water containers were covered with sliding insulation panels to allow sunlight to charge the storage medium during the day and closed to contain the heat at night. Conversely, in summer the insulating panels' reflective surface on the top kept the hot sun from entering the dwelling, and at night they were opened up to radiate the heat back into the atmosphere—a process called terrestrial re-radiation. These systems were somewhat impractical for buildings with multiple stories or complex roof forms, as roof ponds were primarily limited to single-story structures with high winter sun.

Coupling cooler interior spaces, usually located on the north side of the form, to those that were charged with solar heat on the south side was also important design consideration and detail. This process was referred to as "zone-coupling" and could be accomplished by either mechanical intervention with fans for example, or through natural convection—operable openings between the charged and served spaces. For buildings with spatial organizations that aligned internal spaces oriented on the north–south axis, it became difficult for spaces on the far northern end to receive either direct solar radiation or to secure heat from adjacent spaces. Zone coupling was more prohibitive with complex space programs and complicated designs. Richard Crowther was a master at subtly manipulating ceiling planes to control internal natural heat flow within the residence.

3.3 Passive Solar Demonstrations a) Terry House b) Balcomb House c) Bramwell Residence d) Loffredo Residence (courtesy DennisRHolioway Architect.com)

As heat rose, solar charged air naturally convected high in the southern spaces and moved along slightly inclined ceiling planes to more isolated spaces within the dwelling. More simple means that used French doors and transom windows could be operated manually.

One of the most widely published solar projects was the Balcomb House designed by William Lumpkins. Built in 1979, the passive design approach for this house was accomplished with a dominant isolated-gain sunspace passive system thermally coupled to interior adobe walls, stone floor, and in-ground remote rockbeds. The two stories of living spaces adjacent to the sunspace were the beneficiary of this heat source, and were regulated with multiple operable openings.[13] Designed into the roof was a clerestory that brought light down into the center of the house and simultaneously served to support domestic hot water collectors. Engineer Douglas Balcomb lived in and analyzed the house for nearly 10 years and eventually developed a set of solar engineering design procedures for passive solar heating that enabled architects to design with useful performance-based modeling and calculation methods. The solar load ratio (SLR) method, based on the ideas of K. Subbarao in 1982, allowed designers to quantify useful solar energy gain and to estimate the net solar contribution to a space. Later, Balcomb developed Energy-10, an energy and cost design tool, which is still used today. Methods like these were especially useful for the sizing of solar collector arrays, determining the amount of thermal storage, and identifying the solar contribution to energy loads. David Wright designed the Karen Terry house, also located in Santa Fe in 1975, which demonstrated a direct gain passive solar system with cascading clerestories. In Figure 3.3a the stepping glazing, solar shading devices and the mass walls can clearly be seen. Figure 3.3b shows the Balcomb south-facing sunspace that dominates the entire façade, which illustrates the critical relationship between heating load and collector area.

The Bramwell House, located in Florissant, Colorado and shown in Figure 3.3c, was designed by Phillip Tabb and constructed in 1983. There were integrated active and passive systems, which combined to create a unique and synergetic hybrid. All living spaces had a southern façade that either faced directly outside or into the central sunspace creating independent, but connected stand-alone passive systems. Along the width of the building form was a clerestory that brought light and warmth to circulation spaces to the north side of the house. The sidewalls of the sunspace and floors were insulated and made of solid masonry and concrete providing the thermal mass. At the top of the sunspace were solar hydronic hot-water collectors that also acted as a heat-trap for stratified hot air, which was trapped and distributed down to two remote rockbeds beneath the seating area in the living room and bed area in the master bedroom. The sloped glazing was the first use of Southwall Technologies' Heat Mirror insulating glass in Colorado providing an R-value of 6 (U-value of 0.167). The Loffredo Residence located in Lyons, Colorado and shown in Figure 3.3d (1979) was designed by Dennis Holloway and was a good illustration of combined passive solar systems, direct gain, the Michel Trombe wall and sunspace forming a dramatic façade to the contemporary vernacular form of the house. For some time this was the largest residential Trombe Wall in the United States. Douglas Kelbaugh designed a Trombe wall-sunspace-direct gain hybrid for his Princeton, New Jersey house in 1975. Each of these examples illustrated the dominant area intensiveness of passive and hybrid systems, which were by necessity required in achieving high on-site energy contributions to the energy loads. Typically, demonstrations, such as these, provided solar fractions, or the percentage of energy provided by renewable sources, in excess of 70 percent and very often much higher.

In contrast to the solar-dominant work of David Wright, Dennis Holloway and others, Malcolm Wells went underground. His unique *earth-sheltered* works were intended to reduce the amount of conventional building materials, especially forest depleting products, with more massive earth-based materials—rammed earth, green roofs, stone, concrete block and concrete. Earth sheltering, especially on the roof or north sides of the building, added insulation and wind protection. This pioneering work would later inspire interest in green roof projects several decades later. The work of James Lambeth took on a different approach—one that explored delight in solar architectural form.[14] His projects often exaggerated building form for its solar function with trapezoidal plan aspects, and solar oriented sections. He explored the use of mirrors for the melting of snow on entrance walkways. His designs were optimistic, playful and in his terms "danced with the sun."

ARCHITECTURAL INTEGRATION

Ralph Knowles examined the relationship between pure form, urban density, and both seasonal and diurnal rhythms of the sun.[15] These investigations led to his books *Energy and Form: Ecological Approach to Urban Growth* and *Sun Rhythm Form*, which informed the development of his *solar envelope* concept and *solar zoning* guides that he tested through numerous student project insertions into the urban fabric of Los Angeles. Solar access for densities up to 50 units per acre (124 du/ha) was shown to be achievable. Solar access was aimed at protecting roofs, south walls and south lots. The works of Dean Hawkes and Stephen Greenberg investigated solar building positioning relative to suburban lotting schemes of varying orientations in Great Britain (1987). They were able to demonstrate adequate solar siting for all buildings by relaxing the building-to-plot geometry and giving priority to the solar orientation. While the study proved good solar access was possible, it exposed growing shortcomings in solar urban design and multiple building applications. Providing adequate solar access, while responding to flexible site designs for difficult and varying site conditions, was challenging in achieving higher density developments.

The collector tilt angle was seen as an important design consideration in order to achieve the greatest degree of collection efficiency. Because the sun position moves from east to west throughout the day and lower in winter to higher in summer, the optimal collector tilt angle increased solar collector efficiently. Key was selecting the incident tilt angle that resulted in the least amount of sunlight deviation from normal to a collector's glazing surface. High incident angles, especially for glass surfaces, created a high degree of reflectivity and, therefore, a low amount of solar transmission. The concept of a solar window emerged as a way of identifying a spatial and temporal context within which favorable sun angles would strike a collector surface for maximum solar gain. For single-family residential projects, the solar window was usually defined by six hours of sunshine over midday from 9am to 3pm and from summer to winter solstice. In higher densities the solar window was reduced to four hours. Solar hot water systems requiring solar energy year-round were optimized for both summer and winter sun angles. Solar space heating systems were optimized for winter and swing periods when temperatures were colder and the sun position was lower in the sky. The solar window changes with varying latitudes in response to the axial tilt of the Earth. It is higher in the sky in the lower latitudes and lower in the higher latitudes. Solar geometry was recognized as an important design determinant.

Optimal collector orientation and accompanying building siting were other requirements of a system's design. On low-density sites or those with favorable slopes to the south, there was little difficulty in securing good orientation. However with sites of higher density and slopes that were off cardinal directions, siting could be problematic. To reduce the complexity and cost of a building's foundation, it was better to orient a building parallel to contours. The study by Dean Hawkes and Stephen Greenberg illustrated south-oriented collector-building placement, yet the odd and sometimes awkward building-to-plot and building-to-street relationships violated other important urban design considerations. Ideally there should be a harmonious geometric relation among building-to-plot-to-street. Figures 3.4d–g illustrated a student model in Ralph Knowles' studio for the Bunker Hill Solar Access Project (1981), which pair the solar envelope with physical designs.

1970s: SOLAR ARCHITECTURE   61

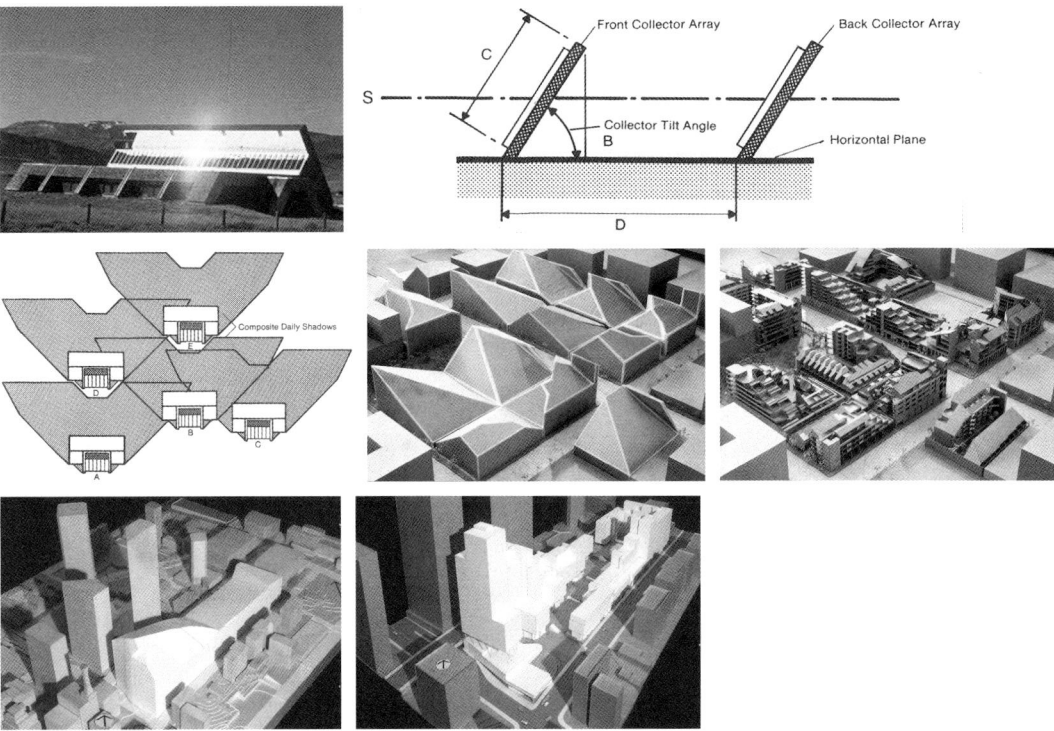

3.4   Architectural Integration Constraints a) Dominant Solar Section b) Optimal Tilt Angle and Spacing c) Shadow Masks and Solar Access d) Solar Envelope e) Development in Envelope f) Solar Envelope g) Development in Envelope (d–g taken from L. Knowles Ritual House, Island Press, 2006)

Jeffrey Cook of Arizona State University was a strong advocate of bio-climatic design, however he became critical of many solar-oriented designs. He attacked what he called the "dominant solar section" suggesting that it was too fixed and inflexible to respond to other important climatic, programmatic, aesthetic, and formal determinants. His concern was the predictable and uninteresting opacity of the north sides of these buildings and the overly angular and, phototropic building section with its transparent southern façades that typified these early solar designs. Double-loaded east–west streets posed inequities as public entrances on either side of the street took on completely different architectural qualities and languages: sunny open-transparent and shaded closed-opaque. The drawings in Figure 3.4a, b and c show the dominant solar section for an office building in Frasier, Colorado, an optimal winter tilt angle, and shadow masks created by composite daily sun angles for low sun angles on December 21.[16] In the United States, growth in alternative energy industries expanded until Federal and State energy tax credits expired in 1985. This, coupled with the availability of cheap natural gas, set back the greening of architecture in America for at least a decade as mainstream architecture engaged with new agendas exploring a variety of theoretical themes. Meanwhile in the 1980s, postmodern schemes tempered the solar architectural aesthetic and thermal functioning of the building.

OFF-GRID AND UNPLUGGED

Off-grid projects were considered buildings designed to be independent from all public utilities, including electricity, water, sewers and energy for heating and cooling. Only on-site resources and alternative methods for water and waste were utilized in order to help enable autonomous sustainable living. Initially, off-grid projects were realized on sites with excellent access to on-site resources, especially sun, wind and water, and in locations far from public utilities. Heating was accomplished with passive solar systems, electricity was generated with photovoltaic systems and/or wind turbines, water was collected through wells or rainwater-harvesting methods, hot water was provided by solar thermal systems, and waste was filtered, recycled and piped to septic tanks, leaching fields or vegetated wetlands. Most off-grid examples were located on remote sites, where there was no access to public utilities, especially electricity, and therefore, it became by necessity economically feasible to incorporate off-grid technologies. As the first photovoltaic residence was not realized until 1979, widespread use did not occur until later in the next decade when cell efficiencies increased and costs decreased. *USA Today* reported in 2006 that there were as many as 180,000 families in the United States living off the grid. According to Lori Riker in her book, *Off the Grid*:

> An almost-invisible grid of infrastructure binds us together. It is a system of electric poles, wire, and substations, with hydroelectric dams and tele-communication towers, webs of highways, and systems of sewage and water extraction from both free-flowing and dammed sources.[17]

Radical works of Michael Reynolds, which began in the early 1970s, pushed the boundaries of residential design with the use of unconventional recycled materials, such as automobile tires, aluminum cans and recycled glass bottles. Figure 3.5a indicates a pile of used automobile tires, and together with rammed earth, they were used in the construction of the "U-shaped" Earthship walls. The roof of an Earthship was heavily insulated—often with two layers of insulation, waterproofing and earth. Further, as photovoltaic technology became feasible and commercially available, Earthships were completely off-grid, consequently realizing the full potential of on-site resources and alternative technologies for passive and active solar heating, water harvesting, and photovoltaic electricity production. Earthships were independent, free-spirited and often looked rather unusual, unorthodox and homegrown.[18] An important consequence of Reynolds' work was the demonstration of a clear and visible relationship between the conditioned rooms or "served spaces" and the various sustainable systems' area and volumetric requirements for providing completely off-grid heating, on-site water and electricity. Figure 3.5b shows the relationship among a single "U-shaped" space, the sunspace, photovoltaic array and cistern requirements for that space. What was important with this comparison was the area and volumetric requirements of the off-grid technologies relative to the needs of a single, livable space.

The photograph in Figure 3.5c illustrates an Earthship located outside of Taos, New Mexico that combined all the alternative systems with a dominant sloped passive solar sunspace for space heating that serves the U-shaped interior spaces formed by tires and rammed earth. The roof was used to capture rainwater, which was stored in the cistern adjacent to the space. Mounted on top of a pole was a photovoltaic collector array for electricity production and integrated into the building form was a thermosiphon solar water heating system.

3.5 Off-Grid Architecture a) Earthship Tires (courtesy of Otis Bradley) b) Earthship Off-Grid Modules c) Earthship (b and c courtesy of Michael Reynolds) d) Advanced Green Builder Demonstration (image courtesy of the Center for Maximum Potential Building Systems, photograph by Paul Bardagjy) e) Beadwall Aspen Airport f) Strawbale Construction

This Earthship was a model autonomous building, which was appropriate to the high desert, hot-arid climate zone of northern New Mexico. It was important to visualize the various off-grid systems' components and understand their operational constraints and integrative characteristics. While unconventional, the Earthships provided valuable learning principles and examples.

Off-grid systems were typically designed by determining resource needs for electricity, water and space heating, and matching these needs with the available on-site resources. High R-values (low U-values) were typically achieved in walls and roofs. Efficiencies of the systems, peak loads and the variability of the natural resources were all taken into account. The beadwall movable insulation system designed by Ron Shore and shown in Figure 3.5e and the strawbale in Figure 3.5f were good examples of heat retention techniques. Furthermore, photovoltaic collector areas were determined by the internal electrical demand for lighting, appliances and equipment, the quality of direct solar radiation and the efficiency of the given photovoltaic cell type. Water harvesting systems similarly required catchment areas, cistern volumes and filtering to match water needs with quantity of rainfall and length of dry periods. It was critical to engineer the systems carefully because there were no public utilities that could act as backup under inclement or drought conditions. Examples of off-grid dwellings were important in showing what can be done with more extreme greening design measures. A primary criticism of off-grid works was their lack of connectivity to outside cultural, institutions and social networks. While being remote and independent, they still relied upon the automobile to connect to schools, grocery stores and other cultural and critical life-support functions.

Another approach to resource independence focused on human-made closed ecological systems, such as those developed by the New Alchemists in Cape Cod and Prince Edward Island. Founded by John and Nancy Todd and William McLarney, their work focused on closed-loop food chains, water and energy efficient bioshelters. They researched intensive gardening, biological pest control, cover cropping, irrigation using fishpond water, perennial food crops, and tree crops. Their most publicized biosphere was the Ark constructed on Prince Edward Island completed in 1976. The "PEI Ark" was conceived as a resource independent research laboratory that incorporated the New Alchemists ideas about biological technology coupled with passive solar architecture, wind energy and energy conserving architectural form. Among other researches performed there was the concept of a "living machine" which was another important green strategy. The pioneering work of the New Alchemists biological analogies for aquaculture, and intensive organic agriculture was also incorporated in the Biosphere II project in Oracle, Arizona in the late 1980s.[19]

Several critical lessons were learned from these early demonstration projects. There was an integral relationship among the functional requirements and needs of users, the quality and availability of on-site energy sources, and the various architectural responses to particular contexts. If resources were abundant and the architecture was responsive, then high percentages of the needs could be met. Conversely, if the architecture was poorly designed and constructed, and the on-site resources were scarce or under-used, then there would be a high dependency on conventional fossil fuel sources. It was important to realize the dynamic and inextricable implications contained within this triad: needs to form to energy.

SOLAR COMMUNITIES

The proliferation and ambition of the demonstrations of single solar architectural examples led to the development of larger-scale solar housing projects and solar communities. It soon became clear that single, isolated solar architectural projects were only able to address certain needs in the quest for energy independence. The next logical evolution was to create attached housing typologies, multiple-unit housing clusters, cohousing schemes and village-scale developments that not only utilized solar technologies, but also addressed other site planning, land use, energy, transportation and infrastructural issues. The earliest projects were conventional subdivision developments with solar thermal systems placed on roofs often after initial construction. This was in part a result of the kinds of government demonstration programs and tax-credit incentives at that time. Later projects were more integrated designs with diverse energy systems. One of the first such communities was established on a quarry and landfill site in Llwyngwern near Machynlleth, Wales, called the Centre for Alternative Technology (1973). The purpose was to demonstrate a wide variety of alternative technologies providing education programs for the public. Programs cover all aspects of green living: environmental building, eco-sanitation, woodland management, renewable energy, energy efficiency and organic growing. Today, the Centre houses 90 staff and resident members, and receives around 65,000 visitors each year. Similarly, The Center for Maximum Potential Building Systems (CMPBS) in Austin, Texas, established by Pliny Fisk and Gail Vittori in 1975, demonstrated regional contexts as bases for responsible resource use relative to materials, energy, water, waste, food, and meaningful employment, Figure 3.5d. Their researches and projects investigated eco-balance along with design innovation.

Issues of housing typology, density and scale affected energy performance especially when compared to single detached buildings. Peter Calthorpe and Susan Benson wrote that adding passive solar systems to single houses does save energy inside the home but does not take into consideration the accompanying land use, infrastructure and transportation demands.[20] They went on to say, that these external considerations have a much greater potential for energy savings than any solar application. In a study conducted in Great Britain, heating requirements for varying housing typologies differed greatly. The single-family detached house required double the amount of energy compared to an intermediate flat. Density not only affected the heating requirements of buildings, but also could reduce the length of streets and corresponding infrastructure. Narrower spacing of housing resulted in shorter streets and corresponding travel distances. In *The Cost of Sprawl* (1974), comparisons among various development schemes revealed that those with higher densities and the use of solar technologies reduced both energy consumption, land and development costs. The most expensive was the single-family detached solar model. The most efficient was the solar townhouse typology.[21]

Village Homes was a 70-acre (30-hectares) subdivision located in the west part of Davis, California. Michael and Judy Corbett planned the community for 225 homes and 20 apartments, community center, orchards, vineyards, greenbelts, parks, swimming pool and other common areas.[22] Construction began in 1975. The gross density was 3½ units per acre (8.5 du/hectare) with 40 percent of the development dedicated to open space. Most of the homes were designed with either active or passive solar heating. Access streets to the houses were narrow, less than 20 feet (6 meters) wide, because there were distributed off-street parking bays provided in the plan. All streets within the plan were oriented along the east–west axis that helped enable good solar access and proliferation of solar architectural designs throughout the community. Alternating the street system was an extensive pedestrian and bike path system running through the green spaces and other common areas. Refer to the site plan in Figure3.6a where the horizontal development bands are clearly seen. One criticism of the development, which occurred well after the initial construction, was that some neighbors were solely concerned about property values and house appearance, and did not adhere to or share the principles of the original vision. Nevertheless, Village Homes was an excellent example of the early solar village planning and identified many of the issues, problems and solutions to developments of this nature.

Wonderland Hills was a solar development constructed in several stages in Boulder, Colorado by the Wonderland Hills Development Company. Phase one was primarily an active solar systems' retrofit to newly built housing development on Boulder's north side. The solar systems were funded through the HUD Demonstration Program Cycle 1 in 1974. The systems' integration was an afterthought, as the development plan had already been designed and the program merely became a demonstration of the solar systems. Subsequent phases incorporated passive quadruplex housing clusters and solar townhouses. A low temperature solar system was added to heat the community swimming pool. The community was linked together with pedestrian and bike paths fostering a more pedestrian-friendly environment. Greater care was given to the integration of systems in these later phases. Figure 3.6b shows a wide view of several of the development pieces around Wonderland Lake. Wonderland Hills Development Company became a leader in the design for cohousing communities throughout the United States. Families interested in cohousing were often likely to be equally interested in alternative energy choices.

Cohousing was a process that emerged in the 1970s that integrated community involvement in the initial design process with fairly progressive concepts of intentional community living. The theory originated in Denmark in the 1960s among families who were dissatisfied with existing housing and neighborhood forms. Kathryn McCamant and Charles Durrett introduced cohousing in America after their visits and studies in Denmark. Cohousing was a process that brought interested residents into the very beginning stages of the planning process, often before actual building sites were selected and purchased. The method allowed for a high degree of participation where community concepts often missing in the available building stock were absent. Included were ideas about multi-general residents, safe pedestrian environments especially for children, provision for community functions and facilities, low-rise but compact designs, and automobiles kept at the periphery. Typically cohousing projects were made up of between 20 and 40 homes. By 2007 there were 200 cohousing communities in the United States. In Denmark, where the concept began in 1972, there are some 500,000 people living in cohousing environments. One of the first such projects was Tinggarden Cohousing built in 1978 and was designed by Karsten Vilbild. It was a 79-unit development with a plan of six clusters of attached rental apartments with a common house and space. The common house was used for dining, meetings, socializing and other community activities. It was considered one of the most successful government-subsidized nonprofit housing in Denmark. Other projects, such as Sun and Wind in Beder, Denmark completed in 1980, employed large rooftop solar collector arrays and a windmill for electrical power.[23]

Most large homebuilders were reluctant to stray very far from what they perceived to be the American housing market preference, which included price-point, conformity and relative spaciousness. Housing costs in the United States increased rapidly in the 1970s. The median-priced single-family home in 1970 cost $23,000 at an average interest rate of 8.5 percent, which represented 17 percent of the homeowner's income. By 1979 the same house cost $55,700 at 10.9 percent interest, or 25 percent of the owner's income.[24]

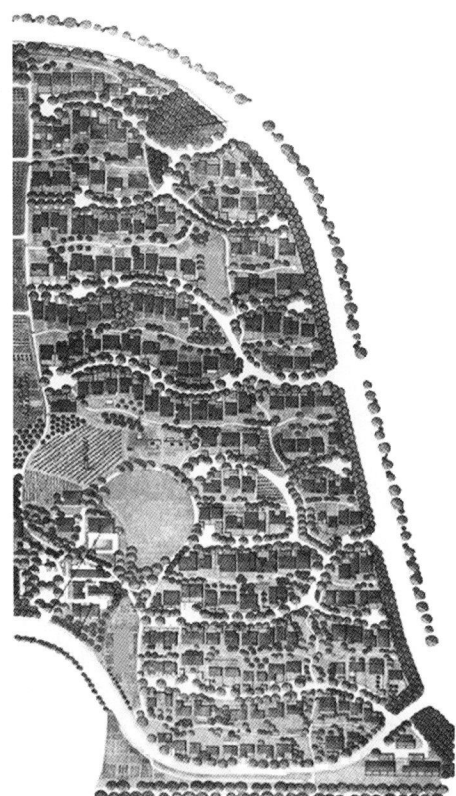

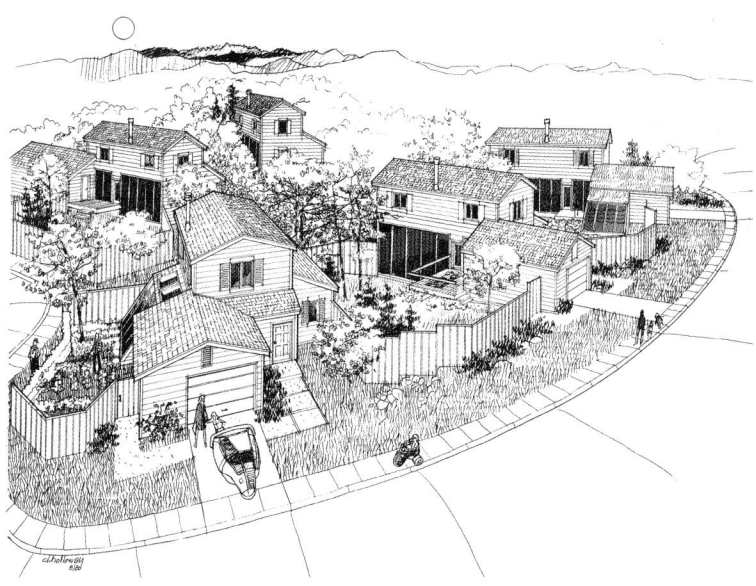

3.6 Solar Communities a) Village Homes (courtesy Mike Corbett) b) Wonderland Hills Development c) Tinggarden Cohousing (courtesy William Sherlaw) d) Mainstreaming Solar Communities (courtesy DennisRHollowayArchitect.com)

The average single-family house size grew from 1,500 square feet to 1,750 square feet (139–163 square meters). Following far more conventional housing delivery methods, the design work of Dennis Holloway for US Homes in Colorado generated model solar homes for the giant homebuilder. Sim Van der Ryn and Peter Calthorpe saw the need for ecological community planning focused in three general areas—the urban tissue, the existing suburban landscape, and new developments beyond the suburbs. They felt it important to see the development of sustainable communities as a connected part of their contexts rather than isolated and self-centered.[25] In *For Everyone a Garden* (1974), Moshe Sofdie put forward the concept of a three-dimensional community that increased density, intensity and access to greenspace.[26] Refer to Figures 3.6a, b and c for varying forms of solar and cohousing communities.

The end of the 1970s finished with a certain optimism. The newly elected Carter administration was supportive of solar and alternative energy development. Carter passed the Solar Energy Research, Development and Demonstration Act, the Federal Non-Nuclear Energy Research and Development Act, and the National Energy Act in 1978, including conservation incentives and tax credits, and limits for the use of oil and gas in electrical generation. Solar technology had evolved from the heat transfer physics of collectors to fully integrated solar communities. For green practitioners there was a shift from form-function preoccupations of modernism to one of form-performance. Where the architecture of the 1960s seemed to spawn bolder, more conceptual and urban concepts of sustainability, the 1970s' architecture was all about the business of responding to the energy crisis revealed at the beginning of the decade. The technological development of solar systems, coupled with the needs and constraints of the systems eventually led to finding architectural ways in which to gracefully integrate them. Solar architecture developed its own language dominated by the solar section, large glazing areas, sloping glass, higher levels of insulation and ways of integrating thermal mass.

WEAVING MODERNISM

Where was mainstream modernism at this time? Labeled by some in the 1970s, it started as "late-modernism" and continued the reductive and functionalist architecture directed toward large commissions for corporate and institutional clients, and by the end of the decade it was tending toward "postmodernism" with a diverse aesthetic that was less rational and formal. It was bracketed by works, such as John Portman's atrium hotel forms found in Atlanta, Georgia at the beginning of the decade to Philip Johnson's Crystal Cathedral in Garden Grove, California at the end of the decade. While the greening of architecture developed technologically and focused on energy performance, mainstream architecture explored slightly different directions often expressing contradictory ideas especially in the context of environmentalism. Modernism was still evolving toward economy, efficiency, and functionalism aided by the expression of technology, mainly structure and cost-oriented material systems.

The early 1970s were characterized with advancements and demonstration programs oriented toward solar heating of skin-dominated residential buildings—those that reduce heat loss around the skin or envelope of the building and compensated with active and passive solar systems. The late 1970s focused more on solar heating for commercial buildings and load-dominated technologies—those that reduced heat loads generated by internal gains, heat generated especially by people, artificial lighting and equipment. This focus was not entirely successful as these larger non-residential building typologies generated greater cooling loads than heating loads, to which the solar systems were not effective. The problems of cooling load reduction through daylighting, solar control with sunshading devices and reflective glazing, and more effective ventilation methods were an easier match to the more recent developments in late-modern architecture.

Much of the solar energy development of this time was regarded as inconsequential to the thrust of late-modernism and the mainstream heroic agendas it embraced. Nor were mainstream housing and commercial markets interested in changing to solar energy applications. Late-modern buildings avoided most of the allusions, irony and self-mockery of postmodernism that was expressed more fully in the 1980s. They also modified the uncomplicated, predictable matchbox shapes of the international style by chamfering or serrating them, by slicing the plan and elevation into angles, or by relinquishing the rectangular prism in favor of pyramidal, cylindrical or free-curved shapes as described by Hugh Hardy and his notions of the evolution of the modern box. Late-modern architecture was nothing if not sleek, glossy and machine-like. It strove to convey the image of the formidable technology of the computer and the satellite, a technology that was not yet practical for everyday use in the building industry even though it appeared overseas in such tours de force as the Hong Kong and Shanghai Bank by Norman Foster (1979–86) and the Lloyds of London Building by Richard Rogers (1978–86).

Centre Georges Pompidou (1977), also known as *Place Georges Pompidou* or *Place Beaubourg*, was located in the center of historic Paris. It was an important building as it not only was a legacy of some of the inspiring images of the earlier work of Archigram, but it synthesized many of the expressions of eco-technology that became commonplace in the 1990s. In 1971 a competition was initiated and it received 650 entries. The team of Renzo Piano, Richard Rogers and Gianfranco Franchini, assisted by Ove Arup and Partners, submitted the winning project. The design was based on the idea of a flexible interior and complex machine exterior. The skin of the building was sheathed in glass that was supported by the steel eco-skeleton with exposed heating and cooling ducts, diagonal escalator, and industrial-like exhaust vents. The structure was to house a museum of modern art, reference library, center for industrial design, and a center for music and acoustic research. Also included were administrative offices, a bookshop, restaurant, cinema and children's activities. It was the technological effects that seemed to endear futurists and engineers alike. They considered the building a "cultural machine."

The piazza in front of Centre Georges Pompidou was very popular and alive. Mimes, street portraitists, musicians and other entertainers animated large crowds and added to the placemaking magic of the Centre. The design of Centre Georges Pompidou was influential in later buildings, which incorporated daylighting, sun control devices, photovoltaic arrays, and water-harvesting technologies that became part of a number of environmental technologies developed with great precision in architectural integration. According to William Curtis, the building was designed "as a vast, serviceable hanger supported by a megastructural steel-tubed frame."[27] Initially, all of the functional structural and environmental elements of the building were celebrated with color-coding: white and stainless steel for the structural skeleton, green pipes were plumbing, blue ducts were for climate control, electrical wires were encased in yellow, and circulation elements and devices for safety were red, which further accentuated the functional and technological expression of the building. The photograph in Figure 3.7b shows the projecting stainless steel trusses and white-painted exhaust vents reminiscent of the tectonic language of a large sea vessel.

Thorncrown Chapel (1980) located in Eureka Springs, Arkansas was designed by Fay Jones and was a radically different expression of technology than Centre Georges Pompidou. Rather than focusing on the exterior façades with high technology, Thorncrown Chapel was a wonderful ethereal marriage inside between light and shadow caused by the crisscrossing wood trusses that transcended as one's position changed through the interior of the space. It was about interiority of experience as can be seen in Figure 3.7c. Sheathed in transparent glass, with 425 windows, and constructed mostly of wood and other materials indigenous to northwestern Arkansas, the design was one large passive solar collector and minimized material transportation costs. It had its own organic aesthetic derived from the Ozarks region and an intimacy that was far different from many late-modern examples of architecture, and especially compared to The Crystal Cathedral (1980) by Philip Johnson, realized at the same time, as seen in Figure 3.7a.

The Crystal Cathedral was a large religious building constructed in Garden Grove, California. The cathedral, founded in 1955, was originally a drive-in theater—an interesting manifestation of contemporary culture in the United States. The purpose-built cathedral seated 2,736 people. The experience of this place was anything but endearing. It was monumental and outrageous, and many visitors viewed it as "spectacular." The thousands of panels of glass glued together and the free space inside created a feeling of grandeur. It was one of the first churches to be conceived as a studio for televised congregational Christian worship.

3.7 Late Modernism a) Crystal Cathedral (courtesy "Shutterstock") b) Centre Georges Pompidou c) Thorncrown Chapel (courtesy of Ed Cooley) d) Citicorp Center (courtesy "Shutterstock")

Critics saw it as a poignant moment in the history of modern evangelicalism that was housed in a dated, opulent architectural form. In 1990 the prayer spire was completed, in 2011 the church filed for bankruptcy, and it was sold and renamed in 2012.

The interest in natural light as demonstrated in The Crystal Cathedral, Thorncrown Chapel and the atrium spaces of John Portman became a logical bridge to the emerging green projects of the 1970s. The 59-story Citibank Center located in New York City was designed by Hugh Stubbins in 1977, and it was a stark reminder of modernism capped with a sloping top originally designed for solar panels as seen in Figure 3.7d. The expression of building technology common to the works of Piano, Rogers and Grimshaw formed another genetic link. The homegrown solar architectural works and skin-dominated systems, primarily created in America in the 1970s, were to soon be joined with the more sophisticated and tectonic load-dominated works of late-modernism in Europe. This was a combination that later informed the development of eco-technology in the 1990s. In between these decades, mainstream architecture went "back to the future" with its self-examining preoccupation with postmodernism, the more historic vernaculars, and hybrid form languages, which to some was a welcome relief to the more rigid modern obsessions previously explored.[28]

Christopher Alexander's, *A Pattern Language*, was published in 1977, and its influence was not felt until the end of the decade and into the 1980s.[29] The structured patterns of recommended practices and design guides spanned scales of application, from paving stones to cities, and provided a design syntax of accumulated design examples that when pooled together created an overall language. Most of the patterns illustrated were time-tested design solutions, many of which had sustainable origins or functions. At the planning scale, such patterns as, "identifiable neighborhoods, web of public transportation, access to water, density rings, and corner grocery store," were important to sustainable community design and the New Urbanism, which developed a decade later. At the building scale, patterns like "building fronts, activity pockets, sheltering roof, south-facing outdoor space, home workshop, and light on two sides of every room," were important to green architectural designs. And the more detailed patterns of "thick walls, interior windows, greenhouse, compost, outdoor room, and sleeping to the east," certainly corresponded with solar energy design practices. In using these patterns as a design tool, it was important to understand a specific context and the needs of a particular place before incorporating the patterns. While many of the patterns addressed climatic issues, there was no clear delineation or grouping of measures for specific climatic regions. Rather than focus solely on renewable technologies, the pattern language was a recipe for an integrative process that also required the function of innovation and design.

The advancements in solar technology and improvements in architectural integration were a direct reaction to building delivery practices that developed under abundant land and resources, vast amounts of energy to process, transport, fabricate and construct, and more energy to heat, cool, light, and power these buildings to heretofore unattainable levels of comfort and dependability. "Energy," according to James Clark Maxwell, was the "go of things."[30] As long as fossil fuels were the primary energy source, they dictated the go of things, which included architecture. The impact of the Oil Embargo and the desire to create greater levels of energy independence led to solar conscious design as an alternative ingredient to architecture of the 1970s. The establishment of the National Renewable Energy Laboratory in 1977 offered the promise for opportunities in alternative technological development. Still three independent strands remained and began to weave into the 1980s—the solar-oriented green, the mainstream modernism and the fledgling postmodern.

In the early 1970s, climate change became a growing concern. It was not clear as to whether this change would bring another ice age or global warming. By the end of the 1970s, scientific opinion had settled on warming, not cooling, which would become evident around the turn of the century. What became known as the Charney Report (1979), suggested that there would be increases in atmospheric concentrations of CO_2 resulting in rising atmospheric temperatures of between 3.6°F and 6.3°F (2°C and 3.5°C).[31] The issue of global warming and its apparent causes were concerns for considerable debate. The first concern was whether or not there really was global warming, which was challenging to the science and accuracy of its reporting. The second dispute was whether these changing temperatures were caused by normal climatic variations or created by human activity, mainly those centered on greenhouse gas production through the burning of fossil fuels. This brought focus to the design of the built environment and the potentially negative effects it may have had on global warming. And third was the estimate of climate sensitivity along with the accuracy and magnitude of predicted changes. By the turn of the century scientists had resolved most of these concerns, yet they became politicized within the public realm.

The International Solar Energy Society (ISES) was a global organization that was originally formed in 1954, but renamed in the early 1970s, and whose purpose was to advance the utilization of solar energy through research, demonstration and awareness to the general public. The Energy Research and Development Administration (EDRA) along with the Solar Energy Research Institute (SERI) were established in 1975. The Department of Housing and Urban Development (HUD) and the Department of Energy (DOE) supported residential and commercial solar demonstrations programs beginning in 1974 and into the early 1980s. The American Institute of Architects Research Corporation (AIA/RC) grew out of an urban design and development corporation to procure grants and contracts. Early work of the AIA/RC headed by John Eberhard focused on energy conservation and solar energy applications to buildings. The first National Passive Solar Conference was held in 1977 that marked a shift from purely solar engineering applications and building science to more architectural applications of the emerging passive solar technologies.

In the late 1970s Lisa Heschong wrote *Thermal Delight in Architecture* that shifted the energy architectural discourse away from tectonic and performance-based considerations to the thermal environment as possessing cultural and sensual qualities.[32] Heschong explained that the central hearth with the warmth and light offered more than energy, but accommodated thermal, psychological social and spiritual comfort. Originally, it was also used for cooking, the smoking of food and protection from wild animals. Similarly, the sauna provided a healing and sensual experience. In Finland, not only was use of the sauna a common practice, but the rolling in snow that accompanied it was also done. Heschong highlighted these oppositions and extremes as contributing to a healthy environment and concluded with the notion that simple pleasures contributed to a sense of delight. These sensibilities seemed to be a harbinger of postmodern architecture, which was to evolve more fully in the 1980s.

An interesting vision of a green future was put forward in a somewhat obscure publication by the Sierra Club called *YV88: An Eco-Fiction of Tomorrow* (1977).[33] The plan was for a transformation of Yosemite Valley as a place where human values and the wilderness enhanced rather than excluded each other. The first thing that happened was that they took out the roads, replanted the linear space and re-introduced the railroad. Next the Yosemite railroad, with new lines, bridges and stations, connected San Francisco to small settlements within the valley. Natural habitats were restored, native animals were re-introduced, water-recycling systems were engineered, windships were designed, and life-support systems were put into place. Estimated annual visitors were numbered over two million. This vision was about the incredibly powerful quality of the natural environment of Yosemite, the creation of new social structures and advanced and imaginative future technologies. YV88, though written in the mid-1970s, was envisioned for 1988. Little did they know how prophetic this vision actually was for the serendipitous decade that was to follow.

ENDNOTES

1   Farrington Daniels was a pioneer of the practical utilization of solar energy-exploring applications in cooking, space heating, agriculture, industrial drying, cooling and refrigeration, and photo-thermal-electric conversions. Farrington Daniels, *Direct Use of the Sun's Energy*. New York: Ballantine Books, 1964.

2   Wilson Clark, *Energy for Survival: The Alternative to Extinction*. Garden City, NY: Anchor Press and Doubleday, 1974.

3   Daniel Yergin, *The Quest: Energy, Security, and the Remaking of the Modern World*. New York: The Penguin Press, 2011.

4   Michael Holtz, *Solar Dwelling Design Concepts*. Washington DC: AIA Research Corporation, 1976.

5   Ken Butti and John Perlin, *A Golden Thread: 2500 years of Solar Architecture and Technology*. Palo Alto: Cheshire Books, 1980.

6   Various energy design strategies are targeted to the varying stages of the design and building delivery process. Jan Kreider, *The Solar Heating Design Process*. New York: McGraw-Hill Book Company, 1982.

7   The office primarily focused on solar architectural projects for five years between 1974 and 1979. The Solar Housing Project was also known as The Stonebraker Solar Housing Project. Joint Venture Architects, Principals: Alan Brown, Roland Hower and Phillip Tabb. Boulder, Colorado, 1975.

8   Othmar Humm and Peter Toggweiler, *Photovoltaics in Architecture*. Basel: Birkhauser Verlag, 1993.

9   Richard Crowther was known for his deep commitment to passive solar projects and an early concern for healthy environments. Passive systems were considered those that did not rely on external mechanical and electrical devices and energy. Passive systems were designed to capture and store energy for one day and night. Richard Crowther, *Sun Earth: How to Use Solar and Climatic Energies*. Scribner Publishers, 1977.

10   Soft energy was less about supply and more about efficient use and a diversity of energy sources. Most important were the socio-political impacts. Amory Lovins, *Soft Energy Paths: Towards a Durable Peace*. New York: Harper Collins, 1977.

11   Robert Boyce, *Keck and Keck: The Poetics of Comfort*. Princeton: The Princeton Architectural Press, 1993.

12   Edward Mazria, *The Passive Solar Energy Book*. Emmaus, PA: Rodale Press, 1979: 28–61.

13   Michael Corbett, "First Village, Santa Fe, NM: Living Proof," *Progressive Architecture*. New York, April 1979: 2.

14   James Lambeth, *Sundancing: The Art and Architecture of James Lambeth*. Louisville, KY: Miami Dog Press, 1993: 10–11.

15   The work of Ralph Knowles was extremely important in bringing attention to the urban scale. His first book, *Energy and Form*, related urban spatial structures with the sensuous movements of the sun. Ralph Knowles, *Sun Rhythm Form*. Cambridge: MIT Press, 1981.

16 The book identifies methods for creating composite shadow masks for buildings on flat and sloping sites. Phillip Tabb, *Solar Energy Planning*. New York: McGraw-Hill Book Company, 1984: 214–21.

17 Lori Ryker, *Off the Grid*. Layton, UT: Gibbs Smith Publisher, 2001.

18 Michael Reynolds, *Earthship, Volume II—Systems and Components*. Taos, NM: Solar Survival Press, 1991: 45–8.

19 Nancy Jack Todd (ed.), *The Book of the New Alchemists*. New York: E.P. Dutton, 1977.

20 This work was important in presenting the idea that there could be greater energy savings at the planning and urban design scales. Peter Calthorpe and Susan Benson, "Beyond Solar: Design for Sustainable Communities," *Resettling America*, edited by Gary Coates. Andover, MA: Brickhouse Publishing, 1981: 313.

21 Real Estate Research Corporation, *The Cost of Sprawl: Environmental and Economic Cost of Alternative Residential Development Patterns at the Urban Fringe*. Washington DC: United States Printing Office, 1977.

22 Michael Corbett, *A Better Place to Live: New Designs for Tomorrow's Communities*. Emmaus, PA: Rodale Press, 1981.

23 Kathryn McCamant and Charles Durrett, *Creating Cohousing: Building Sustainable Communities*. Gabriola Island, BC: New Society Publishers, 2011.

24 Gale Cengage, *American Decades*. Self-published, 2000.

25 Sim Van der Ryn and Peter Calthorpe, *Sustainable Communities: A New Design Synthesis for Cities, Suburbs and Towns*. San Francisco: Sierra Club Books, 1986.

26 Moshe Sofdie, *For Everyone a Garden*. Cambridge, MA: MIT Press, 1974.

27 William J. Curtis, *Contemporary Architecture since 1900*," Third Edition. London: Phaidon Press Ltd, 1996.

28 Jim Leckie, Gil Masters, Harry Whitehouse and Lily Young, *Other Homes and Garbage: Designs for Self-Sufficient Living*. San Francisco: Sierra Club books, 1975.

29 Christopher Alexander, Sara Ishikawa, Murray Silverstein, Max Jacobson, Ingrid Fiksdahl-King and Shlomo Angel, *A Pattern Language*. Oxford, UK: Oxford University Press, 1977.

30 Medard Gabel, *Energy, Earth and Everyone*. San Francisco: Straight Arrow Books, 1975: 16.

31 Jule G. Charney et al., *Carbon Dioxide and Climate: A Scientific Assessment*. Washington DC: National Academy of Sciences, 1979.

32 Lisa Heschong, *Thermal Delight in Architecture*. Cambridge, MA: MIT Press, 1979.

33 Christopher Swan and Chet Roaman, *YV88: An Eco-Fiction of Tomorrow*. San Francisco: Sierra Club Books, 1977.

Chapter 4
1980s: Postmodern Green

Phillip Tabb

> **A new architecture must be formed that is simultaneously aligned with transcultural continuity and with the poetics expression of individual situations and communities.**[1]

Postmodernism was an outgrowth of modernism just as modernism itself was an outgrowth of the Enlightenment of the 19th century. Postmodernism was another one of those terms that was difficult to define and it was as diverse and pluralistic as the theoretical frameworks from which it arose. Derived from artistic and intellectual theory, it approached traditional ideas and practices in non-traditional ways. Whereas modernism was primarily concerned with principles such as identity, unity, authority, objective knowledge, authenticity, reason, and certainty, postmodernism was often associated with difference, plurality, non-linearity, relativism, mutability, skepticism, and social constructivism. Postmodernism in architecture, according to Charles Jencks, celebrated hybridity, which showed the mixture of opposing periods as in past, present and future.[2] It possessed multiple codes combining global technology and local culture or modern architectural elements with vernacular forms.

The postmodernism of the 1980s had an anesthetizing effect on the uninhibited solar architecture of the 1970s, which to a large extent utilized the language of modernism with the emergent alternative environmental technologies. Postmodernism's focus on wit, symbolism, reference, double-coding, and polychromatic aesthetics was in dire contrast to the fixed, overly responsible and performance-based solar predecessors. Instead of solar exaggerated forms, postmodern architecture adapted to local vernacular forms and materials while still appropriating modernist elements and details or departed completely, such as the examples of deconstruction. They were hybrid mixtures of historic, modernist and spurious vernacular languages. While postmodern architecture was seeking greater meaning and aesthetic and symbolic enrichment, one quality that seemed to be missing was "authenticity." According to William Curtis, many of the postmodern buildings shared tendencies toward superficiality, which took earlier precedents for reference projecting a "historical self-consciousness."[3]

Where the greening of modern urbanism was initially focused on solar technology and housing developments in the last decade, new agendas were being hatched with postmodern influences in the 1980s. Climatic design principles were still being systematically considered, but in new ways as expressed in layering found in Donald Watson and Kenneth Labs,

Climatic Design (1983). Postmodern urbanism in response to the placelessness of modernism and globalization began to promote concepts like romanticism, interdependence, self-organizing change, and the modesty of the everyday. Preoccupations emerged with the randomness of interstitial and X-urban spaces, such as Collage City, redefinition that occurred at the edges or boundaries of places, such as Edge City, or the re-tribalizations at the center of the New Urbanism. The lack of legibility and as Nan Ellin suggested, the desire for the familiar and contextually relevant, were missing.[4] The search to resurrect appropriate modernity, critical regionalism and ecological design strategies became variously articulated. The modern urban landscape replete with an inventory of modernist buildings, modern materials and international products was at best given remedial and piecemeal postmodern experiments, which in general ignored the previous and more aggressive solar architectural forms and solar community demonstrations.

POSTMODERNISM

Postmodernism provided a good venue for green architecture to be reexamined and advanced. Both movements were reacting to modernism's negative impact on culture and the environment. The solar architectural works of the previous decade became too predictable, rigid, and inflexible. The strictly tectonic demonstrations were expanded to explore other dimensions of context and languages of form. Architectural theoretician Steven Moore argued; "In the 1970s and 1980s, postmodern environmentalists in Europe and North America routinely characterize modern architecture as both inhumane and inherently anti-nature. In this reactionary view, modern architecture, like modern science and technology that enabled it, was understood be the principal source of environmental degradation, not its cure."[5]

The modernist roots of early green architecture were based on the pursuit of a functional and tectonic order, yet postmodern theory released the rigid functional rules of performance-based design and resituated them to reflection, interpretation and spontaneous expression of coterminous meaning inherent to a particular place or living vernacular. North American postmodern architecture seemed to evolve in two distinct directions. First was with the appropriating of vernacular forms and their revisionist application to contemporary programs, such as the vernacular scaling to "big-box" buildings in commercial shopping malls, or the ornamentation to high-rise structures, such as Philip Johnson's AT&T Building in New York City (1979), and Michael Graves's Portland Building (1983). Second was the focus on the variegated role of local and environmental conditions and causes, which originally generated the vernacular forms. Important to understand was "cause" and then "appropriate contemporaneous form response." The application of indigenous greening principles to specific contexts produced hybrids drawn from cultural and environmental characteristics of a particular place and time, yet interestingly; they maintained continuity with certain modernist spatial, tectonic and material concepts.

While constructed in 1962, the Vanna Venturi house was both an icon and harbinger for postmodernism that fully manifested in the 1980s, Figure 4.1a. It was located in the historic district of Chestnut Hill within Philadelphia, Pennsylvania. Its design was done at the same time that Venturi was writing *Complexity and Contradiction in Architecture*.[6] The primary language of Venturi's design, a simple vernacular broad gabled-roof form, was broken at the ridge with a gap or split pediment that celebrated the hearth and exposed the chimney.

4.1 Postmodern Architecture a) Venturi House (Photography © Vladimir Paperny) b) AT&T Building (courtesy David Shankbone) c) Portland Building (image courtesy City of Portland Archives, Oregon) d) Piazza d'Italia (courtesy of "Shutterstock")

The design maintained axial symmetry and balance with the duality created by the bifurcated street façade, and Venturi saw the house as having a tension between both its large and small qualities. These contributed to the ambiguity and posed playful historical and aesthetic contradictions. This house widely expressed the symbolic form and composition of mass-produced architectural elements that supported the notion of a "decorated shed," which was in dire contrast to the flat-roofed glass box pavilions designed by many modernist architects at that time. Although it was conceived well before any environmental concerns in architecture were commonly known, its design certainly challenged modernist orthodoxy. Its contribution to green postmodernism was somewhat tangential. The Vanna Venturi house did provide a connection to the use of historic vernacular forms with integrated modernist details, which opened the door for a greening of architecture especially at the residential scale.

The infatuation with postmodern high-rise design can clearly be seen with the 37-story Sony Tower, formally the AT&T Building, which was design by Philip Johnson and completed in 1984, Figure 4.1b. Most modern high-rise buildings simplified the form by essentially playing down or eliminating the tripartite base and termination into a single unadorned expression of shaft. Conversely, the postmodern high-rise overly dramatized the base and especially the upper floors and roof. The tops were typically given emphasis, distinction and iconic value to the cityscape. The AT&T building became immediately controversial largely because of its adorned ornamental top. Kate Nesbit described this building as pastiche and having historical fragments that did not possess genuine respect for the past. Aside from issues of image and form, the validity of the high-rise building typology, as a sustainable approach to mitigating sprawl and reducing energy, still remained in question. The challenges posed by transportation, infrastructure, resource utilization and embodied energy were among the issues of high-rise sustainability. Addressing the greening of high-rise architecture occurred with greater urgency and attention at the turn of the century as sustainable urbanism became a global concern, especially in more densely populated regions where high-rise building typologies are far more commonplace—the rule rather than the exception.

Michael Graves had become less concerned with the roots of modernism and had developed a wide-ranging eclecticism in which he abstracted historical forms and emphasized the iconic shapes reinforced with the use of color. He had been a member of the New York Five in the 1970s, whose work was informed by pure geometrical languages and were later criticized for indifference to site and context—a major issue addressed by postmodernists. Grave's departure from the New York Five was an endorsement of pictorial classicism, which was applied to a wide range of commercial, residential, and product designs. Graves was probably best known for The Portland Municipal Services Building in Portland, Oregon constructed in 1982, Figure 4.1c. It was a 15-story municipal office building that incorporated a variety of surface materials and patterned windows that articulated the facades into the illusion of a decorative language.

Another reaction to modernist architecture was expressed in the work of Charles Moore. Constructed in 1963, the houses at Sea Ranch in Sonoma County, California along the Pacific coastline were a play on timber-framed construction and "redwood-cabin Regionalism," as described by William Curtiss. The response was a regional shed-roof vernacular that was used to deflect the strong winds. His work in the 1980s, however, evolved into something more playful employing some of the lessons of Pop Art. Charles Moore and Perez Architects designed the eclectic Piazza d'Italia in New Orleans, 1979, Figure 4.1d. It featured an urban outdoor fountain and stage-set that connected a series of colonnades and screens into an atmosphere of entablatures, color, and form. It was conceived as a new symbolic gathering point and memorial for the New Orleans Italian community.[7]

These example works of American postmodern architecture expressed dissatisfaction with the vapid effects of modernity, and provided a change that redeemed pluralism, complexity, double coding, historical contextualism, and hybridity.[8] They were clever, decorative, ironic and interesting. These works brought out an interesting question regarding the greening of architecture. What were their redeeming qualities and formal and material implications to sustainability?

- Pluralism: a response to modernism's reduced and overly objective and singular levels of abstraction that could not capture the richness of diversity. This included singular models of sustainable architecture. Pluralism in green architecture allowed for multiple design agendas and elements of expression, especially grafting sustainable technologies into vernacular languages. It allowed for modern technologies, materials and details to be appropriated in postmodern and sustainable ways.
- Complexity: modernism's focus on efficiency, function and simplicity reduced the expression of elaboration, variability and scale. Complexity in green architecture could be contradictory where complexity of form created energy inefficiencies, yet complexity of environmental systems could be necessary in order to respond to the multiple building needs, variable on-site resources, and differing systems' requirements. Green architecture was seen less as an object and more as an environment of dynamic and inter-related parts.

- Double Coding: modernism stripped away meaning, symbolism, and reference through abstraction rather than conveying multiple levels of meaning, ambiguity, connotation, juxtaposition, and simultaneous forms of expressions that could be experienced in diverse ways on multiple scales—cosmos, region, neighborhood, dwelling, room and object. Double coding in green architecture suggested the presence of tectonic hybridity in response to multivalent environmental phenomena, and the expression of eclectic architectural languages. It also built on the notions of twin-phenomena or dual function.
- Contexualism: modernism supported the reduction and even elimination of local constituent architectural features in favor of ones that were universal and homogenized. Contextualism in green architecture, was perhaps more easily understood and demonstrated, related to the historical precedents, climatic conditions, and cultural characteristics of a place. This opened the door to the integration of on-site resources and the expressive incorporation of their corresponding technologies as well as local building materials and practices.
- Hybridity: modernism sought a universality and homogeneity of form and function, structure and technology, and materials and details. For postmodernism, hybridity contributed to the complexity, ambiguity, and irony of architectural design. In green architecture hybridity certainly had relevance in the mixes of conventional and alternative technologies, local and universal materials, but also the integration of differing architectural languages—modern, vernacular, critical regionalist, reconstruction and deconstruction.

While the differences between modernism and postmodernism were explicitly delineated, it was interesting to see the ways in which they still were connected. A great deal of attention was given to change in expression, scale, image and to some extent building form, as modernism was taken from the present and put into the past. Postmodernism assumed the role of the more current paradigm. Yet on some levels there was little difference in terms of construction materials and methods, spatial concepts, structural systems, building equipment or tectonic details. Postmodern architecture was released from static and sober expressions to a richer, more ironic and colorful style. Green architecture, by necessity, was required to re-think the materialization of buildings in order to render the sustainable systems' in efficient and functional ways. Issues of form, shape and orientation, and of opacity, transparency and massiveness, for example, needed careful consideration in order to realize the full utility of the emergent sustainable systems.

CONSERVATION, PRESERVATION AND HISTORICISM

Conservation, preservation and historicism were three completely different approaches to postmodern regionalism in the 1980s. There were similarities and shared concerns as each addressed the present building stock in ways that either related, protected, reused and/or upgraded to higher levels of environmental performance. Far from being pastiche, they were perhaps overly serious and respectful of the past, placing historic integrity above accommodation of contemporary programs of use—form follows historic purity. In contrast, Aldo van Eyck argued for an architecture of temporal depth with an inherent continuum that created a form language charged with vital historical associations.

Conservation was referred to as a process where the architectural heritage was prolonged and the integrity of character was maintained through carefully planned interventions. This included the identity, style, form and materials of the building placing a high premium on their retention. Conservation was the ethical use and the managing of change of land or buildings. Within ecological conservation, it involved the sustaining, maintaining and improving the ecosystem. Conservation had the dual agenda of preserving that, which was essential and important and allowing for change and evolution. The term is often interchangeable with preservation, yet conservation promoted restoration for continued use.

Preservation was a more protective practice focused on the built environment especially with privileged structures with historic significance. John Muir, who founded the Sierra Club and expounded the value of American wilderness as part of the country's culture and identity, started the preservation movement. He advocated that these iconic wildernesses be preserved for future generations as part of that cultural heritage and quickly gained the ear of movers and shakers at the time. In architecture issues of integrity, authenticity, and accuracy were a challenge, especially with the need of new programs of use.

Historicism was less a specific practice and was more of a mode of thinking that gave significance to mutable interpretations to local contexts, historical periods and geographical places. The source or essence of architecture could only be defined within the historical context to which it belonged—a systemic affect. Historic innuendos and elements of design were appropriated into new buildings. Another dimension of historicism was the glorification of the moment into what was called "periodization," and the separation of works into distinct categories of time. According to Alan Colquhoun, there were three kinds of historicism advanced through the continual creation of the avant-garde in social, technological and symbolic forms. Two facets emerged, concerns for the past and the direct use of historical forms. For green architecture historicism strengthened the bond to both geographical and temporal contexts, especially where climatic vernaculars were concerned.

Important to green practice was the repurposing or recycling existing buildings with new functions and contemporary uses. Adaptive re-use realized the embodied energy and resources inherent in using rather than destroying our existing stock of buildings. Carl Stein explained that it consumed the equivalent of 17,000 gallons of oil, which takes into account the manufacture and delivery of building materials and products as well as the energy required during construction, to build a new 3,500 square feet (325 m^2) house. The environmental value or the amount of energy saved by adaptive re-use and sustainable upgrades were considered between 1/3 and 1/2 the energy required for new construction.[9]

Architectural restoration, rehabilitation, reconstruction, upgrades and densification were concerns of conservation and were important to the greening process. Restoration focused on the retention of the most important historic features of a particular time while allowing removal of materials from other periods. Rehabilitation emphasized the retentions and repair of historic features including materials, finishes, spatial relationships and character. Reconstruction established limited opportunities to reconstitute a building in new materials and upgrading suggested modernizing buildings to meet present construction standards. This included upgrading to meet higher energy performance levels. These conservation practices occurred in differing ways that were project-specific over time or the life of a building.

4.2 Preservation, Re-creation and Recycling a) Wyoming, Ohio Historic Home (courtesy of Wyoming Historical Society) b) Rainwater Retrofit (courtesy of "Shutterstock") c) Portmeirion, Wales d) Universal Recycle Symbol

Two architectural works that share certain similarities are quite different. The Wyoming, Ohio house located within metropolitan Cincinnati, Ohio was an example of a well-kept and restored early 20th-century Tudor-revival home, Figure 4.2a. In contrast was a new home designed by Ike Kligerman Barkley Architects and located in upstate New York. A cursory comparison reveals that the two-story houses both have strong gable roofs with dormers, stonewalls and chimneys that reach up beyond the roofs. Yet upon closer examination, it becomes clear that they were not constructed in the same era. To modernists this design language may have been sacrilegious, but in postmodernism, it was quite acceptable. Figure 4.2b is a residential retrofit to a conventional house form for rainwater harvesting and non-mechanical ventilation, and Figure 4.2c is a photograph of the Portmeirion Village Center located in north Wales and design by Welsh architect Sir Clough Williams-Ellis (1925–75). Figure 4.2d is the ubiquitous universal recycle symbol designed by Gary Anderson (1970).

CONTEMPORARY VERNACULAR

Some viewed vernacular architecture as simply shelter in response to basic needs—a style of architecture fixed in the past. Vernacular architecture was also considered an area of architectural theory that viewed buildings that were made by empirical methods without the interventions of professional architects. This was to suggest that the design and construction evolved through an intuitive, instinctive, learned and an accumulative intelligence gained by trial-and-error of making and shared time-tested experiences within a given locale. It was an evolving vernacular that embodied a regenerative process. Other notions of vernacular architecture saw the use of locally available resources and traditions to address local needs and circumstances. With both views on vernacular architecture, they tended to evolve over time and reflected the environmental, cultural and historical context in which they existed. Another view of vernacular architecture was explained by the embodied vernacular experience of a place, which evolved a living intelligence and, therefore, was available for translation, transformation and application contemporary cultural use.

A living vernacular was one in which the most useful traditions of a particular place were carried on in time and were recreated as well as re-invented. Older forms and methods were slowly augmented with trial-and-error improvements and the introduction of new technologies. Construction practices, vernacular forms, and specific details were improved. For example, the fire pit evolved into a fireplace with chimney and the chimney evolved to maximize draw of fresh air and expulsion of unwanted smoke. These in turn were amalgamated and refined over time into the overall expression of the buildings. Two contemporary characteristics and challenges were the increase in space size and number of functions and the incorporation of modern technology and equipment. Typical sustainable characteristics that have accompanied contemporary vernacular residential architecture include the following:

- Climate responsive primary and secondary architectural forms and building elements.
- Use of passive solar heating, orientation-conscious design where possible, including new advances in glass technology, and spatial buffering.
- Use of daylighting, natural ventilation, operable windows and sunshading.
- Incorporation of on-site water harvesting.
- Use of high-efficiency heating, air conditioning and control systems.
- Use of energy efficient appliances throughout.
- Use of local, natural, low-embodied energy, and/or not-toxic building materials.
- In more recent instances, the use of photovoltaics for electricity production.

In Australia, Glenn Murcutt was also concerned with the production of environmentally sensitive architectural works, of both residential and institutional type. His motto was, "touch the earth lightly," and connect to nature.[10] The Magney House in New South Wales (1984) used a vaulted butterfly roof that featured water, air and light. Adapted to the hot, dry climate were wide overhangs that protected the glass from excessive sunlight and channeled breezes through the house. A trough, down the longitudinal length of the house, collected rainwater, which fed to an underground cistern. The southern side of the dwelling housed service functions while the northern side was open to daylight, prevailing breezes and vistas to the Tasman Sea (located in the southern hemisphere), Figure 4.4a.

In Nova Scotia, Brian MacKay-Lyons designed with traditional vernacular forms and modernist details. While he began his practice in the mid-1980s, his seminal green designs were done a decade later. He drew inspiration from the local construction culture and regional architectural forms of the shipbuilding towns along the Nova Scotia coast. The Martin-Lancaster House, located in Prospect along the Atlantic coast, was 3,000 square feet (279 square meters) residential complex featuring a composition of simple gable forms including a detached garage and guesthouse, social pavilion and arrival courtyard.

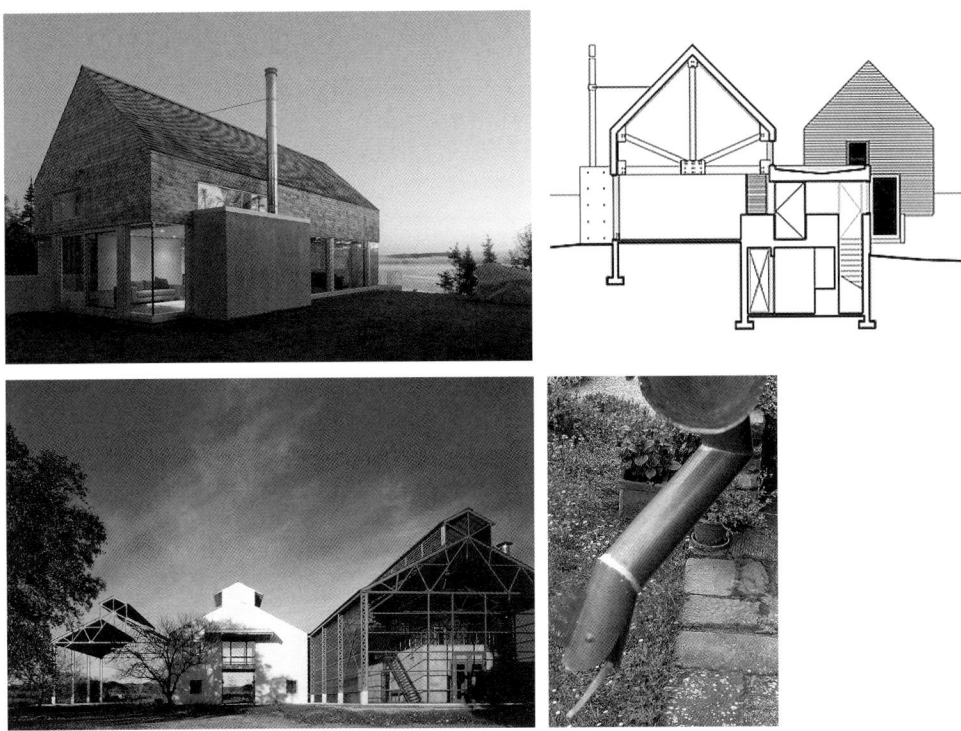

4.3   Contemporary Vernaculars a) Martin-Lancaster House (courtesy of Greg Richardson Photography) b) Martin-Lancaster Section (courtesy of Mackay-Lyons Sweetapple Architects) c) Alamo Cement House (courtesy of Hester + Hardaway Photographers) d) Downspout

Suntempering and passive solar building strategies were used as well as a "zero-detailed" roof in response to the freeze/thaw cycles of the marine climate. Malcolm Quantrill described his work as: "An architecture as 'instrument,' rather than as a predetermined formal or geometric entity, [that] would be open to the possibility of free interpretation or free performance."[11] The profile of the Martin-Lancaster House, pictured in Figures 4.3a and b, illustrates the simple iconic vernacular gable roof, a more balanced form compared to the dominant solar section of the 1970s.

In San Antonio, Texas the firm Lake|Flato developed a regionally driven contemporary vernacular that in their words was a "blend of sustainability and modesty."[12] Primarily working within the Texas climate, their work focused on responses to the unique qualities of a specific site, natural vernacular materials, rainwater collection, large roofs for summer shading, and passive solar heating in winter. Their works were driven by the use of a palette of regional materials, authentic forms and the natural environment. Often they employed rural vernaculars, such as large roof overhangs, rolling barn doors, exposed structure and corrugated metal roofs, silos and wall panels. It was the roof that emerged as the most dominant and important design feature that characterized many of their projects in the hot Texas climate. The Carraro Residence or Alamo Cement House located in Kyle, Texas (1990) was designed using reassembled steel structural parts from the Alamo Cement Plant, which was being demolished and sold for scrap, Figure 4.3c. The industrial vernacular shell was repurposed as an outer skin to provide sunshading and spatial definition for outdoor rooms. The success of this work was measured by the hybridity and reuse of these historic vernacular forms and their utility to contemporary architectural agendas.

The work of Miller Hull in the Northwest of the United States was what they called a "new realism," buildings with simple enclosures and regional gestures, and the use of hybrid materials, such as redwood, corrugated metal, painted steel, and concrete floors.[13] The Hansen Residence in Moses Lake, Washington (1984) was an earth-sheltered, passive solar house or the Novotny Cabin in Decatur Island, Washington (1990) was a simple iconic gable-formed structure with extended overhangs on the east and west sides for sun and rain protection. Their work did not employ any overt sustainable technologies, but rather responded to regional and local site conditions through design, using compact forms and little spatial complexity, passive solar heating in winter and sunshading in summer. A strong determinant was the function of the architecture to create direct engagement with the beautiful conditions provided by the site and the experience of nature. While many of their pioneering projects were completed in the 1990s, they reflected the spirit and intent of many postmodern contemporary vernaculars. The Bridge House (1987), Bainbridge Island, Washington by James Cutter, was another good example of a vernacular form designed to enhance the experience of site and take advantage of a south orientation for passive solar heating and views to Puget Sound. Cutter believed that architecture should pay homage to the site and respond carefully to the ecological demands of the place.[14]

An interesting offshoot of contemporary vernacular practices was the community-oriented design-build projects of The Rural Studio and Yestermorrow that brought together regional considerations to the actual building process in unconventional ways. The Rural Studio, established in western Alabama by Samuel Mockbee, was a program at Auburn University that became widely acclaimed for introducing students to the social responsibilities of architectural practice and for providing safe, creatively designed, low cost, and sustainable buildings.[15] These buildings, designed and built by students, incorporated novel materials which otherwise would be considered waste. For example, Masons Bend Community Center, Figure 4.4b, was a multifunctional open-air structure that used automobile windshields for glazing, rammed earth for walls, and improvised construction techniques. It was considered a hybridized vernacular that consisted of a combination of vernacular, green and modernist elements. Their outreach works were directed to community projects and families living in rural Alabama with incredibly low construction budgets.

The work of Yestermorrow, founded in 1980 in Waitsfield, Vermont, focused on emerging renewable technologies that were self-built and low cost building methods, and combined a design-build school with outreach projects, such as the Waitsfield House in Figure 4.4c. The Yestermorrow School provided more than 150 workshops and courses in sustainable design and construction for students of all ages with the goal of learning through shared inquiry and hands-on experience. Their sustainable design courses included green development best practices, solar systems design, wind power, green remodeling, and green building materials. The significance of Yestermorrow's work was in the collaborative nature of the design process and focus on craft-based sustainable design approaches. The participatory and creative design work by the Archetype, Rural Studio and Yestermorrow, and the contemporary vernacular forms of Murcutt, McKay-Lyons, Lake|Flato and Miller Hull reflected a connection to modernism's functionality and simplicity, but also realized forms that were human in scale, connected participants with the surrounding environment and were climate-responsive. The suburban Parisian sun-tempered house completed in the mid-1980s characterized a vernacular form dressed in postmodern geometric patterns, colors and materials.

4.4 Regional Green Designs a) Magney House (Photo: Anthony Browell courtesy of the Architecture Foundation Australia) b) Masons Bend Community (courtesy Tim Hursley) c) Yestermorrow (courtesy Gary Hall) d) Parisian Postmodern

POSTMODERN URBANISM

Postmodern ideas about the city were reactions to placelessness, rampant sprawl, absence of community, and issues of safety. They promoted either a sense of place, community, stewardship and security on one hand, or excitement, control and escapism on the other. Often the former demanded automatic respect for the existing context and pre-occupation of pre-industrial forms of urban designs. They championed past identifiable forms and metaphors that suggested wholeness, homogeneity and comprehensibility, such as, market squares, city blocks, narrow streets, clearly defined neighborhoods and villages. The latter approached the city as a rapidly changing, unpredictable, accidental and contemporary cultural landscape that often evolved within what Nan Ellin called "betwixted and between" places.

Investigations and metaphors such as *College City* by Colin Rowe (1975), *Learning from Las Vegas* by Venturi, Scott-Brown and Izenour (1977), and *Edge City* by Joel Garreau (1992) are paradigms of urban heterogeneity.

Where solar communities grew from the success of single-application solar technologies on individual buildings, and the interest in proliferating the energy savings through larger demonstrations and higher densities, they tended to lack richness, complexity and diversity in their designs. Other collective postmodern measures such as the New Urbanism movement were largely influenced by the postmodern agenda and reacted to the rampant suburban sprawl, functional zoning laws, and low density, and promoted more compact, mixed use, and neo-traditional settlement designs. The Central Place Theory (Thunen, 1826 and Christaller, 1933) influenced many of the New Urban developments with open markets, greens or plazas in settlement centers. Places like Poundbury in Dorset, UK (Leon Krier), Seaside, Florida (Duany Plater-Zyberk), and the transit-oriented developments (TOD) in California (Calthorpe Associates) were among the notable examples of this new movement. The New Urbanism developed guiding principles, which are still considered today:

> *Neighborhoods should be diverse in use and population; communities should be designed for the pedestrian and transit as well as the car; cities and towns should be shaped by physically defined and universally accessible public spaces and community institutions; urban places should be framed by architecture and landscape design that celebrate local history, climate, ecology, and building practice.*[9]

Two initial schools of thought emerged in the early stages of New Urbanism in the United States. The first was the development of new satellite communities, commonly located in the east and southeast that were based upon traditional town planning practices. These included the organizational planning devices, such as orthogonal grids, city blocks, hierarchy of roads, tree-lined streets, village centers, walkable scale and varying lot sizes and housing typologies. The second was planning and design reforms to conventional housing development practices, most often located on the west coast, that generally included use and density mixes, transportation nodes and modal changes, and formal geometry occurring with larger-scale and relatively functional zoning schemes.

Poundbury was an experimental new town extension of Dorchester, England on land owned by the Duchy of Cornwall.[16] Guided by principles set forth by Prince Charles, it was planned by Leon Krier in 1988–91 as a traditional higher density mixed use urban pattern with focus on pedestrian, rather than automobile, movement within the community. Poundbury was planned for an ultimate build-out of 2,500 dwellings for a population of 6,000 residents. Its design, as can be seen in Figure 4.5a, seemed to be based on more compact and spatially organized German town planning schemes rather than the more organic traditional English villages. The architecture, however, was strictly English. In order to maintain high development standards, a stringent code was developed to communicate the intended character and ensure conformity to the master plan, which was a common practice for New Urban developments. The design implemented many of the ideas that were previously published in Krier's urban design manifesto in the early 1980s. The urban design manifesto outlined a set of critiques of modern urbanism.[17] Among his counsels were the conceptual blueprints for urban growth by *multiplication* rather than by gross *addition*, promotion of *integrated zoning* rather than *functional zoning* with spatial separation of uses, and establishment of pedestrian scaled *urban patterns* such as streets, blocks, squares and outdoor public rooms. Principal ideas of Krier's urban design manifesto included the following:

- Population growth by organic multiplication of livable, walkable urban increments rather than by mere addition and gross expansion at the edge—hypertrophy.
- Implementation of integrated zoning of activities rather than spatially separated "functional" zones.
- Creation of traditional urban patterns, such as, walkable urban blocks and streets, squares, and a mix of public and private buildings.
- Inclusion of dispersed "civitas" included both local and whole community public activities indoors and outdoors.
- Reduction of automobile dependency, promotion of a pedestrian-scale environment and walkable distances within the community.
- Planning of an organic town–country transect and hierarchy of urban form—a legible gradient silhouette.
- Compact urban design with higher density using individuated building blocks that also give structure to and definition for public spaces.

The first highly publicized New Urban development was Seaside, Florida, an 80-acre (32 hectares) destination community located in Walton County along the Florida Panhandle, Figure 4.5b. Designed by Duany and Plater-Zyberk and Company (DPZ) for developer Robert Davis, it incorporated many New Urban planning principles guided by the building code and town plan.[18] Its projected population was 2,000 residents with approximately 490 dwellings, another 95,000 square feet (8,825 square meters) of commercial space composed of a mix of uses including restaurants, grocery store, shops, markets, chapel, school and recreation facilities. Seaside rose to global fame with the filming location of the popular movie *The Truman Show* (1998). The goal of Seaside was to not create an old-fashioned beach town, inner-city neighborhood or an alienating suburban environment, but to create a social atmosphere within a vacation seaside environment. Features included mandatory porches, a discernible center, mixes of use including necessity stores, narrow streets, walking paths, and protection of the beach ecology. The Form-Based Code was an enabling design tool that gave conforming control for the design of the place.

According to Peter Katz, it was initially criticized as being "too cute" or it was not "a real town."[19] Seaside evolved to become an important New Urban model and demonstration of certain planning principles. In regards to not being real, Robert Davis argued that Seaside should not be compared to purpose-made suburban communities or the revitalization of established inner city neighborhoods, but rather it should be contrasted with other seaside vacation developments, which at the beginning of Seaside's construction were piecemeal single-use developments strung along the Florida Panhandle from Pensacola to Panama City. Few places were designed like the historic Grayton Beach Village, located several miles from Seaside, that responded to original seaside community character and integrity, which included buildings derived from the cultural and environmental conditions of that place. In deference to the instant developments along the Panhandle at that time, Seaside evolved in strategic stages or manageable increments over time through the use of the form-based code developed by DPZ.

New Urban development on the US West Coast took on a slightly different form. Not specifically aimed at creating new communities, it was initially directly at improving conventional residential development of that time. These New Urban projects generally maintained revenue-retaining and market-driven elements, but focused on reforms to transportation, the automobile and modifying larger housing development practices with density and use mixes rather than creating all together new or traditional town forms.

  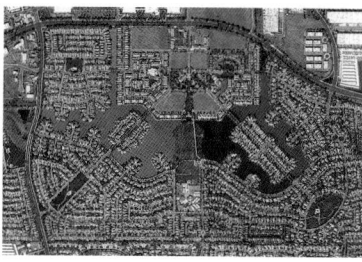

4.5 New Urbanism a) Poundbury, UK (Leon Krier) (© Duchy of Cornwall) b) Seaside, FL (Duany Plater-Zyberk) c) Laguna West, CA (Peter Calthorpe)

Transit-oriented developments (TOD) became a spatial organizing theme for many projects. The Laguna West in Sacramento County, California (1991) was planned by Peter Calthorpe Associates and was considered "a better suburb" and the first TOD application.[20] Planned on a 1,045-acre (422 hectares) site, was a mixed-use development of 3,400 dwelling units with a 100-acre (40 hectare) town center, Figure 4.5c. Criticism of Laguna West was directed to the use of cul-de-sacs, suburban style houses with garages fronting onto streets and automobile dependence despite the connection to transits, which were considered undesirable to New Urbanist principles. According to Philip Langdon, "Laguna West seemed to have been done without passion."[21] Even with its shortcomings, the concept of this transit-oriented development was a welcomed mixed-use residential and commercial development scheme designed to maximize access to public transport, incorporating features to encourage transit ridership. A sustainable premise of the TOD was to provide numerous centers with different commercial and non-residential functions and link them by high quality transit service, and then people would significantly reduce their use of automobiles for both commuting and non-work travel. A major obstacle to the successful implementation of transit-orient developments was the creation of effective and accessible local micro-transit systems through which TODs could connect to larger transit networks. There must be a reasonable walking distance from every dwelling to transit stop or station forming nucleated places within a mile diameter (1.6 kilometers).

The New Urbanism models, according to Ruth Durack, were by necessity fully planned and regulated environments, fiercely resistant to change and any deviation from the rigid encyclopedic rules that govern their form and function.[22] While they incorporated some sustainable planning strategies, such as densification, mixed uses, pedestrian orientation and varying transportation modes, they were far from being truly "green." Their architecture was largely nostalgic, referential and spurious, versus being authentic, climate, resource and energy responsive. Criticisms of Laguna West, for example, were aimed at the extreme automobile dependency and the conforming singularity of style architecture. Many of the more recent homes incorporated four-car garages. However, its improved density of seven-dwelling units per acre (17 units per hectare) and the transit service were considered a success. Andres Duany claimed that New Urban developments were "implicitly environmental," yet more recent developments were beginning to become "intrinsically environmental" incorporating integrated agriculture, transect zoning, and to a lesser degree the inclusion of some renewable technologies. This appeared to be a welcomed evolution among the advancements of solar communities of the 1970s, the New Urbanism of the 1980s, and Agricultural Urbanism of the 2000s.

CRITICAL REGIONALISM

Regionalism was considered by several defining factors. History, culture, climate, customs, geography and physical context gave specific characteristics and meanings to a region, including the love a particular locale or setting. It sensibility looked to the uniqueness of site and location when deriving the formal aspects of any given project. Critical regionalism sought to mediate the spectrum between universal characteristics of a civilization and the particularities of place. Critical regionalism modified this to include avant-garde and the innovative—pushing the boundaries of historical precedents while maintaining some connections to modernism, mainly its progressive qualities. It arose in response to placelessness and the lack of meaning in the modern environment. There was confluence of authentic climatic and regional characteristics with the needs of contemporary culture, and the modern means by which to construct hybrid architecture in response to it.

The researches of Alexander Tzonis and Liane Lefaivre into design cognition and regionalism, contributed to notions that problem solving should de-empathize imported universal solutions in favor of reflective, local and unique qualities of a region. They saw critical regionalism as not needing to exclusively draw from the context, but rather elements of a place could be stripped of context and used in unfamiliar ways. There was a confluence of local (centripetal) and global (centrifugal) considerations in developing a contemporary synthesis. Critical regionalism and the greening of architecture shared a common interest in becoming modern while returning and responding to sources. Critical regionalism addressed questions of sensitivity to local context with the implications of globalization, with new configuration of analytical and discursive techniques with which to give appropriate expression to and emerging contemporary culture. It also considered the specifics of local climates and materials, topographies and building methods.

In his essay, *Towards a Critical Regionalism* (1983), Kenneth Frampton called for an architecture that would strive to overcome placelessness and lack of identity by utilizing a building's geographical context. According to Frampton's proposal, critical regionalism should adopt modern architecture, critically, for its universal progressive qualities but at the same time value should be placed on the geographical context of the building. Emphasis, Frampton noted, should be on topography, climate, and light; on tectonic form rather than on "scenography."[23] He further stressed that architecture was neither a vacantly "international" exercise in modern technology nor a "sentimental" imitation of vernacular buildings, arguing for a propinquity of place cultivated between the universal and local. The "critical" in this proposition of regionalism meant a questioning and critique of the cliché, inappropriately picturesque and superficial. Steven Moore saw in Frampton's call a powerful "proto-environmentalist discourse" that helped legitimatized the next green phase in architecture.

The Säynatsalo Town Hall, Finland (1952), by Alvar Aalto, according to Frampton, was an exemplar Critical Regionalist building. Although it was designed decades before the full thrust of Critical Regionalism set in, it expressed a regional character, created a definite human-scaled place, used a modernist geometrical language, and had embodied local meaning—all tenants of critical regionalism. Scale was further expressed through the use of tactile surface's ability to make legible the architecture and the brick steps on the exterior, leading to the council chambers affirmed the foot as a measure of human scale. Placemaking was certainly reinforced by the placement of the building within the forested setting and with the elevated courtyard form of the building.

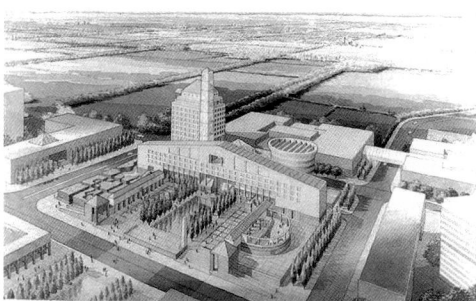

4.6   Critical Regionalism a) Brion Tomb b) Mississauga Civic Centre (permission Kirkland Partnership, Inc) c) MIT Rehan House (© Chant Avedissian / Aga Khan Award for Architecture) d) Sydney Opera House (courtesy "Shutterstock")

The program called for a number of mixed functions designed to generate more varied and intense activities, which would contribute to the vitality of the place. Aalto compared this design with Italy's Palazza Pubblico in Siena, as both used the courtyard spatial structure and vertical civic chambers to symbolize the center of community and the unification of democratic values. Designed for a cold climate the building incorporated a number of green measures that included mixes of use, natural daylighting, sunshading devices, and use of heat absorbing materials.

The US Energy Tax Credit Act of 1978 along with state tax credits was an inducement for homeowners to invest in energy conservation and solar energy devices. The incentives were curtailed in the mid-1980s, and along with the reduction in conventional energy costs, resulted in a slow-down of solar energy industry development and residential applications. Greening of architecture continued in the 1980s, and primarily focused on less ambitious residential-scaled projects, with emphasis on what was referred to as "*skin-dominated*" and "*vernacular-oriented*" sustainability with corresponding technologies. This directed green measures to the energetic interaction between indoors and outdoors adopting contemporary vernacular forms and mediating envelopes or "skins" that allowed for appropriate levels of opacity, resistance, transparency and porosity. There also were more subtle seeds influencing green architectural thought at this time that were less about sustainable technology and more about promoting a variety of postmodern agendas. Brion Cemetery (1978) was a collection of sculptural and somber structures designed by Carlo Scarpa that reflected the human requirements of life and the afterlife characteristic of a cemetery, and critical clues, which connected them to the region, place and time. The Mississauga Civic Centre, designed by Jones and Kirkland (1982) was a good example of postmodern architecture in Canada with its regionally derived vernacular for a load-dominated building typology. The Mit Rehan House (1981) located in Cairo, Egypt and designed by Hassan Fathy illustrated an elegant solution appropriate to a hot climate region. Jorn Utzon's Sidney Opera House (1973) was a good example of contemporary and local architecture. These examples, in Figures 4.6a, b, c and d, are from differing climatic contexts where specific climatic responses to these regions have given appropriate form to the architecture.

POSTMODERN GREEN ARCHITECTURE

Deconstruction, a development of postmodern architecture, began in the late 1980s and was brought into public attention with the Museum of Modern Art's 1988 exhibition *Deconstructivist Architecture* in New York City. The exhibition featured works by Frank Gehry, Daniel Libeskind, Rem Koolhaas, Peter Eisenman, Zaha Hadid, Coop Himmelb(l)au, and Bernard Tschumi. Deconstruction grew from post-structural philosophy and literary criticism, and its development in architecture was characterized with fragmentation, distortion, dislocation of architectural elements, and an interest in surface or skin. A few, though tenuous, connections can be made relative to the benefits of deconstruction to the development of green architecture at this time. Both shared a desire to break from modernism's constricting simplicity and overly reduced language. Where deconstructivism sought unpredictability, confrontation, disconnection from context, and to some degree chaos, postmodern green blended regional context and contemporary programs to the linage of vernacular forms. Neither deconstruction nor green postmodern embraced ornament, yet both had precarious traces of modernism. Deconstruction subverted functionalism and postmodern green reacquired it for environmental purposes.

Relative to the greening of architecture, deconstructivism had mixed influences. Even though it was considered a development of postmodernism, on one hand the exciting and complex designs reinvigorated a waning discipline that was disenchanted with both modernism and postmodernism—over rationality versus superficiality. Deconstruction provided a brief creative outlet from the regressive with explorations with non-rectilinear shapes, fragmentation, distorted forms, and infatuation with design and qualities of surface. They tended to express through more public and high-profile building typologies, such as museums, monuments, and arts facilities, which often was the case for the designs of Gehry, Miralles, Coop Himmelb(l)au, Koolhaas and Hadid. Deconstructivism produced designs that were exciting, spontaneous and often chaotic, and they were generally well received by the public and academic institutions.[24] On the other hand simultaneously, they were complex with inherent energy inefficiency and largely were an expression of conspicuous consumption. Complex forms usually produced greater surface areas generating higher levels of heat loss or gain, additional corners that were susceptible to thermal bridging, increased volumes with greater heating, and cooling and ventilating loads. Complex shapes and geometry usually resulted in higher material costs and increased construction waste. The complex compositions fortuitously allowed, in some instances, the inclusion of sustainable technologies that otherwise might have been considered obtrusive and aesthetically disharmonious to more traditional, as well as modernist, designs.

A common ground can be seen with the example of the Solar House in Breisach-am-Rhein, Germany (1992) by Thomas Spiegelhalter. It was a complex and sculptural arrangement of architectural volumes juxtaposing renewable energy components and exterior space-defining elements. This project was referred to as "Vila Deconstructa."[25] Its systems for using ambient energy and rainwater collection, its integrated conservatory/greenhouse, and its indeterminate form gave flexibility that it could grow and change with the lives of its occupants. While this project was at the residential scale, it was significant because of the architectural language and tectonic character of the design, which was largely driven by formal principles boldly expressing the renewable energy and passive solar technologies. For example, the "L-shaped" photovoltaic collector array provided an installed capacity of 5,400 watts, while at the same time provided protection from sun in summer and wind in winter. And while the rigorous functional and energy conscious programs and tectonic expression were strong, the house was also an organic compositional entity offering flexibility and adjustability. The dynamic geometry, spatial zones and layering of sustainable systems can clearly be seen in the Breisach House in Figure 4.7a.

The form-variability of many of the works of Steven Holl were seen by William Curtiss as a hold-out against the fashions of postmodernism and deconstructivism in favor of personal, mythical, tactile and phenomenological themes. His works were a process of intuition and the sensual properties of materials, but also focused on edge definition and place creation. Frampton wrote that Holl was obsessed with typology and the metaphysical potential of the stripped down "degree-zero" version of the American vernacular, exemplified by his Martha's Vineyard House (1984–88). The Artisan Housing Project designed against a Staten Island, New York warehouse, was intended to express individuation of the artisan's dwellings and to some degree the nature of their craft (1980–84). Figure 4.7b illustrates the iconic geometric shapes and vernacular forms with the spatial separation and expression of each artisan dwelling. To some degree this work was re-invented with the realization of the Hybrid Building at Seaside, Florida a few years later (1985–88), where a vertical layering of mixed-use functions were capped with cubical two-story flats named after the poet, musician, and mathematician.[26]

Antoine Predock was a pioneer in postmodern regionalism with practice primarily oriented to the American southwest, although his later commissions were worldwide. His works were a blend of modernist forms and tectonic detailing with regional character and materials, climate-responsiveness, and site-specific designs. Many of his buildings grew from the ground and gradually culminated with a vertical element, which functioned as a place-marker. Typical examples of this form topology were the Tesuque House (1983), the American Heritage Center in Laramie, Wyoming (1986), and the Nelson Fine Arts Center at Arizona State University in Tempe, Arizona (1985). The Las Vegas Library and Museum (1990), was a good example of Predock's regionalism.[25] In discussing this design he explained, "It's where the confluence of the Spanish trail, the Mormon trail, the Native American trails happened. So the building for me was about the land, and about crossroads and not about fetishizing the Strip (the Las Vegas Strip)."

Another place-enhancing characteristic to some of Predock's works was the use of celestial references, which simultaneously connected his buildings regionally and locally, but within a larger cosmological context. In the Las Vegas Library and Museum this characteristic took the form of a conical-shaped birthday party room, pictured in Figure 4.7c, which had small star-like apertures that resembled the night sky.[27] Incorporating celestial references into architecture was a way of expanding experience and awareness to a larger context within which placemaking could be determined, connected and experienced. Sunpath symbolism, oppositions, such as sun and moon, and the notion of a cosmic dwelling were, according to Paul Oliver, connotations that were important to indigenous and non-Western cultures.[28] For postmodernism, these considerations could be expressed through double coding and certainly would contribute to the pluralistic nature that was so characteristic of postmodern architecture.

4.7 Postmodern Hybridity a) Breisach House (Photo: Friedrich Busam) b) Autonomous Artists' Housing (© Stephen Holl) c) Las Vegas Children's Museum (Photograph in the Carol M. Highsmith Archive, Library of Congress, Prints and Photographs Division)

Phenomenology emerged as a subject of interest to some postmodern architects. Christian Norberg-Schulz was an important figure in the 1980s in bringing attention to phenomenology in architecture through his books *Genius Loci: Towards a Phenomenology of Architecture* (1980) and *The Concept of Dwelling: On the Way to Figurative Architecture* (1985). They provided readily accessible explanations of a phenomenological approach to architecture.[29] Recovery of place and response to the genius loci involved new connections and interpretations to the living traditions of a given locale. The notion of "dwelling," as a quality of place, implied a greater degree of belonging and being present on multiple levels as opposed to purely functional, flexible and disposable characteristics of modern space. The confluence of phenomenology and place-oriented design, as opposed to the heroic object-building, were formative ideas that later would influence sustainable urbanism and ecological architecture. Sustainable phenomenology was an alternative vision of environmental thinking, and was a refocus away from placelessness and over-emphasis of technological sustainability to one of sustainability through the relationship between design and behavior, and between place and participant.

Phenomenology shifted the modernist and postmodernist obsession with the building as object to considerations of the broader concerns and contextual issues of placemaking. Places were being recognized for their qualities for social interaction and encounter, vitality of activity, connections with the elemental qualities, such as sunlight, breezes and the atmosphere of a locale. In his book *Space and Place: The Perspective of Experience*, Yi-Fu Tuan makes the distinction between these two concepts;[30] space was abstract and denoted freedom and movement, while place was about pause and more intimate experiences. Both are important to the greening of architecture. Spatial considerations among sustainable technology components are often necessary in order for them to function effectively. Placial qualities, in contrast, suggested a safe, nurturing and meaningful environment. Michael Brill in 1985 suggested that places, and especially significant places, were imbued with certain formal characteristics, including the existence of a sense of center, orientation, passage and thresholds, differentiated boundary, internal order (interiority), the presence of nature and natural light, discriminating views, diverse materiality and human ceremonial participation.[31]

Placemaking was antithetical to notions of vapid empty spaces, disposal environments and spatially separated functions, especially those requiring the automobile for connectivity. Placemaking, as a sustainable strategy, was directed toward reductions in energy usage, but more importantly toward quality of life, an enhanced participation within a place, and increased familiarity, dwelling, stewardship and reflexive development. As a place, whether it was a dwelling or community, containing a diversity of activities, the ability to change and evolve, and possessing staying power, then it became a context for greater opportunity for supporting sustainable behavior. According to Tuan, "when space feels thoroughly familiar to us, it has become place." And to Edward S. Casey, "the importance of place is a conviction that place itself is no fixed thing: it has no steadfast essence (e.g., gathering, nearing, regioning, thinging)."[32] This was to suggest that placemaking was a dynamic, ongoing and evolving process with no one set of formal structures. However, revalorizing place with a sustainable agenda had specific responses to the local environmental conditions. Interaction and love of the specific natural environment was an important part of this placemaking process.

Postmodern urbanism, as an extension of placemaking, tended to support compact and diverse community-oriented schemes. They reacted to the inhuman and characterlessness of fragmented, disconnected, low density and single use developments common to modernism especially in the suburban landscape. Piecemeal developments between urban concentrations and hinterlands created discontinuity in both the built and natural environments. Ecosystems, natural habitat, riparian zones, natural waterways were interrupted, isolated and in many instances destroyed. Similarly, the fragmentation and separation of uses of the built environment created greater dependency upon automobile use to remedy the dysfunctionality and disconnectedness. Nan Ellin explained, "postmodern urbanism sought to satisfy needs that were not merely functional and to convey meanings other than that of simple building function and tectonics." Charles Jencks argued that the iconic competition within postmodernism, such as the hidden nature and cosmological references became explicit in the ecological and solar images.

Contrasted to the solar dominant architectural and urban forms of the 1970s, the postmodern vernacular designs were a good match for the evolving sustainable agendas. The iconic geometry common to residential architecture, triangle on top of a square (common gable form), tended to be simple, compact and uncomplicated, and had a more formal balance than their solar phototropic counterparts. This balance was important to neighborhood designs where street symmetry was important and efficient aggregation was desired Often these designs were anthropomorphic, which may have contributed to their appeal aesthetically. The vernacular designs were able to employ traditional green elements such as fireplaces, increased windows, dormers, clerestories and greenhouse buffer spaces. Gabled roof overhangs provided protection from precipitation and provided sunshading during the warmer summers. Transparency could be distributed for passive solar functions while remaining true to the overall form of the building.

The 1970s saw a tremendous burst of sustainable systems' innovation and tectonic development. With the sunsetting of state and federal tax credits for renewable technologies and the reduction of natural gas prices, after the mid-1980s the greening of architecture in America all but expired. Postmodernism provided a temporal and theoretical distraction between the singularity of modernism and the hybridity and tectonic pluralism that became prevalent in the 1990s. It also was responsible for a shift away from the focus on technology toward one of comprehensive design. Considered European postmodern architects were James Stirling, Yorn Utzon, Aldo Rossi, Recardo Bolfill, Mario Botta, Leon Krier, and Terry Farrell, who expressed through more urban projects, which was not surprising given the strong predominance and presence of existing European urban environments. Nan Ellin suggested that these works were more played out on the urban "wings" rather than the urban "center stage." Other Western European architects and engineers, Arup, Rogers, Piano, Herzog and Grimshaw began to embrace sustainability and fully integrated it into mainstream building design.

Meanwhile the American postmodernists like Robert A.M. Stern, Michael Graves, Charles Moore, Steven Holl, and Antoine Predock, including Luis Barragan in Mexico were preoccupied with symbolism and what Emilio Ambasz called "metaphysical images dwelling in para-historical domains."[33] They tended to be engaged with suburban projects or those on isolated sites, and offered minimal attention to sustainability. As a result, there began a shift in the innovation and demonstration of sustainable architecture from the United States to Western Europe. The 1980s were not as much a time of sustainable expansion, but rather a time of pause, introspection and reflection. The interests and developments within postmodernism influenced green architecture, yet on the topic of ecological design, Charles Jencks suggested that the outcomes were plural, "different for north and south, the equator and the poles, rich and poor."

An obvious shortcoming of postmodernism in architecture was its struggle for an authentic regionalism informed by local culture in an era of intense globalization. How could a single architecture reconcile these two seemingly opposite tendencies? In addition, postmodernism's inherited bonds to modernism, especially within its material content—structure, systems, and construction—was never really separated or liberated. However, Charles Jencks would argue that these contradictory impulses would give energy to the ambiguous, hybrid and pluralistic nature of postmodern architecture. Kenneth Frampton would frame this opposition critically, particularly if it counteracted placelessness and superficiality. And Nan Ellin's assessment was that modernism and postmodernism both contained universalizing rationality and an emphasis on locality. They were "two sides of the same coin" in her words. Postmodern architecture of the 1980s certainly addressed the issue of developing an appropriate and authentic mix between these divergent considerations: local vs. global, hand-made vs. machine-made, high-technology vs. low-technology, the automobile vs. the pedestrian, and all the way to paper bags vs. plastic ones.

The influences of postmodernism on the greening of architecture were complicit in encouraging an assessment of the previous solar-dominated scheme; a liberated creativity in building design and the incorporation of traditions that previously had been suppressed. To some degree, green architecture was released from its singular purpose—responsible, performance-based and tectonic determinism—in favor of a more balanced, integrated and phenomenal formalism. The Formative Principle in the sense that the formative power reconciled the expression of form, the presence of whole and part, and the associated and embodied meanings largely drove the development of postmodern green.[34] To Glenn Murcutt, architecture was responsible for giving something back, "like light, space, form, serenity, joy." There were new placemaking sensibilities, a revived vitality and scaling to human experience that the greening process demonstrated primarily at the urban fringe or on wilderness sites, and this included many of the New Urban projects as well. New Urbanism gave focused and renewed attention to the image, function, and composition and agglomeration of forms and uses for a place.

In early 1980s the Passive and Low Energy Architecture (PLEA) organization formed to engage in discourse on sustainable architecture and urban design through annual international conferences. The first conference was held in Miami, Florida where leaders in the academic and professional disciplines discussed important issues in the field. While much of the mainstream architectural focus of this time was on postmodernism, threads of sustainable architecture continued to strengthen with research and development at the fringe of popular culture.

96 THE GREENING OF ARCHITECTURE

4.8 Changing Syntax a) Rasin Building (Photo: Jordi Peralta) b) Boolean Matryoshka Doll (courtesy Jaime Pitarch)

In the World Solar Challenge, Sunraycer—a solar powered car engineered by General Motors, AeorVironment and Hughes Aircraft—won the first in Australian 1,867 mile (3,005 kilometers) race from Darwin to Adelaide in 1987. It wasn't until the early 1990s that green architecture was further explored, developed and brought into the mainstream and back onto the urban stage. Like Sunraycer, green architecture began to more closely focus on the relationship between integrated technology and form. The Lloyds of London Building (1986) by Richard Rogers was a harbinger of this re-engagement with complex technology. Frank Gehry and Vlado Milunic further explored these visual and iconic tendencies with the Nationale-Nederlanden Building in Prague (1996), Figure 4.8a. The two tower gestures or body languages performed an urban function protecting views to the River Vltva and providing an anchor to the adjacent small public square.

The Boolean Russian Doll, Figure 4.8b, exemplified postmodernism with its complexity of form, playful ambiguities, moments of symmetry and embedded scalar references. The defining elements were derivative of the single parent object. The artist Jaime Pitarch, referencing the nuclear reactor disaster in 1986, titled this piece "Chernobyl." In the coming decade the pendulum was to swing away from semantic imagery back to an interest in technology with renewed vigor and enthusiasm for its form-giving qualities, functional abilities, performance and tectonic languages.

ENDNOTES

1   Nan Ellin, *Postmodern Urbanism*. New York: Princeton University Press, 1996.

2   Charles Jencks, *The Story of Postmodernism*. New York: John Wiley & Sons, 2011.

3   William J. Curtis, *Contemporary Architecture since 1900*," Third Edition. London: Phaidon Press Ltd, 1996.

4   Nan Ellin, *Postmodern Urbanism*. New York: Princeton University Press, 1996.

5   Steven Moore, "Environmental Issues," *The Encyclopaedia of Science, Technology, and Ethics*, edited by Carl Mitcham. New York: Macmillan, 2005: 262–6.

6   Robert Venturi, *Complexity and Contradiction in Architecture*. New York: Museum of Modern Art Press, 1966.

7   Keven P. Keim, *An Architectural Life: Memoirs and Memories of Charles W. Moore*. Boston: Bulfinch Press Book, 1996.

8   Charles Jencks, *Symbolic Architecture*. London: Academy Editions, 1985.

9   Carl Stein, *Greening Modernism: Preservation, Sustainability, and the Modern Movement*. New York: W.W. Norton & Company, 2010.

10 James Wines, *Green Architecture*. Köln: Taschen, 2000.

11 Malcolm Quantrill, *Plain Modern: The Architecture of Brian MacKay-Lyons*. Princeton: Princeton Architectural Press, 2006: 28.

12 Contemporary World Architects, *Lake/Flato*. Rockport, MA: Rockport Publishers, Inc., 1996.

13 Miller Hull Partnership, *Ten Houses*. Rockport, MA: Rockport Publishers, Inc., 1999.

14 James Wines, *Green Architecture*. Köln: Taschen, 2000.

15 Andrea Openheimer Dean and Timothy Hursley, *The Rural Studio: Samuel Mockbee and an Architecture of Decency*. Princeton: Princeton Architectural Press, 2002.

16 Leon Krier, *Architecture & Urban Design 1967–1992*. London: Academy Editions, 1992.

17 Leon Krier, "Houses, Palaces, Cities," *Architectural Design Profile*, edited by Demetri Porphyrios. London: 1980: 30–33.

18 Andres Duany and Elizabeth Plater-Zyberk, *Towns and Town-Making Principles*. New York: Rizzoli, 1992.

19 Peter Katz, *The New Urbanism: Toward an Architecture of Community*. New York: McGraw-Hill Book Company, 1994.

20 Peter Calthorpe, *The Next American Metropolis*. Princeton: Princeton Architectural Press, 1993.

21 Philip Langdon, *A Better Place to Live*. Amherst, MA: University of Massachusetts Press, 1994: 164.

22 In this essay Ruth Durack suggests that the adopted village model of the New Urbanists and sustainability are contradictory concepts. Further she proposes a far more indeterminate urbanism that is more open, adaptive to change and responsive to inconsistencies. Ruth Durack, "Village Vices: The Contradiction of New Urbanism and Sustainability," *Places*, 14: 64. Fall 2001.

23 Kenneth Frampton, "Toward a Critical Regionalism: Six Points for an Architecture of Resistance," *The Anti-Aesthetic: Essays on Postmodern Culture*, edited by Hal Foster. Port Townsend, Washington: Bay Press, 1983: 26–7.

24 William Curtis, *Contemporary Architecture since 1900*, Third Edition. London: Phaidon Press Ltd., 1996.

25 Othmar Humm and Peter Toggweiler, *Photovoltaics in Architecture*. Basel: Birkhauser Verlag, 1993.

26 Steven Holl, *Anchoring*. New York: Princeton Architectural Press, 1989.

27 Brad Collisn and Juliette Robbins, *Antoine Predock Architect*. New York: Rizzoli, 1994.

28 Paul Oliver, *Dwellings: The House Across the World*. Austin, TX: The University of Texas Press, 1987: 153–70.

29 Phenomenology is the study of structures of consciousness as experienced from the point of view of the first-person. In architecture it is based on the direct experience of building spaces and materials and their sensory properties. Christian Norberg-Schulz, *The Concept of Dwelling: On the Way to Figurative Architecture: Towards a Phenomenology of Architecture*. New York: Rizzoli, 1985.

30 Yi-Fu Tuan, *Space and Place—The Perspective of Experience*. Minneapolis, MN: University of Minnesota Press, 1977.

31 Michael Brill, *Using the Place-creation Myth to Develop Design Guidelines for Sacred Space*. Buffalo, NY: Self-published, 1985.

32 Edward S. Casey, *The Fate of Place: A Philosophical History*. Berkeley, CA: The University of California Press, 1997.

33 Nan Ellin, *Postmodern Urbanism*. New York: Princeton University Press, 1996: 303.

34 According to certain traditions, there are geometric forms with associated mathematical properties that contain particular meanings. The Unity, Generative, Formative, Corporeal and Regenerative Principles are found with the intelligible geometries of pi, the square root of two, square root of three, and Golden Mean Proportion. Robert Lawlor, *Sacred Geometry: Philosophy and Practice*. London: Themes and Hudson, 1982: 32–4.

Chapter 5
1990s: Eco-Technology

Phillip Tabb

> **Almost everything being done in the name of sustainable development addresses and attempts to reduce unsustainability. But reducing unsustainability, although critical, does not and will not create sustainability.**[1]

Postmodern green design expanded in the 1990s to encompass new and improved environmental technologies that boldly expressed and blended into contemporary architecture. The impetus was less about historic and contextual integrity, and more about tectonic expression of form. Sustainable technologies were no longer seen as crude and awkward bedfellows of a building, but rather they were elevated to the same level of consideration, expression and detail as other technologies in architecture. High-tech gained momentum and was being informed by structural, sustainable technologies, and with the interest in greater levels of transparency, light-mass construction, and innovations in glazing systems provided the opportunity for further expression of the "bones" of a building. Engineering and architecture were fusing together. The proclamation of this time was that architecture should naturally be designed sustainably and normalized within the characteristic constraints and parameters of a given project: green should become standard practice.

Advances in building technologies were not only evident in the built works, but in the design and engineering processes that created them. According to Catherine Slessor, the advancement of computer-aided design (CAD) software and ever more powerful computers had enabled engineers and architects to create complex and unprecedented structures. The computer began to open the way to the potential of new concepts of form, order, prototyping, mesh-networking and digital asset libraries. It employed algorithmic techniques to virtual design. Marcos Novac explained, "technology is allowing us to change the common structure of probabilities and to stabilize formations that were previously so unlikely as to be delegated to the realm of dreams and miracles.[2] Another of the important contributions of computers to the design process was prototyping—the process of creating 3D computer models of a design that could be subjected to computer-based testing, computational methods and performance analysis. This was particularly useful in performing energy analysis for sustainable systems.

The emerging green architecture tended towards larger and more varied building typologies that required inherent *load-dominated* energy design measures and *eco-centric* technologies for reduction of unwanted heat gains from solar radiation and internal sources, such as gains from artificial lighting, equipment and people, mechanical ventilation, elevators, and modern air conditioning systems. As the sustainable technologies evolved, they tended to move from fixed building elements to more dynamic systems, eco-technologies, responding to the changeable nature of onsite resources, diurnal cycles and inclement conditions. Among the more important architectural examples and prominent architects and engineers of this time, especially in Europe (Calatrava, Foster, Grimshaw, Herzog & De Meuron, Miralles, Piano, and Rogers, to name a few), the tectonic qualities of a building's design became an opportunity for architectural integration, including the expression of the sustainable systems. These buildings tended to exist within urban settings rather than around the fringe or on isolated building sites. Beyond their sustainable utility, these buildings were saturated with technology making a statement that did not look back to the future, but rather projected the future. They were high-tech, lightweight, low-mass, highly glazed, often delicate, bold and heroic. Green architecture was no longer small and parochial.

HIGH-TECH ARCHITECTURE

Honesty of materials, integrity and efficiency of systems the use of advanced technology, especially structural elements, were generally considered the driving determinants to high-tech architecture. Structural expression was found both inside and outside of buildings. Early high-tech buildings were referred to by architectural historian Reyner Banham as "serviced sheds" due to their additional exposure of mechanical services in addition to the structure. By the 1990s, these buildings were no longer "sheds," but rather were bold and often monumental expressions of architecture, and often considered sculpture rather than simple corporeal structures. High-tech architecture found a sympathetic partner with certain building typologies, such as bridges, airports, train stations, communications towers, sports stadiums, high-rise structures, museums and other large-scaled public buildings. Utility, science and art were combined and elevated to generate a renewed and re-invigorated version of Vitruvius' "commodity, firmness and delight" or, before him, Plato's "truth, goodness, and beauty."

Contemporary high-tech architecture had its roots as early as the late 1970s with Centre Georges Pompidou in Paris and in the mid-1980s with the Lloyds of London Building (1986) by Richard Rogers. High-tech's influence was felt even before with examples like the Seagram Building by Mies van der Rohe in 1958 or the CBS Building by Eero Saarinen in 1965. These buildings according to William Curtis were derived from a "techno-romanticism" or from considerations arising from "natural inevitability of forms," such as expression of structure, function, and daylighting assembly. The postmodern skyscrapers or tall buildings were re-examined and given language with focus on an open plan, honest articulation of structure on the exterior and integral to the façade, expressing rather than hiding mechanical services and equipment, and establishing geometric order rather than symbolic references. High-tech also meant beauty in tectonic form, high-craft and attention to detail. Curtis exclaimed that the expression of technology was a long-standing modern architectural theme tended to reflect either "utopian character" or illustrate the "mechanics of engineering."[3]

Most of the characteristics of high-tech formalism were brought together in the Alamillo Bridge, designed by Santiago Calatrava. It was constructed as part of infrastructure improvements for the Expo 92, which was held in Seville, Spain. The bridge spanned the Canal de Alfonzo with a single, asymmetrical pylon cantilever composed of 13 cables. The three tiers supported motor vehicles, pedestrians and bicycles approximately 656 feet (200 meters) across the Guadalquivir River as shown in Figure 5.1a. Catherine Slessor suggested that Calatrava used his structural principles to achieve a "fertile basis for structural expression," which also served both social and symbolic functions. It was so elegant, dramatic and original, and was considered a major work of architecture.[4]

Cesar Pelli designed the Petronas Towers in Kuala Lumpur, and for a time, they were the two tallest buildings in the world for six years, only to be surpassed by the Taipei 101 in Taipei, Taiwan (2004), the Shanghai World Financial Center in Shanghai, China (2008) and the Burj Khalifa Tower in Dubai (2010). The twin towers were constructed to a height of approximately 1,483 feet (452 meters) in 1998 and were in part financed by Petronas, which is short for Petroliam Nasional Berhad—a Malaysian oil and gas company. The design was intended to express the Malaysian culture and heritage through its repetitive geometry, arabesques, scalloped façade, and complex eight-fold plan forms, thereby expressing some postmodern agendas. The twin shapes, connecting the sky-bridge and pointed towers gave it a monumental and modernist affect, certainly with a lasting profile and identity.

The London City Hall, which now is headquarters of the London Greater Council, was designed by Foster + Partners in the late 1990s and opened in 2002. The building was formed into an unusual bulbous shape intended to reduce its surface area, with large amounts of glass for daylighting and view, and positioned with a phototropic orientation to induce self-shadowing. The surface area of a cube with the same volume has 25 percent more surface area. The 10-story structure leans toward the south, which reduces the southern façade surface area along with the reverse-step overhanging the floor plates that provide shading from the high midday and summer sun. The north side of the building receives little to no direct sun during these times, and therefore was glazed in transparent glass to enhance daylighting and views to the River Thames. Inside the spherical structure is a large atrium space with helical staircase connecting each of the floors. There are two layers of transparency—one from the exterior to the occupied spaces and the other to the atrium interior. The skin of the sphere uses an insulated aluminum panel system, and an innovative glazing system that incorporates daylighting, shading and natural ventilation. The building utilized a borehole system from below grade where naturally chilled water is circulated through the structural beams in summer. In winter the water is heated before being circulated throughout the atrium. These measures were intended to reduce heat loss and gains, although energy use measurements have shown this building to be fairly inefficient.[5]

Renzo Piano's Tjibaou Cultural Center (1998), located in Nouméa, New Caledonia, incorporated local Kanak traditions and vernacular forms into an ensemble of iconic shell-like structures. The 10 pavilions were positioned along a ridge in response to the tropical climate with open cup-like forms taking full advantage of lagoon breezes on the leeward side and protection from the stormy windward side of the Pacific Ocean. While the structures reference the indigenous forms of New Caledonia, they were quite tectonically sophisticated. According to Patrick Nuttgens, it was difficult to imagine this set of structures being in any other location as they seemed to fit with the traditions of the place, and yet they were modern in technology with mastery of materials.[5] The conical structures formed a vernacular-tectonic and appropriate symbol of the place.

Among the high technologies of this time was cogeneration, also referred to as combined heat and power (CHP), and the heat by-product was used in absorption chillers for cooling.

It was not a new technology, and one that was extensively used in denser contexts and institutions with multiple buildings, such as university campuses. The Public Utilities Regulatory Policies Act of 1978 encouraged cogeneration technology to connect with public utility networks to purchase and sell electricity. Micro-cogeneration was a net-metering offshoot of CHP and was applied to single buildings and coupled with renewable technologies.

The development of the high-tech movement in architecture brought attention back to a focus on building fundamentals and material elements of design—structure, mechanical systems, material systems, fabrication, joinery, and attention to detail. The introduction of low emissivity glass (Low-E) in 1993 increased the conservation of energy for all building types. High-tech created a predictable break from postmodern capriciousness and a logical bridge to the inclusion of environmental and ecological technologies. This suggested that a building's tectonic function included two related ideas—environmental technology in response to specific onsite resource conditions and a systemic approach to the dynamic process of these onsite resources. The pair of Clinical Sciences Research Center structures by Foster + Partners at Stanford University illustrated two differing ways to accomplish sun control within the same project—horizontal lattice devices on the southern structure and the stand of bamboo along the northern structure, Figures 5.1e and f. The increasing design complexity for high-tech building technologies was addressed with the introduction of digital technologies. Further, these new technologies provided advanced tools and design methodologies that facilitated new and emergent forms in architecture.

5.1 High-Tech Architecture of the 1990s a) Alamillo Bridge (courtesy "Shutterstock") b) Petronas Towers (courtesy "Shutterstock") c) Caledonia Pavilions (Renzo Piano Office Workshop) d) London City Hall e) Stanford Center f) Stanford Center g) German Pavilion

VIRTUAL ARCHITECTURE

"Virtual" came from the Latin, *virtus*, which meant "to martial courage" and extended to cover a large range of other meanings, including "potentiality," and it was used in modern language to include things simulated through electronic medium. This development along with other global factors led to a post-industrial revolution as posited by Klaus Daniels.[6] A shift in such variables as location of work, communications, and high-technology facilitated this change that was further exacerbated by world population growth, globalization of the economy and the emergence of the worldwide information networks. While many tangible advantages and positive possibilities were opened with the development of the computer, certain cautions emerged against virtualization, including increased inactivity, identity theft, and loss of tactile reality and localization. The information age opened the gate to far greater magnitudes of information and knowledge surpassing the options for action.

The impact of the computer and its widespread use of digital programs in the practice of architecture had created, above all, new formal languages. Designs with fractal complexity, iterative explorations, compound curvilinear forms and unusual shapes could now be modeled, engineered, tested and fabricated into building components. Computer-aided design (CAD) methods changed the "paper" design process of working sketches, diagrams, plans, sections, isometrics, watercolor renderings and hand drawn perspectives to one of managing the development of a single holistic three-dimensional virtual model. In addition, certain green technologies were highly attractive and compatible with these numeral methods and digital explorations in architectural form. In addition, computer simulation programs, such as DEROB, NBSLD, Blast and DOE-2, were commonly used by engineers to calculate building energy requirements with dynamic space and daylighting analysis. Lawrence Berkeley National Laboratory developed daylighting software: Superlite and Radiance.

The digital inventions, such as those of Marcos Novac, explored "where no man has gone before." These explorations were less about creating actual architecture and more about pushing the limits of the imagination, creating virtual architectural environments. Novak introduced the concept of "liquid architecture," a fluid, imaginary landscape that only exists in the digital domain. Further, he suggested a type of architecture cut loose from the expectations of logic, perspective, and the laws of gravity, one that did not conform to the rational constraints of Euclidean geometries.[7] Notions of algorithmic urbanism and design suggest the fusion of biology, digital technology and urbanism with explorations in proliferation of self-organizing systems and changeable forms. Figure 5.2a, a futuristic architectural design, was an example of a digitally expressed exploration of architectural imagery. The film *The Matrix*, directed by Larry and Andy Wachowski, brought to the cinematic world a new generation of images made possible through digital technology, Figure 5.2c.

The Guggenheim Museum in Bilbao, Spain was a landmark structure designed by Frank Gehry in 1997. The museum housed modern and contemporary art featuring permanent and visiting exhibitions of Spanish and international artists. Its form relied upon a dynamic interpretation of the ectypal elements of architectural form, mainly floors, walls, ceilings and roofs and fenestrations.[8] It was a complex composition of sculpted concave and convex planes that according to William Curtis, were capable of evoking multiple associations, musical and nautical as well as the simple function of catching and reflecting light.

The museum was the first project in the redevelopment of the former trade and warehouse district along the south bank of the Nervion River. Referred to as an "ark" of cultural identity, the museum was considered a single moment in architectural history, which most likely was due to its uniqueness of form enabled by the computer and contrasted by its historic context. The use of the Computer Aided Three-dimensional Interactive Application (CATIA) and visualizations were instrumental in enabling the design and fabrication of the complex surface and titanium cladding. The computer simulations were also used to create the building's structural system.

From a sustainable viewpoint, the urban insertion of a building of this nature, both in terms of program and design, invigorated the city of Bilbao. The museum project focused on responsible environmental conservation development, on minimizing the environmental impact of building operations and preserving the nearby ecosystem, promoting conservation and striving towards a more eco-efficient working environment. While certain green measures were adopted, such as recycling, provision of an isolated area for hazardous waste, energy use management, environmental training and education, the CATIA systems were not extensively used to model energy performance and demonstrate more advanced eco-technological systems.

The sweeping changes from analog mechanical technologies to global-scale digital technologies were considered the driving force behind a radical economic, social and cultural revolution that would dominate the next century. British computer scientist Sir Tim Berners-Lee and Belgian engineer Robert Cailliau introduced in France in 1990 the use of Hypertext Transfer Protocol (HTTP) to link and access information as a web of nodes to which users had access. In 1992 the World Wide Web (WWW) was introduced to the public, and by the end of the decade over half of American households were connected to it.[8] Fiber-optic and satellite technologies accelerated this process and the world became more connected and increasingly online practice focused throughout the 1990s. One of the benefits of this new technology was the research-based precedent for sustainable design. The Internet provided access to sustainable development, projects, literature, organizations and blogs (portmanteau for *web log*). The 1990s saw the advancement and proliferation of the early Mobile Telephone Service, the first generation (1G) analog cellular network, second generation (2G) digital cellular networks, third generation (3G) broadband data to present fourth generation (4G) native-IP networks.[9] This added telecommunications capabilities to off-grid building sites.

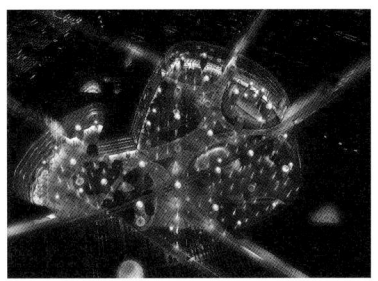  

5.2 Virtual Architecture a) Digital Architecture (LAVA Laboratory for Visionary Architecture) b) Guggenheim Museum, Bilbao (1997) (courtesy "Shutterstock") c) The Matrix (1999) (courtesy "Shutterstock")

ECO-TECHNOLOGY

Eco-technology, much like the earlier high-tech counterpart, evolved along similar lines with comparable intentions. However, eco-technology harnessed and subtly manipulated natural forces to leverage their beneficial environmental effects and expressed them explicitly. The natural ecological flows were in a constant state of flux including the functions of resource collection, use and discharge that informed the mutable and tectonic function of the environmental systems.[10] This suggested, for example, that there was a shift in thinking from a static and fixed view of climate and site to a more dynamic and interactive one, which included the changeable nature of solar energy seasonally and diurnally with its movement across a site, the variable nature of both prevailing winds and microclimate, the sporadic nature of rainwater with its wet and dry periods, the potential for recycling waste, and the beneficial relations between built works and landscape.

Sustainable architecture tended to focus more on the immutable formal and material characteristics of a building's design and associated technologies, where systems were matched with a singular purpose. Ecological architecture, on the other hand, addressed the more holistic, systemic and dynamic flows of the larger environment toward a combination of systems in response to ecological processes. Common among the principles of eco-technology in architecture were the three mutable and interactive cycles that described the flow of energy and resources in terms of their collection and capture from the environment, their distribution and use within the building, and their discharge back into the environment. This assumed that a built work's insertion into a site would be done so with minimal disruption and disfigurement of the pre-existing ecosystem. New ecological developments were equated to what were called "pioneering communities," that required greater initial amounts of energy and resources in order to create them. Later they evolved to "climax communities" with a more balanced and interactive relationship with their surroundings. Established neighborhoods, for example, were considered climax communities, with mature systems in place and greater balance with the three energetic cycles.

- Collection and Storage Cycle—*Flows in*: considered the source for natural resource flows and includes ambient environment, direct solar radiation, geothermal temperature flux, wind and breezes, down-flow precipitated water, seasonal and diurnal climatic changes, on-site agriculture, and waste and other onsite products as fuel.
- Use and Distribution Cycle—*Flows throughout*: renewable resources obtained from the immediate site considered necessary and available for human comfort, function, consumption and utility. This cycle included systemic distribution and the cascading affect from higher to lower grades of resource use, such as solar electricity to solar heat.
- Discharge, Decompose and/or Recoverable Cycle—Flows out: considered a recoverable resource from waste or a material in an entropic state that was no longer available for human use. This cycle assumed a healthy reintroduction of waste, including pollutants from land, air and water, back into the environment. This flow included the use and reuse of buildings and building materials over time.

Examples of ecological architecture included Renzo Piano's Tjibaou Cultural Center (1998) located in Nouméa, New Caledonia combined the local vernacular with the contemporary iconic shell-like structures.[11] The Milwaukee Art Museum Quadracci Pavilion (2001), by Santiago

Calatrava, was another graceful expression of green technologies, featuring elaborate wing elements, which opened and closed for improved solar control. Constructed in a city with a strong craft tradition, the pouring of concrete into one-of-a-kind wooden forms made the structure hand-built. The blending of the powerful, harmonic and sensual form and structure, with the shading devices, created a vibrant and animated example of green architecture.

The Wilkahn Factory was a German manufacturer of modern office furniture. Like many of the projects of Thomas Herzog, it was a hybrid design—a blend of high-tech structural elements and the use of natural materials. The building was designed in 1993 on a site of green rolling fields near Bad Munder, Germany. The green features included double-glazing, operable cross ventilation, and photovoltaic arrays. The use of a translucent insulated panel system, enabled daylight, dispersion of glare and the admittance of a soft natural light. In contrast to Herzog's hybrid architectural language was the work of Enric Miralles as exemplified with his National Gymnastic Centre (1993) in Alicante, Spain. The exterior of the building was a complex composition of angled walls, structural columns and braces coupled with reverse trusses supporting cantilevered roof canopies.

The British Pavilion in Seville, Spain and designed by Nicholas Grimshaw and Ove Arup for Expo 92 was another powerful climate-responsive structure. It was a 75,347 square feet (7,000 square meters) single-volume building characterized by structural clarity a kit of parts. The lightweight prefabricated structure incorporated many adaptable environmental control features and cooling devices for this extremely hot, dry climate including a large water wall on the east façade, water-filled containers on the west wall, S-shaped solar collection and roof shading devices, and translucent membranes.[12] Another significant demonstration by Grimshaw was the Eden Project in Cornwall, UK, that featured a constellation of domed skins that could be inflated or deflated to adjust the insulation levels responding to outside temperatures. The Tropical Biome, or "Pillow Dome," was the world's largest enclosed multiple greenhouse complex covering more than four acres (1.6 hectares) of land, containing over one hundred thousand plants representing five thousand species from many of the climate zones of the world. The tectonic language was reminiscent of some of the earlier projects of Archigram and Bucky Fuller with the skin made from hexagonal and pentagonal inflated cells supported by steel frames.

Rather than using fixed architectural elements to control the heating of the sun, a new generation of mediating technologies emerged. The Headquarters of SAP Americas in Newtown Square, Pennsylvania used a light sensor system, while the New York Times Company Headquarters designed by Renzo Piano and FXFowle Architects had a draped shade system that could adjust to the movement of the sun and changing conditions of the sky. Kroon Hall (2009) at Yale University, designed by Hopkins, was elevated as an "ultra-green" building, with 50 percent reduction in energy use as compared to other comparable sized modern buildings. Its design utilized solar energy through the long slender south side of the building, earth sheltering of the lower floor, daylight illumination for most of the interior spaces, and a rooftop mounted photovoltaic array providing about 25 percent of its electrical needs. The Federal Environmental Agency, located in a former brownfield site in Dessau, Germany (2005) designed by Sauerbrush Hutton as a compact building incorporating a large rooftop solar collector array, passive solar atrium/pedestrian streets, an increased envelope insulation level for the undulating façade and most importantly a geothermal heat exchange system that ran underneath the structure.

5.3 Ecological Architecture a) Quadracci Pavilion (courtesy Douglas Krinke) b) British Pavilion (Photo: John Linden) c) Eden Project (courtesy "Shutterstock") d) IT Company Office Building

Daylighting, one of the oldest green strategies, was an important natural resource utilization approach that accompanied most of the high-tech and eco-tech projects. Several considerations were critical in the design for an effective system. The objectives were to create as much useful natural light as deep into the building and to minimize glare, respond to changing light conditions, match appropriate systems to varying building types and internal lighting needs, and reduce heat gain especially in summer. The combination of new glazing types and systems, multi-layered walls, light-shelves, mirrors and shading devices were commonly used. Generally these systems generated only secondary form responses to an overall building design, but in the example of the Quadracci Pavilion by Calatrava, the shading device system was a primary form determinant and element of expression that was matched with the daylighting was light-sensitive artificial lighting. Light pipes were apertures designed to bring light from the roof into the interior of a building where perimeter glazing could not effectively reach. Optical fiber technology was not developed until 2004 and has had limited success. Hybrid systems appeared to be the most effective approach to lighting with vertical glazing, skylights, clerestories, atriums, light pipes, light shelves, movable shading devices and high efficiency artificial lighting systems.

Dynamic contexts reflected changing land, water, ecological and climatic patterns and their interactions were difficult to predict. These coupled with changing social and global economic systems added to the complexity for development. In their book, *Dynamic Sustainabilities*, Leach, Scoones and Stirling outline four nuanced approaches to sustainability.[13] First was for the need to transform thinking of fixed and conventional approaches to sustainable development to those of dynamic and variable patterns that were located and context-specific.

Second was the need to transcend increasing preoccupations with issues of risk, uncertainty either real or perceived, and the presence of incomplete knowledge. Third was to work with wider assumptions and contexts of sustainability with multiple framings and scales of application. And fourth was to go beyond the illusionary rhetoric about sustainability and ground it in normative processes and interventions that included qualities of human wellbeing, social equity and environmental integrity.

Eco-technology in the 1990s featured single buildings and mutable technologies that interacted with their immediate environments. So the early demonstrations of eco-technologies were limited to the micro-contexts, as demonstrated by the Quadracci Pavilion, British Pavilion, Eden Project or the Kronsberg IT Office Building. The projects typically demonstrated movable sun control devices, daylighting, advanced skin designs, and more efficient mechanical systems. In some instances photovoltaic electricity was used. And many of the eco-tech projects at this time incorporated rooftop photovoltaic arrays. It was a decade later (well after the millennium) that ecological architecture expanded into more extensive ecological and urban systems, and the relationship between building and context became larger-reaching and increasingly blurred. Urban and ecological systems found correlations, similarities and dynamic interactions.

LOW-TECH HYBRIDS

Emerging from the residential projects of the previous decades, low-tech demonstrations of ecological sustainability develop throughout the 1990s. They continued to target onsite resources, skin-dominated energy flows, and hybrid systems' responses within integrated architectural designs. Low-tech solutions in the 1990s were often distributed, small-scale tectonic designs and passive measures aimed at specific onsite resources. Definitions for low technology suggested relatively unsophisticated technology directed toward common and non-specialized systems. Low-tech was sometime referred to traditional designs, building products and construction practices. Where high-tech architecture often utilized complex engineered structural systems, stainless steel members and joinery, titanium skins and sophisticated glazing systems, and they tended toward a more lightweight, transparent and machine aesthetic that adhered to a strict code of honesty in expression. High-technology was most often applied to public and larger-scaled structures. Low-tech utilized more insulated envelopes, heavier mass buildings that were often hybrid mixtures of multiple technologies applied to residential-scale buildings. As hybrids, they often used a combination of both high and low technologies. Use of photovoltaic technology seemed to cross both low- and high-tech projects providing similar challenges and opportunities for both.

The photovoltaic effect was credited to French physicist Alexandre-Edmond Becquerel in 1839. The photovoltaic effect referred to photons of light exciting electrons into a higher state of energy, allowing them to act as charge carriers for an electric current. The commercially available photovoltaic systems in the 1990s made it possible to achieve off-grid solutions that were coupled to passive solar, solar hot water and rainwater harvesting systems. As the price of solar cells dropped, their demand for buildings and other uses located away from utility lines increased. The tilt angle and orientation of collector arrays considerably influence the electrical production. Two system types emerged—grid-connected systems where overflow energy production by the photovoltaic cells went into the electric utility grid, and battery storage systems for projects located far from utility grids.[14] Different chemicals were combined to make storage batteries for photovoltaic systems. Some combinations were low cost but were low in power storage, while others were able to store more power at increased costs. Sealed lead-acid batteries offered the best balance of capacity per dollar and were a common battery used in stand-alone power systems. Gel-cell batteries offered longer life at higher cost. Since photovoltaic cells produced DC power, an inverter was necessary to convert to AC power for lighting and most residential appliances.

Ackert Architecture designed the Monier Residence (1989), located on a four-acre (1.6 hectares) site near Perth, Australia. The 2,500 square feet (232 square meter) award-winning design was part of the "Monier Design Competition," and incorporated a host of green low-tech design measures that enabled it to be utility independent and off grid. The sustainable measures included an electric wind turbine, solar water heater, 75 feet long (23 meters) rammed earth wall, large areas for natural ventilation and light. Another example was the Casey Family weekend retreat (1998) located in the Hill Country outside of San Antonio, Texas designed by Lake|Flato. The project was fashioned after a "Jacal," which was a Mexican term referring to a low-tech lean-to cedar pole structure and was designed to be completely off-grid. According to Lori Ryker, the owners wanted to contrast their normal urban lives with a retreat that was simple and allowed their family to experience the natural landscape of the rock ledge upon which the house was sited and the Bear Creek below.[15] Key sustainable features were a passive solar heating system, a 5,000-gallon (19,000 liters) rainwater cistern, photovoltaic system with battery storage for water heating and electricity use, a Rumford fireplace, composting toilet, pulley system for adjusting window flaps, and propane for refrigerator and stove. The remarkably simple 925-square feet (86 square meters) structure was constructed with thick limestone walls, large 450-square feet (42 square meter) screened living space, and site-harvested cedar posts and braces.

The LivingHomes designed by Ray Kappe, as seen in Figure 5.4d, illustrated prefabrication at the silver LEED certification level. At the Museum of Science + Industry located in Chicago was a two-year exhibition of a smart home designed by Michele Kaufmann that showcased sustainable practices along with modular construction, Figure 5.4e. One hundred shipping containers were recycled and mounted on a structural metal grid for the Student Hostel in Havre, France designed by Cattani Architects, Figure 5.4f. Prefabrication, modular construction and repurposing components continued to provide interesting and challenging sustainable building practices.

Low-tech approaches to sustainable design, although not new to the 1990s, continued to be realized in hybrid combinations. With the commercialization of photovoltaics and wind turbine energy, many were able to function completely off-grid, which was particularly welcomed with projects in remote locations. Photovoltaic electricity was being used for emergency telephones along remote roadside locations, traffic lights, outdoor lighting, calculators, wristwatches, and other utilitarian uses. They also included many of the following low-technologies: double glazing, cross ventilation, daylighting, light shelves, passive heating, water-harvesting and water-saving devices, ceiling fans, whole-house fans, fixed overhangs or shading devices, super-insulation, moveable insulation, solar cookers, thermosiphon solar water heaters, and green roofs. The constellation of sustainable measures and architectural integration were an evolution for green architecture for the 1990s. In his book, *Low Tech, Light Tech, High Tech* (1998), Klaus Daniels explained that, "the ideal and 'quasi-intelligent' buildings of the future will 'breathe' and will have modifiable room dimensions."[16]

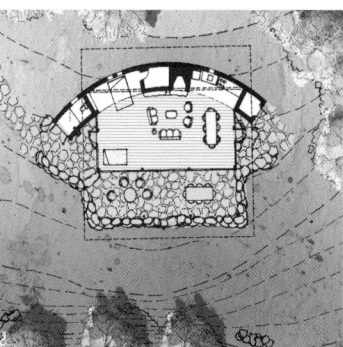

5.4   Low-Tech and Prefabricated Buildings a) Casey Jacal Retreat b) Jacal Floor Plan (courtesy Lake/Flato Architects) c) Porch House (Photo: Frank Ooms) d) LivingHomes (courtesy Ray Kappe) e) Science Museum + Industry mkSolaire (permission Michelle Kaufmann Studio) f) Container Student Hostel (courtesy "Shutterstock")

Daniels suggested that both high-tech and low-tech solutions would be highly interactive and flexible, and applicable to both residential-scale and larger-scale building types. The only shortcoming with this vision was the absence of thermal mass, which is a necessary component for a properly functioning passive solar heating system.

Prefabrication and modular technology were initially created to reduce construction costs by manufacturing buildings and components within a controlled environment, which were then transported to the actual building site. Later prefabrication was sequestered by avant-garde designs that required greater precision, materials processing and careful construction control of component parts, such as the Court Yard House designed by Frank Gehry for the German firm

WeberHaus. More recently prefabrication has become a revival strategy for sustainability. And according to Michelle Kaufmann, modern green prefab offered a more efficient way of building with less construction material waste, and generally resulted in smaller building designs.[17] The work of Living Homes showed that prefabricated residential design could achieve LEED platinum certification. The Porch House designs by Lake|Flato were aimed at achieving lower costs, much shorter construction timelines and integrated sustainable measures. They were designed in prefabricated blocks that could be added on to for increasing space requirements. Yet, generally they accommodated small spatial programs that were easily added incrementally. Modules were 17'-0" (5.1 meters) wide and varied in length. Onsite construction was intended to respond to specific programmatic, climatic conditions, and green details.

LITERAL GREENING OF ARCHITECTURE

Green architecture naturally evolved to include the literal greening of buildings. The earlier earth-sheltered works of Malcolm Wells and others certainly contributed to this approach.. Earth sheltering was not a new dwelling concept as it was linked to the beginnings of human habitation within caves and construction of sod shelters. Thatch was a roofing material that provided protection from precipitation, but also had excellent insulating properties. The ivy hanging gardens of Ivry-sur-Seine, France (1980), were designed by Jean Renaudie, Figure 5.5a, and they provided additional insulation with dead air spaces around the walls of the structures. The development of garden features, such as, pergolas, wall trellis and other structures enabled climbing plants to be used on vertical surfaces.[18] Jean Nouvel's 23-story Residential Tower in New York was what he called a "vision machine" with forested interior (2008).

Green roofs and façades became areas of focus for many sustainable projects in the 1990s with emphasis on horizontal and vertical vegetation. Green roofs served several purposes for a building, such as harvesting rainwater, providing surface water absorption, increasing roof insulation, creating a habitat for wildlife, and helping to lower urban air temperatures that mitigate the heat island effect. The concept of the green wall dates back to 600 BC. with the Hanging Gardens of Babylon. More recently, larger green wall applications have been utilized with innovative hydroponics technology. Building shell vegetation applications have contributed to the improvement of the thermal conduct (insulating properties) of buildings, to increased biodiversity as well as to their aesthetic and social aspects, but also helped to reduce air-polluting substances such as fine dust particles and carbon dioxide. Patrick Blanc was credited with creating the modern living wall.

Green roof technology provided shade and removed heat from the air through evapotranspiration, reducing temperatures of the roof surface and the ambient air. The green roof was also a source of oxygen and provided a habitat for some birds, especially in urban areas. Starting from the top, an extensive green roof had a layer of plants, which were typically sedums. These were low-growing, shallow rooting, drought tolerant plants. There were many different varieties of sedum, with different coloration and different flowerings, so that a roof could have a varied appearance, rather than looking like an entire mono-crop of a single variety. The plants were in a growth medium, an engineered mixture of lightweight soils, vermiculite, and other materials that provided a good environment for the sedum. Thatch roofs were popular in Germany, The Netherlands, Denmark, Belgium and Ireland, yet there were more thatched roofs in the United Kingdom than in any other European country.

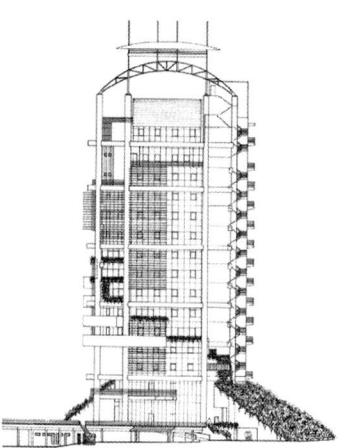

5.5 Literal Greening of Architecture a) Hanging Gardens (© www.discoverparis.net) b) EDITT Tower (Copyright T.R. Hamzah and Yeang Sdn. Bhd. (2012)) c) IBM Tower (courtesy Kim Yeang) d) ACROS Fukuoka (courtesy Emilio Ambasz, Architect) e) Vertical Farm (courtesy "Shutterstock")

Good quality straw thatch could last for more than 45–50 years when applied by a skilled thatcher. Thatch had properties that were naturally weather-resistant, and was a natural insulator, as air pockets within straw thatch insulated a building in both warm and cold weather.

Green walls were typically either freestanding independent structures or an integral part of a building's façade. Vertical gardens or living walls reduced cooling loads in summer by shading building surfaces; this "blanket effect" also cut heating loads in winter, with the green layer acting as extra insulation. As the plants grew, they trapped carbon dioxide and produce oxygen, and soaked up such exterior pollutants as lead and cadmium. Green walls absorbed noise; helped reduce the heat island effect, keeping cities cooler; and provided habitat for birds and insects. Green walls were enabled with hydroponics technology, which were closed systems of terrestrial plants and polyamide felts that mimicked cliff-growing mosses and provoked capillary action for gravity movement of the nutrient solutions. Green façades were typically live plants rooted to the ground while living walls were considered modular systems with various kinds of growth media.

The researches of Dickson Despommier at Columbia University illustrated the vertical farming concept developed in 1999 that focused intense growing within high-rise structures year around.[19] Despommier saw the dense urban environment as a "black hole" that sucked vital nutrients where nothing was produced. His arguments for vertical farming were directed toward providing necessary food for feeding future generations where population increases were projected to exceed the planet's capability of crop raising on existing arable land. Placing farms closer to actual resident populations was another sustainable measure, increasing accessibility and reducing transport energy and costs.

The literal greening of architecture was exemplified by the design for the IBM Tower (1992) in Kuala Lumpur by Hamzah & Yeang. Similarly, their EDITT Tower in Singapore (1998) shown in Figure 5.5b, demonstrated a regeneration project with a continuous vertical landscaping eco-system spiraling around and throughout the tower to facilitate ambient cooling. In addition, the 26-story building was designed to collect rainwater and the integrated photovoltaic panels to provide 40 percent of the building's energy needs.[20] It was planned to have 55 percent water self-sufficiency and 40 percent energy production for the photovoltaic system. The design featured what was called "organic components" and flexible building elements, such as moveable partitions, removable floors and mechanically jointed construction. The project won the 1998 competition for Ecological Design in the Tropics. A criticism of this approach involved the challenge of the maintenance of the vertical forest and the vertical stack effect of potentially fast moving air. In areas of low rainfall, the lack of on-site water could also be problematic, however in areas of high precipitation it could be an expression of regional identity.

The ACROS Fukuoka (1995) was designed by Emilio Ambasz & Associates and demonstrated an impressive 14-story south-terracing vegetative façade-roof of 35,000 plants. The mixed-use complex preserved and revitalized the 24-acre (10 hectares) Tenjin Central Park. The interior featured an exhilarating atrium, a Cultural Information Center, and arts related functions. The California Academy of Sciences in San Francisco designed by the Piano Building Workshop (2008) was another example that featured multiple green venues, including an undulating living roof with 1.7 million native living plants, use of recycled materials, and large photovoltaic canopy. These works ostensibly represented a host of similar projects that took on the literal greening of a building including green roofs, green walls, greenhouses, sky gardens, and high-rise farms. The applications were also considered living tectonics and in some instances, edible landscapes applied to both buildings and urban designs.

Literal greening of architecture provided a softer and even nostalgic aesthetic and natural architectural language especially compared to the more precise high-tech, light weight and eco-tectonic works of this same time period. An interesting design challenge became the fusion of the natural medium of green walls and roofs with the more Euclidian geometries and modern materials that accompanied the contemporary building forms. This clash of natural materiality and tectonic language could be clearly seen with the EDITT Tower, ACROS International Hall and Vertical Farming proposal where the architectural ordering and tectonic systems tended to dominate the natural systems with large, rigid, unnatural forms. However, the emergence of digital software enabled the more complex undulating curves and building roofs that were more reflective of natural landforms.

HEALTH CONCERNS

The relationship between building materials and products and human health became a concern of green architecture. In his book, *Cultural Creatives* (2000), Paul H. Ray introduced the notion of a large and expanding global consumer market for goods and services that were sustainable, healthy and virtuous, which defined a large demographic segment.[21] Later the term Lifestyles of Health and Sustainability (LOHAS) was assigned to this market that estimated 50 million people at the turn of the century. The concern for products, materials, machinery, energy, transportation, socially responsible money, services, also included buildings. In 1997 former President Clinton issued an executive order banning cigarette smoking in all interior spaces of federally owned buildings, rented or leased. Effective in 1998 was the US Department of Transportation ban on smoking on all commercial passenger flights. Health was becoming a larger consumer concern and its relationship to architecture was gaining attention.

Sick building syndrome was a combination of ailments created in the workplace or home caused by poor air quality and outgassing of toxic chemicals and gasses. The causes were generally due to inadequate ventilation, the presence of chemical and biological contaminants, such as volatile organic compounds (VOC) and molds, and infiltration of outdoor pollutants. Molds in high quantities were hazardous to health causing allergic reactions, fungal infections or mycotoxin toxicity.[22] Radon gas can accumulate from certain types of soils, such as phosphate ores, mining wastes and masonry buildings. It was particularly problematic when present in super-insulated buildings where exchange with outside air was dramatically reduced. Radon was a colorless and odorless gas produced from decaying uranium and was the second most frequent cause of lung cancer according to the Environmental Protection Agency. Energy efficient insulating materials often contained toxic flame retardant chemicals, including polystyrene, polyisocyanurate and polyurethane. Formaldehyde, emitted from particleboard was determined to cause a host of health problems. Carbon monoxide was created from wood-burning stoves. While green building practices were moving toward reducing outside air infiltration rates through higher levels of insulation and tighter construction, this was in turn disabling the natural discharge of toxic gases.

An alternative ambit to eco technology can be seen in the pioneering work of William McDonough and Michael Braungart who were authors of *Cradle to Cradle*.[23] Their work focused on the benign effects and minimal environmental impacts of building materials, products, and equipment. With mainly corporate clients, such as, Gap, Herman Miller, Nike, and Ford Motor Company, their work incorporated a blend of passive solar heating and cooling, daylighting and other energy efficiency techniques with incorporation of sustainable building products. Their principal contribution to green architecture was not about formal expression of design or green technology, but with the health and embodied energy implications of building materials. Since the health effects of the greening of architecture had more to do with the materialization of buildings and less about form, it did not carry with it a form-language or visible image of this particular function, perhaps with the exception of green roofs or walls, which do have an evident image. The elemental qualities of form (fire, water, earth, air and light), however, did contribute to health and wellbeing as exemplified in Tadao Ando's Church of Light (1989) in Ibaraki, Osaka. These elemental qualities were considered the basic or essential sources of the given physical world possessing transcendent attributes as well.[24]

5.6 Healthy Buildings a) Vidar Clinic (courtesy Max Plunger) b) GAP Cherry Creek Offices (courtesy William McDonough + Partners)

The GAP Headquarters Cherry Creek Offices (1997) in San Bruno, California were designed with undulating 69,000 square feet (6,410 square meters) of green roofs, covered in wildflowers to evoke the surrounding terrain, daylighting and operable windows to bring the outdoors inside of the building, and the three connected bays had usable office space organized around two-story atriums. Located on 12 acres (4.9 hectares) of land, the design was intended to reflect the ecology of California's coastal prairie. The plan was organized to position all offices with clean air and within 30 feet (9 meters) of a perimeter window and a high efficiency dimmable artificial lighting system was provided to augment the natural lighting. Each bay had incorporated within it two-story landscaped atriums with shaded clerestories. The building was considered 30 percent more energy efficient than what was required by the California State law. Interior finishes were done with low-toxicity paints, carpets and tile adhesives and well as formaldehyde-free particle board, Figure 5.6b.[25] The model photograph shown in Figure 5.6c depicts individual healing retreats and a recuperative hotel designed for the Mado Hamlet at Serenbe Community, Georgia by students at Texas A&M University. The retreats were designed to support varying approaches to healing environments—from high engagement with nature to a more serene inward contemplative focus.

The Vidar Clinic was an anthroposophical hospital that opened on 1985 and was designed by Eric Asmussen as part of the Jarna Community outside of Stockholm, Sweden. The healing functions of the buildings there, and in particular the Vidar Clinic, were based on Rudolf Steiner advice. According to Gary Coates the design emerged from seven healing principles: 1) unity of form and function; 2) experience made perceptible and tangible through contrasts and polarities; 3) the formative process and patterns of metamorphic relationships; 4) intimate relationships to nature; 5) the interplay, mediation, continuity and multiple functions of walls; 6) color luminosity with pigments made from local plants; and 7) the dynamic variability of spatial experience.[26] These healing design determinants underscored the importance of architectural form promoting active living, and the design of their ectypal elements: continuous walls, up-down and in-out spaces, incorporation of natural lighting, ventilation and passive solar heating, and the interactions with the visual and physical surrounding landscape. The term "anthroposophy" came from Rudolf Steiner, meaning that spiritual and healing derived from direct experience through clairvoyance and inner development, and the objective knowledge of being human. It intended to extend the scientific method into spiritual realms, which included architecture and the expressive language of form.

Concepts for healing gardens and healing places, such as the earlier mentioned Findhorn Garden in northern Scotland, emerged as green strategies. In the past, gardens have been used in the healing process, such as the Japanese Zen garden or the monastic cloister garden. While any garden may possess healing qualities, a healing garden was defined as a garden within a therapeutic setting design to enhance the healing process. In her book Healing Gardens (1999), Clare Cooper Marcus identified the role of nature in the therapeutic process that were generally targeted to acute care, psychiatric, and children's hospitals, nursing homes, and hospices.[27] The work reported in the book was in part determined from an emergent process called "evidence-based design" (EBD), where credible data derived from research were used in order to influence the design process. Through this research, it was found that viewing natural scenes, either images on the walls or actual views outside, could increase stress recovery for patients and it exhibited shorter post-operative stays in hospital. The EBD approach became popular in the healthcare industry in an effort to improve patient and staff well-being, patient healing, stress reduction and safety.

Certain design principles emerged from the practice of creating healing environments. Carol Venolia, in her book *Healing Environments* (1988), listed nine qualities for healing environments of which several were directly related to architectural design.[28] These included enhancement of the connections to nature, provisions for privacy, safety, varying stimuli, settings with a balance between familiarity and flexibility, and to be beautiful. It was interesting to compare these healing principles and objectives applied to sustainable architecture. A common denominator seemed to be the beneficial relationship between building and nature in terms of elemental qualities—sun, natural light, water, fresh air, vegetation and views. The relationship between indoors and outdoors, especially in the context to these elemental qualities, was central to a healthy environment. According to Sydney and Joan Baggs in their book, *The Healthy House* (1996), in creating a healthy living environment the concept of the "house of the future," replete with sterile interiors, synthetic materials, electronic gadgetry, electromagnetic fields, and indoor chemical pollution, should be replaced with a more holistic design that fosters natural energies and the healing quality of place.[29]

Active Living was another health effect of environmental design, especially targeted at the planning scale. Active Living was a growing field that emerged from the early work of the Centers for Disease Control and Prevention (CDC) with the release of the Surgeon's General Report on Physical Activity and Health in 1996. Barriers to active living were fears about crime, road safety, pollution, lack of spaces for recreation, and problems with access. To counteract sedentary lifestyles, inactivity and obesity among children and adults, it promoted the integration of greater levels of physical activity into routines of everyday life. Active Living by design became another green strategy that produced positive health effects applicable to both architecture and urban design. At the planning scale causal measures included living-in-place, mixed-use development that encouraged multiple functions, access to elementary schools, bicycle and pedestrian movement with safe sidewalks, crosswalks and exterior spaces to enjoy, such as plazas, parks, playgrounds, walking trails and access to nature. At the architectural scale the visible and convenient placement of stairs, not elevators, and access to indoor and outdoor spaces contributed to active living. Health and wellness were viewed as long-term sustainability strategies and necessary, as well as inseparable, dimensions to the greening of architecture.

A final rather important health concern was in the design for hazards mitigation against the effects of flooding, hurricanes, tornados, volcanic eruptions, earthquakes and other natural disasters. As the world population continues to grow, many people continue to settle in areas of high risk. The science of hazards mitigation focused on assessment of risk, monitoring vulnerable locations, creating more effective emergency services, local preparedness, and implementation of land-use planning and design measures for new building designs and retrofitting existing buildings with directed focus on locating, siting and structural systems' engineering.

GREEN CERTIFICATION PROGRAMS

The critical interaction between architecture and technology moved from preoccupation with the logic of mass production, functionalism and fixed tectonics to the introduction of flexible and highly interactive and mutable technologies addressing multiple engineering agendas. According to Catherine Slessor, "high-tech architecture" evolved to blend the daring feats of structural engineering and expanded the tectonic vocabulary to include sustainability.[30] And the added considerations regarding human well-being and healthy building materials, along with the advent of the merit-defining certification programs, such as the Leadership in Energy and Environmental Design (LEED), EarthCraft, ENERGY STAR, Energy Right, and Green Built programs, further propelled architecture toward a new millennium of greening processes and matriculation into ever expanding realms and scales of application especially within the mainstream.

The LEED certification programs consisted of a suite of programs developed by the US Green Building Council in 1998 and now encompass projects worldwide. The certification process covered five area programs in green building design and construction, interior design and construction, building operations and maintenance, neighborhood development and home design and construction. Within the programs were four priority ratings that certified silver, gold and platinum in increasing order of green performance. The credit areas included sustainable sites, water efficiency, energy and atmosphere, materials and resources, and indoor environmental quality. A few additional points were awarded for innovation in design. While students and professionals alike became LEED certified, not everyone embraced it as an effective means for promoting sustainable design.

Frank Gehry, for example, saw LEED as a political instrument, and stated that, "a lot of our clients don't apply for the LEED certification because it's complicated and in their view, they simply don't need it."[31] LEED was also considered a time consuming and costly process, and sometimes did not meet expectations that led to certification. Not all points were created equally, although they're often measured equally. For example, the presence of bicycle storage and changing rooms earned a similar number of credits toward LEED certification as the installation of solar collection panels. Dave Reid observed, "Buildings built in dense walkable neighborhoods are by default more 'green' than a LEED certified building in the middle of sprawl."[32] While the LEED system may have its flaws, there was no doubt that it had led businesses into investing in green design making companies more aware of sustainable measures. LEED certification also had a marketing benefit to an increasingly aware consumer. The priorities for green merits for New Construction and Major Renovations can be seen with the following LEED allocation of points with site and energy commanding more than 60 percent of the possible points.[33] The Innovation in Design section was rather open ended and was intended to provide projects opportunities to achieve exceptional performance in categories not specified by LEED.

- Sustainable Sites: 26 possible points.
- Water Efficiency: 10 possible points.

- Energy and Atmosphere: 35 possible points.
- Materials and Resources: 14 possible points.
- Interior Environmental Quality: 15 possible points.
- Design Innovation: 6 possible points.
- Regional Priority: 4 possible points.

The Academic Building at Cooper Union College in New York City was designed by Thom Mayne of Morphosis Architects, and was recognized with the first LEED Platinum Certification in New York City, Figure 5.7a. The building was organized around a vertical sky-lit piazza or atrium and an undulating lattice envelope, which defined the perimeter of the building. The double skin was made of perforated stainless steel panels that were offset from the glass walls. The skin and in-between space provided a reduction of solar radiation in summer and a dead-air insulating space during winter. Seventy-five percent of the occupied spaces utilized natural daylighting. The green roof contributed to increased insulation levels, reduction of the heal island effect, and storm water harvesting. Energy was produced by a cogeneration plant that provided waste heat recovery, electricity and cooling for the building. The new building was located on a re-building site and demolished building materials were recycled to the extent possible. It was the combination of the sustainable design measures, the social spaces and urban connectivity that contributed to its high LEED certification.[34] In addition to its obvious green attributes, it had an aggressive and generous design that was well-fitted into its surroundings with genuine civic and academic value.

The innovative work of Ray Kappe in southern California focused on prototype housing schemes at the LEED Silver Certification level. His residential designs were contemporary, warm and inventive with a focus on low-cost, modular and environmentally friendly designs. Kappe designed for LivingHomes, who was the developer of these standard prefabricated homes designed to make living more healthy, sustainable, affordable and accessible. Typical home sizes varied from 2,200 to 2,600 square feet (204 to 242 square meters), which were targeted slightly above the national average for single-family detached houses at that time. The primary green design features were defined by what they termed the Z6 or six areas of zero performance—zero energy, water, waste, emissions, carbon and ignorance. The designs incorporated a green roof, options for photovoltaics, solar water heating, automatic window shades and cistern for water reclamation.

In contrast to the design work of Morphosis and Kappe, a 2,352-square feet (218 square meter) Reid Heritage Home in Guelph, Ontario was the first production home to receive Platinum Certification in Canada. As can be seen in Figure 5.7b, it was a plain, rather common suburban design replete with gable roof, the entrance porch with imported arch, dominant street-facing two-car garage, large concrete driveway, and multiple exterior materials (stucco, brick, wood panel, lapped siding, and asphalt roof shingles). Despite its unremarkable design, it still performed at the Platinum level featuring triple-glazing, double-wall construction, energy efficient lighting, natural ventilation (no AC), rainwater collection, solar hot water collectors, and photovoltaic panels. This brings up questions about LEED or any certification system, for that matter, and their relationship to the promotion of not only environmentally responsive design, but "good" design as well. It seems clear that LEED does not necessarily generate a formal response or contagious architectural language.

5.7   LEED Platinum Buildings a) Cooper Union (courtesy "Shutterstock") b) Reid Heritage Home (courtesy Ashley Ferraro)

An outgrowth of the pioneering work of William McDonough was the development of *The Hannover Principles: Design for Sustainability* (1992), prepared for the City of Hannover, Germany EXPO 2000, The World Fair.[35] Many of the principles were quite general and difficult to specifically apply to architecture, but they did codify the environmental ethic to which buildings should aspire and realize towards sustainable ends with both short and long-term consequences. Underlying constants were concerns for health and wellbeing, safety, human rights, concepts of waste amelioration, the relationship between the built environment and nature—from the most urban to the wild. These themes persisted in green architecture and have evolved to greater degrees of technological complexity in order to enhance this relationship, particularly with the more complex building typologies. These principles were clearly present in most of the pavilions constructed for the Fair and for Kronsberg District, which was a sister demonstration.

Amendments to the Clean Air Act of 1990 focused on acid rain, urban air pollution and toxic emissions. The Pollution Prevention Act of 1990 focused attention on reducing pollution at source rather than waste management or pollution control. It promoted efficiency in the use of energy, water and other natural resources. The Energy Policy Act of 1992 addressed energy efficiency, conservation and management. In the early 1990s the US Environmental Protection Agency created the Energy Star program in an attempt to reduce energy consumption through promotion of energy efficient products. In the United States the aggregation of these legislative acts along with *The Ecology of Commerce* (1994) by Paul Hawken, *Mind and Nature* (1988) by Gregory Bateson, *Ecological Design* (1995) by Sim Van der Ryn and Stuart Cowan, and *Green Architecture* (2000) by James Wines who all underscored the importance of ecological thinking and the relationship between the built environment and the natural flows of nature. Building science with its predictive capability played an increasingly important role in the development of green architecture with focus on detailed analysis of building materials, envelope engineering, building physics, chemistry and biology, structural design and components, and energy and environmental control systems. According to Robert Hastings, Europeans began to take interest in the American passive solar development. Many architects and building researchers traveled to the United States to personally visit passive solar housing projects. As a consequence, passive houses began to appear across Europe, from Scandinavia to Italy.[36] The United Nations Conference on Environment and Development held in Rio de Janeiro in 1992 addressed patterns of pollution, replacement energy for fossil fuels, public transportation, and water scarcity. The Kyoto Protocol was an international treaty signed in 1997 by the United Nations Framework Convention on Climate Change and was aimed at preventing dangerous anthropogenic interference with climate systems.[37] In 1995, Chicago experienced a five-day heat wave that led to approximately 750 heat-related deaths, and in 1996 in the Great Midwest there was the lowest cold outbreak recorded with temperatures of below -60°F (-51°C). These events contributed to an increasing concern about global climate change as greater speculation focused on human activity as the major cause.

The Clinton Administration announced a government initiative called the Partnership for a New Generation of Vehicles (PNGV) in which the government worked with the American auto industry to develop a clean car that could operate at up to 80 miles per gallon. What emerged was the hybrid prototype that was commercialized later in the decade. A small selection of all-electric automobiles were introduced in 1997 in California by major auto manufacturers, and despite user enthusiasm, the programs were dropped after two years. Toyota introduced its first Prius, a hybrid four-door car, in Japan in 1997 and in the United States in 2000 with gas mileage as much as 40 miles per gallon. In 1990 the average combined city and highway gasoline mileage in the United States was approximately 19 miles to the gallon, which represented more than half of what was being introduced in the market with these new hybrids.

The 1990s represented a shift from preoccupation with historicism and architectural meaning to one of tectonic expression, dynamic performance, health considerations, and hybrid applications in design. Where the health and ecological dimensions gave rise to a more qualitative sustainability, the high tectonics and hybrid applications implicitly contributed to an evolving and more normative green form language. The turn of the century brought with it growing concerns about the environment and a renewed interest in the greening of architecture, largely due to increased evidence of global warming and the rising price of crude oil. But more importantly, it brought greater awareness of the complexity and pervasive nature of the environmental problem. Connections, relationships, interfaces and systemic processes emerged in addition to fixed notions about ecological technology and previously focused greening efforts on single buildings. By the new millennium sustainability had accumulated a wide range of green technologies for single buildings in response to the complex contextual and ecological processes of a given place. Low-tech, light-tech and high-tech solutions focused on a host of green measures that were highly integrated into building designs and languages. Green principles and sustainable technologies had become more effective at reducing unsustainability. The greening of architecture had taken on the blueprint of an *"eco-logical"* paradigm and buildings began to reflect this especially in Europe where larger applications were considered.

ENDNOTES

1. John R. Ehrenfeld, *Sustainability by Design: A Subversive Strategy for Transforming Our Consumer Culture*. New Haven, CT: Yale University Press, 2008.

2. Michael Benedikt, http://www.zakros.com/liquidarchitecture/liquidarchitecture.html, accessed February 2012.

3. William J.R. Curtis, *Modern Architecture since 1900*. New York: Phaidon Press Inc., 1997.

4. Eco-technology refers to increasing technological efficiency, reduction of negative environmental impacts, harvesting of beneficial onsite resources, and incorporation of non-toxic, permanent and effective materials and products. Catherine Slessor, *Eco-Tech: Sustainable Architecture and High Technology*. London: Thames and Hudson, 1997: 7–12.

5. Patrick Nuttgens, *The Story of Architecture*. London: Phaidon Press Ltd., 1997.

6. Klaus Daniels, *The Technology of Ecological Building*. Basel: Birkhauser Verlag, 1997.

7. Michael Benedikt, *Cyberspace: First Steps*. Cambridge, MA: The MIT Press, 1992.

8. Francesco Dal Co and Kurt W. Forster, *Frank O. Gehry: The Complete Works*. New York: The Monacelli Press, 1998.

9. Mobile phone technology was developed as early as 1946 by Bell Labs allowing mobile users to place and receive calls from automobiles. The first mobile web access was developed commercially in 1996 by Nokia. It is estimated that there will be 982 million smart phones sold in the year 2015. Source: http://en.wikipedia.org/wiki/History_of_mobile_phones, accessed February 2012.

10. Kenneth Yeang, *Designing with Nature: The Ecological Basis for Architectural Design*. New York: McGraw-Hill Book Company, 1995.

11. James Wines, *Green Architecture*. Köln: Taschen Press, 2000: 11–15.

12. Catherine Slessor, *Eco-Tech: Sustainable Architecture and High Technology*. London: Thames and Hudson, 1997.

13. Melissa Leach, Ian Scoones and Andy Stirling, *Dynamic Sustainabilities: Technology, Environment Social Justice*. London, UK: Earthscan Publications, 2010: 3–5.

14. Othmar Humm and Peter Toggweiler, *Photovoltaics in Architecture*. Basel: Birkhauser Verlag, 1993.

15. Lori Ryker, *Off The Grid: Modern Homes and Alternative Energy*. Layton, Utah: Gibbs Smith Publishers, 2005.

16. Klaus Daniels, *Low-Tech, Light-Tech, High-Tech: Building in the Information Age*. Basel: Birkhauser Verlag, 1998.

17. Michelle Kaufmann and Cathy Remick, *PreFab Green*. Layton, Utah: Gibbs Smith Publishers, 2009.

18. Raymond Sterling, William Farnan and John Carmody, *Earth Sheltered Residential Design Manual*. New York: Van Nostrand Reinhold Publishers, 1982.

19. The vertical farm is a fascinating idea that suggests a completely new building typology replete with an interesting cast of mixes of use. Dickson Despommier, *The Vertical Farm: Feeding the World in the 21st Century*. New York: Thomas Dunne Books, 2010.

20. Kenneth Yeang and Arthur Spector, *Green Design: From Theory to Practice*. London: Black Dog Publishing, 2011: 8–12.

21. Paul H. Ray and Sherry Ruth Anderson, *The Cultural Creatives: How 50 Million People are Changing the World*. New York: Three Rivers Press, 2001.

22. G.B. Leslie and F.W. Lundau, *Indoor Air Pollution: Problems and Priorities*. Cambridge, UK: Cambridge University Press, 1994.

23 William McDonough and Michael Braungart, *Cradle to Cradle: Remaking the Way We Make Things*. New York: North Point Press, 2002: 174–6.

24 Liliana Gomez and Walter Van Herck, *The Sacred in the City*. London, UK: Continuum International Publishing Group, 2012: 142–3.

25 Source: http://www.mcdonoughpartnrs.com, accessed February 2012.

26 Gary J. Coates, *Erik Asmussen, Architect*. Stockholm: Byggforlaget Publishers, 1997.

27 Clare Cooper Marcus and Marni Barnes, *Healing Gardens: Therapeutic Benefits and Design Recommendations*. New York: Wiley & Sons, 1999.

28 The nine characteristics of a healing environment are to stimulate positive awareness of the self, enhance connections to nature, allow for privacy, to be safe from physical harm, provide varying stimuli, encourage relaxation, allow for human interaction, contain a balance between familiarity and flexibility, and to be beautiful. Carol Venolia, *Healing Environments: Your Guide to Indoor Well-Being*. Celestial Arts, 1995: 11.

29 Sidney and Joan Baggs, *The Healthy House: Creating a Safe, Healthy and Environmentally Friendly Home*. Sydney, Australia: Harper Collins Publishers, 1996.

30 Catherine Slessor, *Eco-Tech: Sustainable Architecture and High Technology*. London: Thames and Hudson, 1997.

31 Source: http://inhabitat.com/frank-gehry-defends-his-criticism-of-leed/, accessed February 2012.

32 Natural Resource Defence Council Staff Blog, April 28, 2010.

33 The Leadership in Energy and Environmental Design (LEED) was an internationally recognized green building certification checklist developed by the US Green Building Council in 1998. It was a merit-defining process for a broad range of green buildings of varying architectural and aesthetic value.

34 Source: morphopedia.com/projects/cooper-union, accessed February 2012.

35 William McDonough Architects, *The Hannover Principles: Design for Sustainability*. Charlottesville, VA: Self-published, 1992.

36 Robert Hastings, "Passive Solar Heating in the Built Environment," *Springer Reference 2013*. Source: http://www.springerreference.com/docs/html/chapterdbid/301267.html, accessed February 2012.

37 The Kyoto Protocol sets binding targets for participating countries for reducing greenhouse gas emissions through national measures. It was adopted in 1997 and entered into force in 2005. Source: http://unfccc.int/kyoto_protocol/items/2830.php/, accessed February 2012.

Chapter 6
2000s: Sustainable Pluralism

Phillip Tabb

> Emerging backlashes—from nature, from social movements, from politics—reveal
> this widening gap between standard policy approaches and dynamic systems.[1]

The turn of the millennium brought a combination of optimism, skepticism and fear. The Y2K, or what was referred to as the "millennium bug", was a computer-related problem. There was concern that computer systems would break down, causing innumerous difficulties and even severe disasters in the energy, economics, security, and transportation sectors. Terrorism, especially the 9/11 tragedies and, subsequently, the war in Iraq, which started in 2003, were other sources of grave anxiety. The 2008 global financial crisis created a significant decline in economic activity leading to recession. Concerns about climate change and global warming continued to grow with the increase of science pointing toward greenhouse gas accumulations from human related activity. This included the receding of Arctic glaciers and Arctic cap along with droughts in southwestern Australia and increased species extinctions, including the Black Rhino from West Africa.[2] The US National Oceanic and Atmospheric Administration released a report in 2010 that delineated 10 key indicators of climate change, which included troposphere air temperature, sea surface and air temperatures, sea level, quantity of sea ice, ocean heat content, overland temperature, humidity, snow cover and glacier size and movement. Natural disasters, such as the Indian Ocean tsunami (2004), hurricane Katrina (2005), Kashmir earthquake (2005), cyclone Nargis (2008), the Haiti earthquake (2010), the Tohoku earthquake and tsunami (2011), superstorm Sandy (2012), and the Haiyan typhoon (2013), all contributed to greater awareness and reoccurring dangers of our inescapable relationship with the natural environment.

The apparent gloom and doom experienced during the beginning of this century brought awareness and focused attention to the possible causes of global warming, which included the carbon dioxide emissions from fossil fuel burning power plants and from burning gasoline for transportation, methane emissions from agriculture, from deforestation especially within tropical forests, and an increase of chemical fertilizers on croplands. As a consequence, there was a greater accumulation of atmospheric gasses that in turn expanded the global greenhouse effect trapping long wave radiation and increasing ambient air and ocean temperatures and reducing ice and snow cover.

6.1 Solar Decathlon a) National Mall (2002) (courtesy of US Department of Energy. Office of Energy Efficiency and Renewable Energy) b) CHIP SCI-Arc/CALTECH (2011) (© Southern California Institute of Architecture)

According to Derek Markham, the effects of these changes were evidenced in an increase of devastating storms worldwide, rise of sea levels, crop failure, species extinction, an increase in evaporation, and disappearance of coral reefs.[3] While there was greater public acceptance that global warming was indeed occurring, the debate shifted to the question of its source—natural cyclical causes or the consequence of human activity. The Intergovernmental Panel on Climate Change in 2007 concluded there's a better than 90 percent probability that human-produced greenhouse gases such as carbon dioxide, methane and nitrous oxide have caused much of the observed increase in Earth's temperatures over the past 50 years.[4] Despite all the negativity, at the beginning of this century there were positive moments in which the green movement was one of the beneficiaries.

For green architecture, the turn of the century brought renewed concerns and an increase in environmental awareness that human activity relative to architecture and planning could be reformed and curtail some of the negative effects of climate change. This turn of the spiral of the greening process incorporated greater considerations of urbanism, ecology and scales of engagement. The landscape for green architecture expanded to include the full transect spectrum from urban through rural buildings, with applications globally. Further, green architecture became a context for the nesting of many sustainable measures and technologies on multiple levels. The US Department of Energy's first Solar Decathlon was held in 2002, which was an international competition held biannually to promote energy performance, efficiency and aesthetics in residential design. This gave a diversity of ideas of what sustainable architecture might be with a plurality of approaches emphasizing, function, performance, tectonics, scaler-integrated interrelationships, and appearance within deepening situational specific contexts.

POLY-SCALER SUSTAINABILITY

Charles and Ray Eames' *Powers of Ten*, a film released in 1968, was a short documentary of orders of magnitudes and relative scales of the cosmos.[5] Zooming out and then in with the positive and negative powers of 10, the film depicted the vast scaler differences from the observable universe to carbon proton quarks. The significance of this film was in the expression of the enormous vastness of existence at varying scales. For architecture and planning the span of scales, from the molecular composition of floor carpeting to regional transportation systems, were large enough to produce distinct layers that required differing sustainable approaches. There emerged three important considerations; first was the delineation and differentiation of specific scales, second was the identification of the sustainable strategies appropriate to each scale making up the built-environment, and third was identification of the ways in which each scale interacted and nested with one another.

Susan Owens, in her book *Energy, Planning and Urban Form* (1986), described sustainable strategies operating at varying scales of development, from regional to local scales, with varying spatial characteristics and structural variables.[6] This was to suggest that differences in the spatial characteristics and structure of a place could contribute to a wide variation in energy efficiency. Some of the sustainable issues overlapped, repeated, and co-existed across scales while some were distinct or present within a particular scale. For example, water was an issue that existed at the regional through systems' scales although handled in different magnitudes. Onsite resource utilization was primarily confined to the building scale although in some instances applicable to the cluster scale and renewable energy farms. Transportation energy was affected by configuration, density of built form and mixes of use that were applicable to the settlement and neighborhood scales. As an outgrowth of Owens' research, nine descending or cascading scales of consideration for sustainable measures included the following:

- Global scale—increasing efficiency with transportation of natural resources, food, manufactured products, and capital, especially in rail, shipping and air transport sectors—reducing gaps among relationships of labor, production and consumer markets.
- Regional scale—reducing travel distances and trip frequencies, creating efficient flows of water, energy and materials, providing waste management, recycling, varying transportation systems, agriculture, biodiversity, and habitat preservation. Responding to potential natural disasters.
- Settlement scale—with considerations of size, shape, density, land use mix, spatial structure, power production, infrastructure systems, internal movement systems, transportation fabric, green space and recycling.
- Urban design scale—density of built form, mixes of use, cogeneration, repurposing existing building stock, infrastructure architecture, urban agriculture, solar access, daylighting, public transportation, and provision of pedestrian places, access to green space and network systems.
- Neighborhood scale—density, mixes of use, district heating and cooling where applicable, pedestrian orientation, schools and activities for children, integrated agriculture and community gardens, and recycling.
- Cluster scale—density, district heating and cooling, cogeneration, site planning, landscape and open space design, water retention, filtration and re-use, land use mix, and pedestrian movement.
- Building scale—siting, orientation, climate responsive form, onsite resource utilization, passive solar heating, natural ventilation, conservation, geothermal heating and cooling, dynamic systems, reuse, upgrades, retrofits, use of healthy and non-toxic building materials.
- System scale—integration and component aesthetic considerations, efficiency, synergy, hybridity, and intelligent and adaptive control systems.

- Products scale—involving manufacturing, materials, and methods of non-toxic building materials, energy efficient and low embodied energy, made relatively locally, long lasting, low maintenance, affordable and recyclable.

A transect was a geographical section from the most urban-to-rural delineating a spatial disposition of transitional development, and was a good marker across these sustainability scales. Density, land use mix, geometric order, and proximity played a crucial role in the context-defining characteristics of place, and provided a framework for the scales of application of sustainable strategies. The transect shown as a sectional map, identified the distribution of differing geographical and ecological features of a region or site. Later it was adapted to articulate urban characteristics as well, which included the gradient signifying the density of built forms to the correspondent amounts of open space. In 1971 planner Andrew Thorburn published a copy of his diagram of a transect often found in English villages, *The Thorburn Transect*.[7] Rather than expressed in distinct and differentiated zones as you later see in the New Urbanism models (Krier and Duany), it was more a counteracting and seamless gradient between the built elements of the settlement form moving outward and the landscape and natural elements of a region emanating from the edge moving inward to the most dense areas at the village center.

A *transect* was essentially a geographical cross-section between the most urban part of a settlement center or core to the most rural area at the edge. It articulated the agglomeration of people, buildings, roads, other urban elements, and natural features of the place in a hierarchical spatial fashion. The *threshold of dispersion* occurred at the edge and was a concept that defined when these urban elements were too far from one another to really form any kind of meaningful relationship. When this occurred, there was a threshold where these elements were outside of the bounds of the settlement and were considered to be rural and individuated. The term transect was borrowed from ecology, which described changes in habitat and plant distribution over an ecological gradient or zone, usually defined by two edges from the ridge of a wooded hill through a meadow to a water source below. In the urban context the transect delineated the sectional transition from the more focused, dense, diverse and intense parts of the urban fabric gradually decreasing in incremental stages to the most open, tranquil and natural land uses beyond the settlement. Many in the New Urbanism movement have generally articulated a five or six-zone transect model, and in the case of Duany Plater-Zyberk, they have embodied it into their planning codes and practices. Their six zone classifications were urban core, urban center, general urban, suburban, rural and natural. And according to town planner Andres Duany, all possible environments can be mapped into this model. In other words, human habitation can be modeled into this hierarchal spatial system and locational organization offering coding, and urban design guidelines for each of the zones. Missing were clear sustainable strategies targeted for the differing zones.

The transect was a good structure for the identification of appropriate modes of sustainable design. Specific planning and design strategies could be assigned to particular areas along the transect. Sustainable measures were often in direct conflict with one another, such as solar access for passive solar heating, which more easily was accommodated in lower densities with more generous building spacing, and public transport, which functioned more efficiently in higher densities and populations with shorter travel distances.

6.2 Scales of Greening a) Product Scale b) Single Building Scale (courtesy Himin Solar Co., Ltd) c) Urban Design Scale (SHAU Architects / Design by SHAU Architects for Green Campus Company, Delft) d) Ecological Scale (Aeter Architects)

Access to public transportation in low-density contexts was often uneconomical and prohibitive, and solar access for long periods of the sun-lit winter day (six hours or more) was difficult to achieve in dense environments due to increased shading of collection devices. Energy, for example, had three major sectors of end use, which were the production, transportation and building sectors, and they influenced each of the transected scales. A ballooning or exaggeration of any of the areas along the transect would establish the kind of settlement pattern that framed the primary sustainable needs and corresponding strategies, such as dominance at the high density end of the transect as in Hong Kong, China or at the low density end as in Houston, Texas. Proponents of the New Urbanism have applied form-based zoning codes along the transect as a means of controlling designs and maintaining balance among these sectors. This application was a good beginning, but did not address sustainability across the full range of scales from ecological region to products. However, progress has been made when considering how advancements in agricultural urbanism, sustainable urbanism, transect strategies along with infrastructure, biometrics and green architectural design each have contributed to gluing together into a more seamless framework for the entire spectrum for sustainability. Continuity among scales was advancing with products like the new generation hybrids, green buildings, new urban forms and more connected ecological zones as illustrated in Figures 6.2a, b, c and d with the 2012 Prius hybrid, the Sun-Moon Mansion in China, The Why Factory Green Dream in Barcelona, and the ecological scale project for Hong Kong by Aeter Architects.

BIOMETRICS

Biometrics was one of the strategies of sustainability applicable across many of the sustainable scales. This was possible partly because of the connection between sustainability and the basic axioms of biology—cells are the basic unit of life, new species are a product of evolution, genes are the basic unit of heredity, organisms regulate their internal environments to maintain stability, and living organisms consume and transform energy. Inspired through biology, *biometrics,* or alternatively termed *biomimicry,* developed as an interpretation of the landscape through science and the art of exemplifying nature's forms and processes in architecture and urban design. According to Michael Pawlyn, biomimicry contained sustainable principles and initiating inspirations, such as superefficient structures, high strength biodegradable composites, self-cleaning surfaces, low energy and waste systems, and water retention methods. *Biophilia,* named by Edward Wilson, further suggested an affiliation with other life forms and living systems, and the "memorymarks" that were instinctual for survival. Translating to architecture, this would support adaptive designs that enhance access to resources, food, views, and direct exposure to nature.[8] Conceptually, these were useful green planning and design models, but taken too literally, copying nature was naïve especially as applied to complicated contemporary space programs, dense urban districts and historic contexts. Form was celebrated as the result of a process, and part of the attraction of biometrics was the embedded form-process, form-structure, and form-harmonics. Given these inherent qualities, there was a natural crossover to a green architecture in which anthropomorphic, zoomorphic and biomorphic qualities were given to an architectural form-language that was largely enabled with new software modeling programs and fabrication methods.

Biometrics varied greatly across the spectrum of sustainable scales. Examples of biometric architecture were created throughout contemporary architectural history, such as the works by Rudolf Steiner, Antonio Gaudi, Bruce Goth, Herb Greene, Jorn Utzon, Eero Saarinen, Santiago Calatrava, Frank Gehry, and Coop Himmelb(l)au. Biological forms influenced projects like the Sagrada Familia, TWA Terminal Building, Sydney Opera House, Barcelona Fish Pavilion, and Herb Greene's Prairie House, Figure 6.3a. Principle design features included: proportional geometry, harmonious fields, physiognomics, skeletal structures and shapes, organic plasticity, morphological growth patterns, and biological forms. The Las Vegas Springs Preserve, which began in 2005 designed by Tate Snyder Kimsey Architects and Lucchesi Galati Architects, was intended to demonstrate building and living in the desert on a 180-acre (73 hectares) site built around the original water source for Las Vegas. It functioned with nature trails, wetlands habitat, museum, outdoor theater, and botanical gardens.

Nobel Textiles was a collaboration between Nobel-winning scientists and London designers to create textile designs inspired by Nobel Laureates. One proposal was for a lightweight urban agriculture structure based on molecular biology and metabolic living cells. The result was a flexible architecture that was coupled with energy harvesting canopies and membranes inspired by photosynthesis. The Beijing National Aquatic Center in Olympic Park, Beijing was an example of cellular architecture, and the Beijing National Stadium in the form of a bird's nest were constructed in 2008 for the summer Olympics. The JVC New Urban Entertainment Center in Guadalajara, Mexico was planned by Coop Himmelb(l)au in 1990–2001, and was conceived as a marketplace for the future. Its program integrated conventional forms of entertainment and commerce with new facilities based on the creation and exchange of knowledge and intellectual discourse. The contemporary program included 16 cinemas, seven restaurants, and

6.3 Biometrics in Architecture a) Herb Greene Prairie House (courtesy Robert Alan Bowlby) b) JVC New Urban Entertainment Center (© Coop Himmelb(l)au / Armin Hess, Isochrom.com) c) Metropol Parasol Building (courtesy Fernando Alda)

seven bars making up the three million net square feet of space (278,709 square meters). The structure appeared to be soaring with the combination of the form and transparent skeletal vertebrate structure as depicted in Figure 6.3b.

The Metropol Parasol (2011) was a remarkable redevelopment project for the Plaza de la Encarnacion within the dense medieval inner city fabric of Seville, Spain designed by Jurgen Mayer-Hermann. The work was a compelling result of an international competition in which this project came in first place. Like the Bilbao Museum in Bilbao, this structure became an icon and international place-marker creating a new and dynamic urban intervention. The waffle parasol form was made of bonded timber construction with a polyurethane coating, and was reported to be the world's largest wooden structure. Programmatically the project was layered and housed an antiquarium for Roman and Moorish remains, central market, public square, restaurants, multiple bars, underground parking, and many panoramic terraces. The contrast and integration of historical and contemporary mixed uses, of memory, leisure and commerce, identified this work as an unprecedented landmark. Locally, the building was known as *Las Setas de la Encarnacion* translated to "Encarnacion's mushrooms." It was clear, as seen in Figure 6.3c, that the morphed diaphragm structure had reference to organic biological forms like shade trees and mushrooms, and was in such contrast to the plaza's surrounds.

The conflation of landscape and built structure was investigated within a larger context with theories of *Landscape Urbanism* developed in the late 1990s. The principal post-urban themes were designed to achieve urban effects through interdisciplinarity, systemic ecology of place, adaptable territories, fluidity and spontaneous feedback of morphological development, and most importantly, through horizontal fields of urbanism (agrophilia).[9] According to James Corner, there were four inter-practical underpinnings to Landscape Urbanism that included ecological and urban practices which occurred over time, staging context of horizontal surface and geography with decentralization of industry, the working process across the range of scales, and the active realm of the imagination. There was a shift away from the object in space to the projective practice with systems of distribution and density of a more organic and fluid urban form. While treating the urban environment as an ecological model had sustainable implications, Landscape Urbanism's tolerance of low-density and automobile-driven environments, promoting a new kind of suburbanization, was inspired by ecology, but in practice was not entirely ecological.

Landform architecture drew its inspiration from the geology, topography and geography of the land. And as architectural reconstructions of nature, they sequestered their qualities of more fluid, adaptable, and responsive forms.[10] The California Academy of Sciences in San Francisco was designed by Renzo Piano and was among the largest natural history museums in the world.

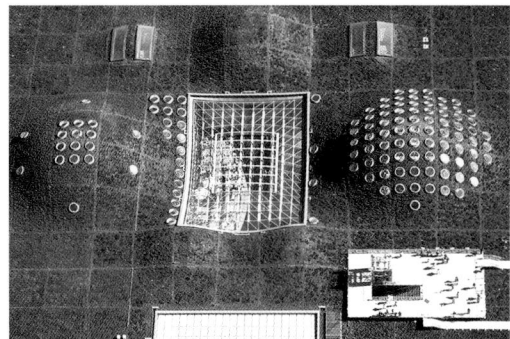

6.4   Landform Architecture and Landscape Urbanism a) California Academy of Sciences b) Mineralogical Urbanism (permission Vicente Guallart) c) Vegetal City (permission Luc Schuiten Architecture) d) Olympic Sculpture Park (© 2007 Benjamin Benschneider / All Rights Reserved)

It exemplified landform architecture with its undulating forms modeling the nearby land, expanded pods, and a seamless green living roof. Programmatically it consisted of an aquarium, planetarium, natural history museum, theater and lecture hall, two restaurants, garden and aviary along with science labs, administrative offices and library. The 197,000-square feet (18,302 square meters) project reopened in 2008 and achieved a LEED Platinum certification. The programmatic complexity was housed within an envelope that was remarkably conventional, except for the undulating green roof. Among the sustainable strategies were less water usage, recycled rainwater, utilization of photovoltaic electricity, incorporated a two-and-a-half-acre (one hectare) green roof, high percentage of natural daylighting, use of recycled concrete and steel, and the walls with insulation made from scraps of recycled denim. Vanke Center located in Shenzhen, China was a mixed-use proposition designed by Stephen Holl for a "horizontal skyscraper" as long as the Empire State Building is high, and it was completed in 2009. Kenneth Frampton observed that the megaform was significant because of its topographic, horizontal thrust of its overall profile.

Examination of biometrics, landscape urbanism and landform architecture all found inspiration in nature, biology, geology, and ecological processes. Biometrics tended to be more self-absorbed and focused on isolated object exemplifications inspired by biological references, while often ignoring existing contextual patterns. Stan Allen argued that, "despite advances in fabrication technology, a large gap still exists between the fluid, curvilinear forms generated by the software and the intractability of materials and construction logistics."[10] Contradicting approaches between nucleated forms of the New Urbanism and the temporal mutability and horizontal extensity afforded by Landscape Urbanism demanded differing concepts of placemaking and sustainable measures especially within the transportation sector. Embodied in the tenets of each of these directions were intrinsic sustainable objectives and measures that were usually afforded by the more dispersed and less dense contexts, such as climate-sculpted forms, utilization of onsite resources, and innovative structure and enclosure materials. The synthesis of these directions provided unprecedented images and new meanings, such as the roof of the California Academy of Sciences (Figure 6.4a), the mineralogical and vegetal landforms in Figures 6.4b and c, and the remaking of the urban territories exemplified by the Seattle Olympic Sculpture Park by Weiss-Manfredi as in Figure 6.4c.

INFRASTRUCTURE ARCHITECTURE

Between-place contexts supported a new kind of architecture, one that had systemic fabric-oriented qualities. Sites for infrastructure architecture tended to be situated circumferentially around dense urban centers and between defined suburban residential districts. These environments were typically linear, complex, often chaotic, and spatially fragmented with multiple land uses, functionally zoned and separated from one another, such as industrial factories, power plants, water treatment facilities, brownfields, sports and entertainment facilities, business parks, automobile dealerships, shopping malls, rail lines, watersheds, and a patchwork of residual land, and they tended to be dominated by automobile highway networks. Given the piecemeal and inhabitable nature of this territory, sustainable strategies tended toward increased levels of connectivity for ecological and pedestrian zones, increased mixes and integration of uses, densification, placemaking, and far more sinuous forms. The new urban insertions and adaptive reuse projects for this development context typically followed linear watersheds, transportation routes, and other infrastructural systems. Katrina Stoll and Scott Lloyd in *Infrastructure as Architecture* claimed that there was an increasing demand for integrated solutions that must respond to new, complex and fragmented urban landscapes. Stoll and Lloyd further suggested infrastructure architecture created a new fluid landscape for cultural spaces connecting "spatial peaks" with stretching "regional fields."[11] Stephen Graham and Simon Marvin argued for a "splintered network infrastructure" as an emerging pattern, replete with wires, tunnels, conduits, water networks, streets, highways and what they called "infrastructurally mediated flow, movement and exchange."[12]

The 2014, Asian Games Stadium (2002) in the port city of Incheon, South Korea, was a competition winning design by Populous Architects, and was an example of the grafting of infrastructure architecture into in-between land, movement systems and green spaces within a complex urban site. The primary focus and destination for the project was the stadium having more than a 60,000-person capacity, and this will be the site of the 17th Asian Games in 2014. All the various facilities associated with the stadiums were fitted between the eight-lane Highway 110 and six-lane street and subway line that lead to the city center. Far from being simply object buildings, the large-scale increments appeared, as a dynamic layering that seemed to liberate architecture into an amalgamation and syntax of pure motion. Among the sustainable features were strong connections to surrounding parkland, the creation of open accessible buildings, and the open-air sun-shaded roof over the stadium seating.

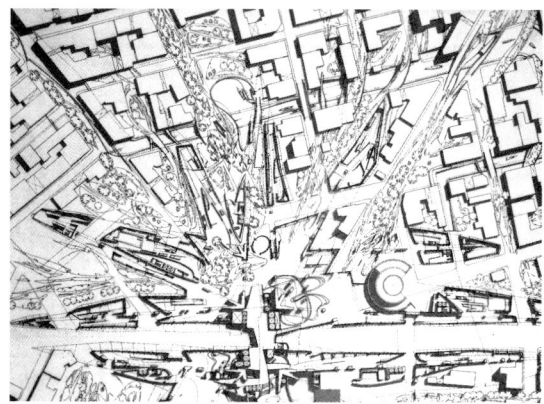

6.5   Infrastructure Architecture a) 2014 Asian Games Stadium (© Populous) b) Namba Parks (courtesy: The Jerde Partnership. Photographer Hiroyuri Kawano) c) High Line Park (1934) d) High Line Park (2011) (photograph: Iwan Raan) e) Michael Sorkin Insertions (courtesy Michael Sorkin)

It was intended that the design be transformed into a park after the sports festival and games. The Dalian Shide Stadium in Dalian, China (2009) designed by NBBJ was a large stadium and infrastructure proposal on a reclaimed site that included innovative green design for stadium architectural typologies. The exterior was designed with an open structure clad in living walls, the large LED panels are powered by photovoltaic and wind turbine-generated electricity, water was designed for reuse and recycling, and the stadium was designed to be shaded with a creative flexible system of cables and fabric.

The Namba Parks completed in 2003 in Osaka, Japan was an amazing example of an infrastructural oasis within the city center. Designed by Jerde Partnership, the parks and 30-story structure replaced the former Osaka Baseball Park, and were planned with one story of activities underground and eight stories above ground. The program called for a combination of retail, and offices with a rooftop garden complex. Included in the project were a number of different restaurants, and amphitheater for live entertainment, and spaces for vegetable gardens and wagon shops. In 2007 a second phase of activities, that nearly doubled the size of the original design, were added that included a cinema complex and specialty stores. The sensuous form was designed to connect to local streets that encouraged passers-by to easily engage in the natural amenities especially with the varied outdoor functions that included stands of trees, clusters of rocks, cliffs, streams, waterfalls, ponds and multiple terraces. The site for the project was less than a 10-minute walk from Namba Station. Far from being an "object building," this infrastructure architecture became an integral, connected and flowing part of the everyday urban, natural, and cultural processes of Osaka. Namba Park was one of four Asian development projects given the Urban Land Institute's ULI 2009 Award of Excellence.

Another example, New York City's remarkable High Line Park (2009 and 2011) designed in three sections by landscape architect James Corner Fields Operation with architects Diller Scofidio + Renfro, was a competition winning proposal created as an aerial greenway elevated above the ground for one mile along Manhattan's West Side.[13] It transformed the 1.5-mile (2.4 kilometers) section of the former New York Central Railroad spur running through the Chelsea Neighborhood. Originally it was a massive public–private infrastructure project done in the 1930s called the "West Side Improvement" that elevated dangerous freight trains 30 feet (9.1 meters) off the street level thereby avoiding conflict with pedestrians and cars on the ground below. Inspired by the Promenade Plantée in Paris, nine entrances give access to the elevated platform and to the pebbledash walkways that expanded and contracted along the park. The design was described as part promenade, town square, part botanical garden, and an urban and nature integration or "*agri-tecture*." While the recycling of the freight rail line into a park was extremely beneficial to the environment, a sense of community was created and real estate development spurred adjacent to the line was a positive consequence of the success of the project. As an infrastructural design, High Line Park provided safe connectivity, pedestrian movement, a destination for adjacent economic development, and urban agriculture. In addition there were positive environmental effects, including reduction of the heat island effect, increase of organic filtration of airborne pollutants and an increase in biodiversity.

These urban infrastructural projects were reminiscent of the visionary urban designs of Michael Sorkin and his neurological network insertions, such as the master plan for Chungcheong, South Korea (2005). The works of Sorkin's studio were consistent in their weaving of contemporary biometric forms and relations of proximity within an existing contextual backdrop. According to Sorkin, urbanity was seen as opportunities for an urban morphology of fresh possibilities and ecological consciousness. The visionary urban designs illustrated in *Wiggle* (1998) were decidedly dynamic, moving, sometimes place-oriented and other times were complementary and rejuvenated infrastructural propositions.[14] Part of the importance of this work was the shift away from object buildings to the focus on the more illusive, in-between, connective and infrastructural urban sites—they intertwined, wove, re-directed, engaged, rejuvenated and laced the urban environments into which his insertions were emplaced.

Supporting these later green developments of infrastructure architecture were the ideas of urban designer Nan Ellin in *Integral Urbanism* (2006) that shifted attention away from nostalgic urbanism, hypermodernity, the spotlight of singularity of focus and reliance on technology for sustainable urbanism.[15] Ellin argued for an integral approach to urban design that celebrated seams, fabric, thresholds, infrastructure, and people places, dwelling not in the past or future, but rather focused on revitalizing the present. The ideas were complicit with those of Jane Jacobs with application to the borders between geographic territories. Ellin's call for an integral design revealed the current state of fragmentation, disconnectedness, incompleteness and lack of wholeness. Proposed were new lenses through which to view the urban landscape highlighted by two primary concepts—re-integration and present time, which were nuanced by hybridity, connectivity, porosity, authenticity and vulnerability. These qualities of integral urbanism were particularly relevant to sustainable planning and design objectives, especially at the infrastructure scale.

SUSTAINABLE URBANISM

The greening of architecture after 2000 proliferated globally with more complex, larger programs and broader reaching considerations as illustrated in James Wines's book *Green Architecture* (2000).[16] Sustainability included urbanism and communities of buildings with their connecting urban and rural spaces, while green architecture evolved to greater levels of integration and sophistication of renewable technologies and climatic form responses. At the threshold of the millennium were the works at Expo 2000 in Hannover, Germany, that explored both these scales of design. The German Pavilion, designed by Josef Wund, was a lightweight and daylit structure that featured concave curved glazed facades. The central meeting place at EXPO 2000, designed by Thomas Herzog, was sheltered by four elaborate umbrella shells erected with hybrid timber and steel construction. While green design focused on single buildings advancing form, new materials and technology integration, projects of much larger scale began to emerge. Many of the buildings of the Expo were saved or repurposed, such as the Expo Plaza, Netherlands Pavilion designed by MVRDV and the Nepal Pavilion.

Adjacent to the Hannover Fair was the new urban project of Kronsberg, Germany, planned by Arnaboldi, Cavadini and Hager. It was an eco-district planned for a greenfield area with high ecological standards. This was a sister project to the exposition, which went beyond focus on individual buildings to demonstrate a transit-driven sustainable community for 6,000 dwellings.[17] The medium-density design incorporated two-story to five-story buildings with renewable technologies, and cogeneration with district heating and cooling. The strong grid layout allowed for super blocks with compact mixed use building types and varying courtyard designs for resident activities, community gardens and water retention. In its center was planned a central square surrounded by shops, galleries, and cafes. A light rail line connected Kronsberg to Hannover city center as seen in Figures 6.6a and b. Adjacent to the transit line was planned a linear business park composed of a series of buildings with high-tech sustainable technologies and architectural languages.

Babcock Ranch located in southwest Florida and planned in 2006 was home of a new 17,000-acre (6,879 hectares) site development by Kitson & Partners, and boasts that it would be the largest 100 percent solar city in the United States. Its design, for 45,000 residents, featured a large nature reserve with open space, agriculture, a network of neighborhoods, hamlets, villages and dynamic town center. Located near Fort Meyers, Florida and next to the 73,000-acre (29,542 hectares) Babcock Ranch Nature Preserve and operating ranch, it will provide 6,000,000 square feet (557,418 square meters) of commercial, high-capacity fiber optics, and electric vehicle transportation system. The solar energy electricity features 100 percent source capacity and smart grid technologies. This amenity-driven development was a shift away from golf course communities previously planned by Kitson to sustainable functions, living and technologies. When complete, Babcock Ranch will have a high school, middle school and around five elementary schools placed within the centers of the hamlets and villages.

The antithesis to Babcock Ranch and its horizontal form, Crystal Island located in Moscow, Russia was designed by Foster + Partners in 2007, and concentrated the program into a dramatic project for a singular spiraling tent-like city for 30,000 residents rising to 1,476 feet (450 meters), Figure 6.6f. The design included a breathable "smart skin" and thermal buffer for the main building, shielding the interior spaces from Moscow's severe weather. The skin was engineered to be sealed in winter to minimize heat loss, and opened in summer to naturally cool the interior. The building design included various solar thermal systems, daylit interiors, wind turbines and an innovative ventilation system. Dramatically, the helical geometry synthesized both horizontal (urban) and vertical (architectural) spaces as the tower superstructure, with its sustainable technologies and materials, transitions to lower densities, gracefully grafted into the urban fabric of the river-formed peninsula below. A blending of both green architecture and sustainable urban design were clearly present in this monumental work.

Another large-scale project by Foster (2007), Masdar City in Abu Dhabi, has been planned in striking contrast to Crystal Island. Masdar City was designed as an emerging global hub for renewable energy and clean technologies in the Middle East with the target of LEED Platinum certification, in which energy will be entirely derived from renewable sources. It is intended to use 80 percent less energy than conventional development and be carbon neutral. Its regionally derived urban design for 50,000 residents incorporates integrated mixes of use, traditional narrow streets, window shading, courtyards and wind towers. Rather than the more heroic high-rise building typology that is more recently typical in the Middle East, Masdar City was designed with compact medium-density, interconnected streets and blocks, "thick-walled" buildings within a "clean-tech" automobile-free environment. Unlike many of the more spectacular green projects of this time, Masdar City was modest climate and culturally appropriate for its geographical location. Figure 6.6d shows Masdar City Center designed by Laboratory for Visionary Architecture (LAVA) during the day, while Figure 6.6e shows the same place at night.[18] The dynamic diurnal design features umbrella-like forms, called "pedals from heaven," that are intended to close during the day for solar shading and open at night for terrestrial reradiation. Transbay Transit Center in San Francisco was a visionary transportation and housing development designed by Pelli Clarke Pelli. It served as a central city hub for long-distance busses. Visionary works of Atelier Castro Denissof Casi in Paris showed green high-rise buildings along the River Seine, Figure 6.6c. Sustainable urbanism to some extent had come full circle similar to some of the early visionary works of the 1960s with these ambitious planning-scale works that showed broader and more diverse expressions of sustainable measures and technologies for completely different cultural and climatic contexts.

6.6 Sustainable Urbanism a) Kronsberg District (courtesy Karin Rumming) b) Kronsberg Street c) Paris Urban Landscape (Atelier Castro Denissaf Casi, international consultation for "Le grand pari de l'agglomeration parisienne" d) Masdar City Center (Day) (LAVA Laboratory for Visionary Architecture) e) Masdar City Center (Night) (LAVA Laboratory for Visionary Architecture) f) Crystal Island, Moscow (© Foster + Partners)

Typical among the issues addressed by sustainable urban designs were higher levels of nucleation, increased densities, greater mixes of use including location of commercial functions, varying building typologies, reduced numbers of single-family dwellings, narrower and more pedestrian-friendly streets, increased connectivity, integrated transit, greener water and infrastructure systems, provision of some alternative energy source-technologies, and incorporation of higher percentages of open space and linked systems of natural areas. Patrick Condon argued that the key to success for sustainable urbanism was found in the ability of the community to integrate all of these systems and planning measures.[19] The individual strategies were welcomed, but it was the interrelationship among them that provided the greatest opportunity for sustainable living—a proposition shared by Nan Ellin, David Grahame Shane, and Douglas Farr.[20] As an outgrowth of these earlier sustainable urban demonstrations, there were planning approaches practiced at this time including Smart Growth, developments advancing greater sustainability with the New Urbanism, and the introduction of Agricultural Urbanism. The Global Recession (2008–2012) slowed development at this scale.

AGRICULTURAL URBANISM

Agricultural Urbanism and *Agrarian Urbanism* were green approaches applicable to both architecture and urban design scales. According to Janine de la Salle and Mark Holland, it was an emerging design framework for integrating a wide range of sustainable food and agricultural systems into communities. In other words they said: "it is a way of building a place around food."[21] Down the center of the Bronx Grand Concourse was planned in 2009 for a four-mile farm intended to transform a predominantly 180-feet-wide traffic-oriented corridor into a self-sustaining boulevard. The goal of the Edible Concourse was to show how urban agricultural practices could be implanted into dense urban environments—while tackling the very real issue of access to affordable, healthy and locally grown foods in the Bronx. The project was a proposition about simple interventions that could be accomplished incrementally over time. The work of Luc Schuiten, pictured in Figure 6.4c, promoted the concept of a "vegetal city," which saw a city-wide eco-transformation over time of biological systems of organization rather than a technological one. Popping up in many urban areas were guerrilla farms such as the one in London created by John-Paul Flintoff pictured in Figure 6.7a.

Sky, a proposal for a livable, sustainable and agricultural development designed for a 571-acre (231 hectares) site in Florida's panhandle, was envisioned by developers Julia Starr White Inc. and planned by Duany Plater-Zyberk & Company. Over 25 percent of the land was intended to be dedicated for farming. The rest of the development scheme was designed to accommodate 624 dwellings, an equestrian complex, farmers market, general store, conference center and open space. The built portion of the development was organized in a fan-shape of housing pods with interior green spaces that resemble the more dense blocks realized at Kronsberg. Sustainable measures included incorporation of geothermal water circulating loops, alternative energy technologies such as photovoltaics, fuel cells and biomass systems, load management techniques, and advanced wastewater treatment facilities.

The Southlands project in Tsawwassen in the south delta of British Columbia was a working development based on concepts of sustainable design where integrating local food and agriculture were a central focus of community life. Designed by Duany Platter-Zyberk & Company, the project design was compact, with a variety of residential uses, neighborhood shops and services, education and recreational facilities. According to Andres Duany, "Agrarian Urbanism," was an evolving approach that wove various food-related activities, such as small farms, shared gardens, farmers' markets, and agricultural processing, into the development model of walkable mixed use traditional small town design.[22] However, it's application extended beyond simply new satellite settlements to include existing urban centers as well. Community allotments have for centuries been associated with neighborhoods, hamlets, and villages worldwide.

Millican Reserve, a three-hamlet sustainable community planned by Lake|Flato and Phillip Tabb, is being developed south of College Station, Texas on a nearly 2,500 acres (1011 hectares) of land along Peach Creek. The development was planned for approximately 1,500 dwellings and was targeted to a broad spectrum of resident users including singles, young families, professional and university faculty, and retirement families. A large function of the development was intended for the provision of equestrian activities with a public arena, stables, barns, paddocks and riding trails for the local residents. In addition, integrated agriculture was included and connected the Texas A&M University researchers. At the entrance to the development was planned a ring of contemporary vernacular buildings being designed by Lake|Flato to set an image for the place and simultaneously provide specific amenities for the community that includes a country store and gas station, farmer's market, outdoor amphitheater, petting zoo and the equestrian center. The three hamlets were themed with wellness, equestrian and recreational organizing activities. In the Rocky Mountains near Eden, Utah was planned an exciting community for Summit Series—a group of young entrepreneurs who envisioned a dynamic place for the hosting of events for focused business practices, technological innovation and the raising awareness for charitable causes. Landscape architects Hart Howerton prepared the first phase of the master plan, and a village plan, designed by Phillip Tabb, featured a ridge-straddling pedestrian village with powerful geometric center, photovoltaic farm, and community gardens. There were also provisions for skiing in and out of the village center in winter (Figure 6.7e).

More integrative examples of Agricultural Urbanism included Serenbe Community located in southwest Atlanta (2004), which was planned by Phillip Tabb for a total build-out for 2,500 residents with 35 acres (14 hectares) of organic farming and preservation of 70 percent of the land. By 2012 there were approximately 250 residents with three restaurants, equestrian stable and arena, small grocery store, Montessori school, and a number of shops and commercial services. Serenbe was the recipient of the inaugural ULI Sustainability Award in 2008. Measures cited for the award included the 70 percent land preservation, integrated agriculture, its compact form and mixes of use, the highly connective circulation networks and seven miles of hiking and bicycle trails, vegetative constructed wetlands, and adherence to the EarthCraft building standards. The community employed a unique four-hamlet constellation in which the hamlet's spatial organizations were omega-shaped with natural areas in the center as pictured in the masterplan and Selborne Hamlet in Figures 6.7c and d. Themes for the four hamlets were cross-programmed and interrelated to create greater diversity, larger markets, and increased critical mass. Selborne Hamlet focused on visual and culinary arts, Grange Hamlet integrated agriculture, market store and equestrian activities, Mado Hamlet will promote health and wellness, and Hamlet 4, still to be planned, will be oriented to additional commerce, retail and education facilities. These non-residential themes contribute to the sustainable amenity within the community.

6.7 Agricultural Urbanism a) Guerrilla Farming in London (courtesy Geoff Pugh) b) Serenbe Farm to Table c) Serenbe Community Master Plan d) Selborne Hamlet e) Summit Village, Utah

Serenbe currently features a 25-acre (10 hectares) certified organic farm, equestrian center, 100 farm animals and approximately 70 percent of the 1,000 acres (404 hectares) of land as open space. The produce from the farm serves the community and the three onsite restaurants. Saturday morning was a time for the Serenbe Farmer's and Artist's Market and for local farmers and artisans to show and sell their goods, and is part of a Community Supported Agriculture (CSA) network. Serenbe has a remarkable sense of community that was partly due to the physical design, but also is a function of the needs and desires of the residents. There was an active and diverse community who enjoyed both the rural and urban amenities of this place. Created by founder Marie Nygren, the name, *Serenbe*, derived from a portmanteau or the blend of two root terms: *serenity* and *be* or *being*. So, embedded in the very name was an affirmational or intentional quality that guided the development process. Serenbe posed an inherent contradiction as it sought to be a development model with the useful transfer of universal sustainable principles and planning practices that may inform other projects especially at edges of metropolitan areas, yet it's success, in part, was due to the unique and sometimes magical place-specific design responses that made its original qualities difficult to replicate. Many of these local design responses have contributed to Serenbe's community character, friendly atmosphere, and evolving sustainable living practices.[23] Like the urban growth models of Paul Krugman, Serenbe engages a constellation of nucleated hamlets.[24] Located at Serenbe in 2012 was the 2,300-square feet (214 square meters) Home and Garden Television show home (HGTV) that attracted 8,000 visitors, and the 1,500-square feet (140 square meters) "Bosch Experience Center" was a net zero house designed by Steve Kemp. Both projects demonstrated a host of green measures with southern regional and climatic designs.

Agricultural Urbanism combined with other sustainable urban strategies and green architectural measures could be a harbinger for future development practices, as well as a potential improvement over the present food production, distribution and grocery store system. New agricultural practices, such as urban agriculture, farmer's markets, organic agriculture, permaculture, small plot intensive or SPIN farming, community gardens, replenishing seed banks, and the 100-mile (1.6 kilometers) diet could all add to a growing interest in bringing healthy food closer to urban life. According to Janine de la Salle and Mark Holland, our relationship with food is an inextricable measure of our culture and this culture connects back to nature. "Chefs, farmers, planners, politicians, designers, and citizens—we all have a role to play in shaping and participating in the new food culture." Like many of the sustainable urban projects, agriculture urbanism was demonstrated on sites adjacent to metropolitan cities or in somewhat isolated locations. A next step might be to bring to more urban contexts and the existing stock of buildings the best practices gained by these early demonstrations. Blending density, mixes of use, workplace environments, alternative transportation systems, and agriculture would certainly provide opportunities for reducing unsustainability. Demonstrations like Sky, Southlands, Millican, Summit and Serenbe have successfully occurred at the edge of urban areas. Yet the greatest challenges for agricultural urbanism still remain within the suburban and urban contexts.

Figure 6.8a illustrates a 500 KWp photovoltaic farm in Possidente, Italy, which is a remarkable juxtaposition of high-technology PV arrays and low-technology vineyards. Figure 6.8b is a wind turbine farm positioned right next to a residential area in the UK. Each suggests a new set of environmental opportunities, issues and challenges. Large energy farms like these have not gone without criticism as they often fall into functional zoning, are removed from living areas, and dominate the natural landscape. Many of the arguments against the commercial viability of wind and photovoltaic electricity amount to the fact that neither can be used as base load power applied at large scale, yet as energy demand increases, the deployment of autonomous renewable systems become more feasible. While technological farms such as these provided solutions to alternative electricity production, they brought up both ecological and aesthetic concerns. For example, studies in the UK indicated that onshore wind farms were not causing long-term damage to bird populations, but the construction of them did cause serious harm to some species while the wind farms were being built.[25] One study conducted in West Texas showed that wind farms were the cause of a slight raise local surface temperatures.[26]

6.8   Technological Farms a) Photovoltaic Farm in Italy (© Sig Solar) b) Wind Turbine Farm in USA (courtesy "Shutterstock") c) Hydro Electricity in Thailand (courtesy "Shutterstock")

Despite their apparent shortcomings, according to the Worldwatch Institute, approximately 18 percent of global electricity comes from renewable sources that include hydroelectricity, geothermal and biomass. Grid-connected sources of solar photovoltaic and wind power saw the greatest increases in renewable energy growth. In the United States net electrical power from non-hydroelectricity sources of renewable energy grew from 3 percent in 2008 to 6 percent in 2012.

ECOLOGICAL FOOTPRINT

The greening of architectural and urban projects accelerated worldwide throughout the first decade of the new millennium, and an increasing number of prominent buildings received LEED platinum certification as a measure of their "greenness." In 2000 the Living Building Challenge (LBC) created an advocacy tool and performance-based certification program that promoted the most advanced green buildings that included varying scales of consideration, including new building construction, renovations, infrastructure, landscapes and neighborhoods.[27] Their rigorous measurement standards for sustainability addressed seven performance categories: site, water, energy, health, materials, equity and beauty, which were subdivided into 20 imperatives. The standards included such topics as urban agriculture, car-free living, net zero water and energy, embodied carbon footprint, conservation, rights to nature, inspiration and spirit. The program was originally launched by the Cascadia Green Building Council in 2006 and supported project primarily in the United States and Canada. The first projects receiving full certification or "living" status were the Omega Center for Sustainable Living in Rhinebeck, New York by BMIN Architects, and the Tyson Living Learning Center in Eureka, Missouri in 2010 by Hellmuth and Bicknese Architects. The Living Building Challenge was seen as an extension of LEED, which was designed to mainstream green building, but the LBC's aim was to demonstrate models at even higher environmental standards than LEED platinum.

By 2012 the greening of architecture arrived at a theoretical position that was informed by relational, multifarious and copious environmental thinking. The concept of an *ecological footprint* and the *carbon footprint* it included, gained momentum within the green movement as it expressed the measure of human activity, and to a large degree the making of buildings, relative to the regenerative abilities of the Earth's ecosystems. The carbon footprint was defined as "a measure of the total amount of carbon dioxide (CO_2) and methane (CH_4) emissions of a defined population, system or activity, considering all relevant sources, sinks and storage within the spatial and temporal boundary of the population, system or activity of interest."[28] The ecological footprint concept and calculation method was developed as the PhD dissertation of Mathis Wackernagel at the University of British Columbia in 1992. Accounting for this method was quite complicated, as it required the assessment of the biology of both sea and land relative to the construction and use of a corresponding built environment.

Two communities under study revealed very low ecological footprints, and therefore demonstrated high ecological standards. BedZED (Beddington Zero Energy Development), a 99-dwelling housing development in Hackbridge, London designed by Bill Dunster (2002), featured energy efficient dwellings and 15,000 square feet (1,394 square meters) of integrated commercial space (Figure 6.9b). The effective performance was due to the 100 percent use of onsite renewable energy production, energy efficient green architectural design with passive solar heating (conservatory sunspaces), extensive green lifestyle program, construction was with low-impact building materials and an onsite car-sharing club. The project discouraged automobiles, while promoting walking, public transport and cycling. Despite its green designs, many of the systems were experimental and suffered some difficulties, mainly with the Living Machine, wood chip boiler and the passive systems. The bold expression of the solar south facades, vaulted roofs and wind cowls gave it a distinct image.

The Findhorn Ecovillage in northern Scotland began in the 1980s, and it was determined to have the lowest ecological footprint in the Western industrialized world according to the Sustainable Development Research Centre in 2006. Findhorn was the largest intentional community in the United Kingdom and had half the UK average ecological footprint.[29] Contributing factors for the low footprint were onsite agriculture, home renewable energy use, and high efficiency home appliances and products with relatively low use. It has 90 benign buildings, four wind turbines, photovoltaic electricity, solar water heating, a biological Living Machine sewage treatment system, district heating, and a large community supported agriculture system. The organic garden at Findhorn was quite extraordinary and was so from its very inception.[30] Within a year of its planting, the garden grew to 65 different types of vegetables, 21 kinds of fruits and 42 different herbs, and it was overflowing with life. Today, it serves the local community and accompanies a major adult sustainable education program. Building within the Ecovillage has been designed for zero-carbon construction using natural and not-toxic materials, breathable wall systems, local stone, straw bale, and Earthships developed by Michael Reynolds. The Findhorn Ecovillage propitiated not only environmental sustainability, but social, economic and spiritual sustainability as well (Figure 6.9d).

Another performance matrix was Zero Net Energy (ZNE), which was defined as a building with zero net energy consumption and zero carbon emissions annually. Buildings producing a surplus of energy over a year were Energy-Plus Buildings. There were several types of ZNEs, which included: zero net site energy use, source energy use, energy emissions, cost and off-the-grid use. A low ecological footprint example was the rural Healthcare Centre in Dharmapuri, Tamilhadu, India that was design by Flying Elephant Studios in 2011. This elegant and affordable solution featured use of local materials, passive solar heating, and a dual-purpose, low-tech butterfly roof for sunshading, natural ventilation and water collection that was physically separated from the compact high-tech internal conditioned spaces. The double-envelope design integrated highly produced interior health facilities and construction in the inner core and local vernacular materials including rubble stone plinth walls, thatch sunscreens and Tetra Pak roof on the exterior. The Bosch House located in Serenbe Community was a ZNE demonstration with a Southern vernacular form (Figure 6.9e). And the Zero Energy House in Chicago, designed by Zoka Zola, illustrated a contemporary language with a low ecological footprint (Figure 6.9f).

Net-positive impact was a goal and a place of responsibility that suggested not just achieving unsustainability, but going beyond it to be truly sustainable. Designing for net-positive architecture required two important processes. The first step was designing with maximum sustainable measures appropriate to a given location and site, which produced more energy than was needed where the surplus was fed back into the utility grid. It included integrating conservation practices in addition to utilization of onsite renewable resources. Second was the ability to analyze and validate project systems' performances and positive impacts on the environment.

6.9 Low Ecological Footprint a) Omega Center Rhinebeck, New York (courtesy of Omega Institute) b) BedZED Housing, London (courtesy Zedfactory) c) Flying Elephant Healthcare Centre (Architects—Flying Elephant Studio. Photography: Manoj Sudhakara) d) Findhorn Ecovillage, Scotland (courtesy Findhorn Community) e) Bosch Net Zero House, Serenbe f) Zero Energy House, Chicago (courtesy Zoka Zola)

The Omega Center, the Tyson Living Learning Center, BedZED, the Findhorn Ecovillage, Bosch Net Zero House, Zola Zoka's Zero Energy House, and Flying Elephant Healthcare Centre were considered among the most ecological projects to date, and interestingly, they referred back to earlier architectural forms and technologies. Yet ironically, the architectural language of these projects were more like the green architectural works of the 1970s, largely due to the projects' scale and programs, orientation to solar energy, location on more remote sites with the exception of the BedZED project, and less about the more futuristic, high-tech, biomorphic or infrastructural images of the examples common in the first decade of the 21st century.

Nearing the end of the first decade of the new millennium, the breadth of the global environmental problems could not be ignored nor could they sustain the singularity of focus of isolated and sedentary buildings, even if they were sustainably heroic or even environmentally remarkable. Among US environmental issues considered in 2012 were legislations focused on nuclear waste management, clean energy standards, infrastructure and jobs, lighting standards, and the controversial climate change and global warming. The greening of contemporary architecture, from the formal integration of skin and load dominated technologies to comprehensive urban designs was no longer a simple disciplinary issue. Circumstances were too complex, invasive and ubiquitous. It should be noted that carbon footprint remains a process of reducing unsustainability, and is not necessarily a process of creating sustainability, which logically brought forward the following question. What combination of strategies should be the next generation focus?

NEXT GENERATION GREEN

Over the past 50 years of sustainable development, green architecture and alternative technologies evolved, but remarkably, they continued to respond to similar needs—individual and cultural—and the same external constraints and conditions despite the advancements in technology, materials and architectural form. Energy and resource conservation and use, response to climate, need for maintaining comfort, and reduction of automobile dependence and carbon footprint still remained and are continuing challenges for future greening efforts. Critical questions that need to be addressed are: "What is to be sustained and for whom, and what is gained or lost in the process?" Answers need to be guided from unsustainability, to balanced sustainability and finally to beyond sustainability evolving from scarcity, to maintenance and eventually to producing renewable abundance. In 2002 Edward Mazria established the Architecture 2030 Challenge to transform the US and global building sectors to reduce climate change, fossil energy consumption, and greenhouse gas emissions through building design, construction and development planning.

In the past sustainability focused on clean technology and corresponding design measures that incorporate them or render them more efficient. While these remain important, the emergent new generation of green architecture seemed to project the following 15 defining characteristics given the evolutionary patterns of the past and an accumulation of the more current greening advancements.

- Natural—an architecture that fully engages with the beneficial characteristics of nature, utilizing non-toxic materials, natural light, water, ventilation, heating and cooling, enhances views, night sky, possessing a biologic aesthetic inspiration and providing an environmental structure of experience.
- Resilient—designs that become more permanently fixed but flexible, elastic, diverse, transformable, and re-usable. While it suggests responsiveness to momentary pressures, it also is adaptable to change, and systems of perpetual evolution.
- Conservative—energy and resource conservation first on all levels of environmental design increasing resistance to unwanted energy flows, reducing inefficiencies, waste, loads and conspicuous consumption.
- Surface Tectonic—with design measures directed to the skin, free façade, transparency and membranes performing adaptable environmental functions, such as sun filtration and ventilation modulation, electricity production, and thermal control.
- Hybridic—sustainable approaches become more pluralistic, diverse and synergetic employing multiple integrated methods, including high-tech, low-tech, light-tech and prefab and onsite mixes. Multiple energy sources and technologies are considered and hybridized.
- Twin Phenomenal—architectural and systems' designs perform multiple functions and are synergetic and efficient through duality of function, utility and province, as well as responding to critical local and global contexts.
- Dynamic—sustainable systems become more sensitive and interactive to changing environmental conditions, varying cultural trends, and characterized with adaptive, spontaneous and refreshive behavior.
- Infrastructural—spatial opportunities exist for emergent infrastructure architecture that is fluid, multifunctional for between places, systemic urban designs, cross

- programming, power generation, smart grids (intelligent networks), eco-boulevards, and electromobility.
- Regenerative—regions, cities, neighborhoods, buildings, building products, construction waste, household products, and materials are continually recycled, restored, repurposed and/or reused.
- Urban—focused on multiple buildings, infrastructure, urban, suburban, and exurban applications for both new and existing developments, exploration of the sustainable megaform, and especially focus on compression, increased density and the existing stock of buildings and infrastructure.
- Scaler—sustainable strategies are interdisciplinary, interrelated, nested and span all scales of design from nanoscopic to building products to architecture to regional planning to macroscopic eco-zones. Energy, resources and people permeate and interact at all these varying scales.
- Connected—scales of consideration, sustainable measures, circulation systems, smart grids, natural ecological areas are interrelated, cross-fertilized and integrated to create a greater synergy of effect. Nucleated places are constellated, cross-programmed and networked.
- Integrative—urban functions become less fragmented with reduction in functional zoning, work and agriculture are integrated to residential districts, and sustainable technologies become mainstream. Interstitial spaces become more organized, densified and connected.
- Diverse—sustainability is applied and expressed in varying ways due to climatic, cultural, historic, scaler, geographic, economic, typological and temporal conditions and differences.
- Global—the greening of architecture becomes a global phenomenon that permeates everywhere from rural to urban, East to West, new and existing, high-tech to low-tech, and within extreme places. It continues to influence and become accessible to the mainstream, normative and everyday facets of life.

Natural architecture was either made with local material blending into a particular natural environment, or it served to heighten the engagement with nature and the elemental qualities of a site through the formal intentions of its design. Natural architecture was often described as "home grown," but now went far beyond that simple vision to include works such as those of Herb Greene, Malcolm Wells, Glenn Murcutt, Fay Jones, and Thomas Herzog. Biometrics, landscape urbanism, landform architecture, and land art all found inspiration from nature and there are embodied principles applicable on all scales for the greening of architecture. Enhancing the relationship between inside and outside was considered a function of natural architecture.

Resilience, from the Latin *resili*, literally means to "spring back," to return to the original form, and the ability to absorb and release energy. In the greening of architecture, this suggested the ability to recover from natural fluctuations and conditions of external change, especially with inclement weather experienced at extremes. This also referred to subtle changes within interior conditioned spaces as well as the dynamic urban condition. It was the ability to survive, adapt and grow in the face of unforeseen changes. It referred to the capacity of a system to absorb disturbances and restore normalcy. One moment a building could become like a thermos protecting against extreme weather, the next it could open and interact with the beneficial weather conditions.

Conservation has long been an integral and necessary sustainable strategy. Renewable resources have been designed to matched and/or augment conventional ones and were determined by the magnitude of need for energy, water, space heating, cooling and building materials. Therefore, the reduction of needs and consequent loads, were an important way of conserving these resources. Tighter construction, providing greater levels of insulation (even hyper-insulation), simpler building forms, installing more efficient equipment and resource conserving devices still remain important objectives with today's green architecture. Conservation does not focus on *source*, but rather on *demand*.

Surface tectonics in architecture draws attention to the mutable qualities and functions of a building's envelope where the greatest luminous, thermal and energetic interactions occur. Skin-dominated sustainable approaches required a complexity of considerations in response to the dynamic and variable external–internal interactions, such as the bio-climatic and environmental modulation and membrane interface described by James Marston Fitch. These included the flows in and out along with protection of sonic, atmospheric, luminous and biological environmental effects. In addition there were the normal functions of fenestrations, which were to provide for view, natural ventilation, daylight, passive solar heating, and means of egress in the event of fire, and for doors the passage of people, goods and services in and out of the building.

Hybridity crossed many aspects of contemporary culture that expressed from clean energy systems and mix use building typologies to hybrid automobiles and TODs, but also including the combination of qualities of universal and local characteristics of a place. In biology, hybridity referred to the offspring of two distinctly individuated systems where the combination of desirable characteristics were combined or sequestered. It also could include cross-programming of spatial activities, such as integrated farm, farmer's market, farm store, restaurant and dwellings nearby. Other commercial and essential non-residential activities can fall into this cross-programming process. Tectonically it referred to the cross-breeding of differing systems and fuel sources to create a new hybridized system, like cogeneration, that often employed the principle of alternation.

Twin Phenomenal sustainability relied on multiple and simultaneous functions of urban, architectural and systems' components. At the urban scale a single building would be designed to contribute of a larger urban design agenda, such as creating public space or terminating an axis, turning a corner, and at the same time responding to the particular functions and internal needs of the building. The synergetic effect would produce both independent and common results. At the architectural scale, secondary forms and building elements would perform multiple functions. For example, a projecting stair core (positive form) could be paired with a recessed entrance (negative space) to help create a better sense of entry. And at the systems scale, individual components would have multiple functions, such as sun control devices providing shading, mounts for photovoltaic arrays, and the funneling of breeze to operable windows to help induce natural ventilation.

Dynamic sustainability implied highly interactive social–technological–ecological systems with connected narratives that recognized the importance of adaptation, flexibility and agility, and also addressed forms of uncertainty, ambiguity and the notion of incremental rather than revolutionary change. In their book *Dynamic Sustainability*, Leach, Scoones and Stirling proposed four properties of sustainability, and these were not considered unsustainable concepts.[31] They were sustainability through stability, durability, resilience and robustness. This model posited reflexive learning, trans-disciplinary interactions, plural interventions and flexible adaptations. At the tectonic level, this referred to the immediate responses to changing fluctuations in weather, light and the external conditions of a site—the ability of a building to respond, adapt and change to these external conditions, including the evolving and transforming urban environment.

Infrastructural sustainability was critical in managing energy flows, water, waste, recycling, materials extraction, and transportation of materials, goods and people. Within the urban context, the infrastructural zones were typically leftover linear spaces along waterways, freeways and in-between nucleated districts. It really was giving new order, function and meaning to these spaces in-between where employment, regional commerce, agriculture, transportation, wildlife corridors, and ecological zones could repair discontinuities, mix, and connect to nucleated settlements from hamlets to city centers. In digital computing infrastructure architecture connoted the low level hardware, networks, and system software, sometimes referred to as "middleware," that supported the applications software and business systems of an enterprise. Within the built environment this definition might suggest that the middleware was the environmental support systems, water, waste, movement, materials etc., that supported a humanist conception of infrastructure contributing to living human communities.

Regenerative sustainability was an important concept regarding the process of transformation, renewal, restoration and the function of continuity of use and repurposing. Regenerative design was a biometric offshoot of ecosystems that revitalized their own sources of energy, materials and waste. The restorative process was one that was intended to creative greater health, strength, efficiency and power. This placed a great deal of focus on the existing stock of buildings worldwide and the infrastructures that support them. Regenerative architecture sought to evolve beyond unsustainability and a net zero footprint, to a new level that actively contributed, produced or gave health and greater wellbeing to an environment. Unlike the recently constructed massive Ghost Cities of China that were rapidly constructed and completely unoccupied, regenerative sustainability promoted organic incremental creation, occupation, growth and regeneration.[32]

An *urban* focus recognized the shift in world population from rural to urban contexts. The Urban Millennium, according to Ron Wimberley, Libby Morris, and Gregory Fulkerson, was estimated to have begun in May of 2007, which marked a world proportional shift from rural to urbanized areas, even though they heavily rely on one another.[33] This brought to the forefront the need to develop new sustainable strategies for both demographic sectors. Urban architecture, fabric and tissue not only needed to respond to internal needs and immediate environmental contexts, but they needed to respond to cultural complexities, urban densities, and ecological cycles. Ole Bauman, the director of the Netherlands Architecture Institute described the situation, "We are keen to participate, but we don't know what it sustainability means." Green projects are still disconnected efforts, which do not reach the scale of interventions needed."

Sustainable measures crossed multiple *scales* comprising the built environment especially from site design, building and neighborhood, but also to larger urban components. It was not only important to address the individual articulated scales, but to enhance the relationship among the various scales—creating ways in which sustainable needs and measures were nested seamlessly to one another. The way in which geometric shapes could harmonically fit together, as shown in Robert Armon's model of the Platonic solids in Figure 6.10a, illustrated the nesting connections of each unique volume and differing families of numbers (two, three, four and five).

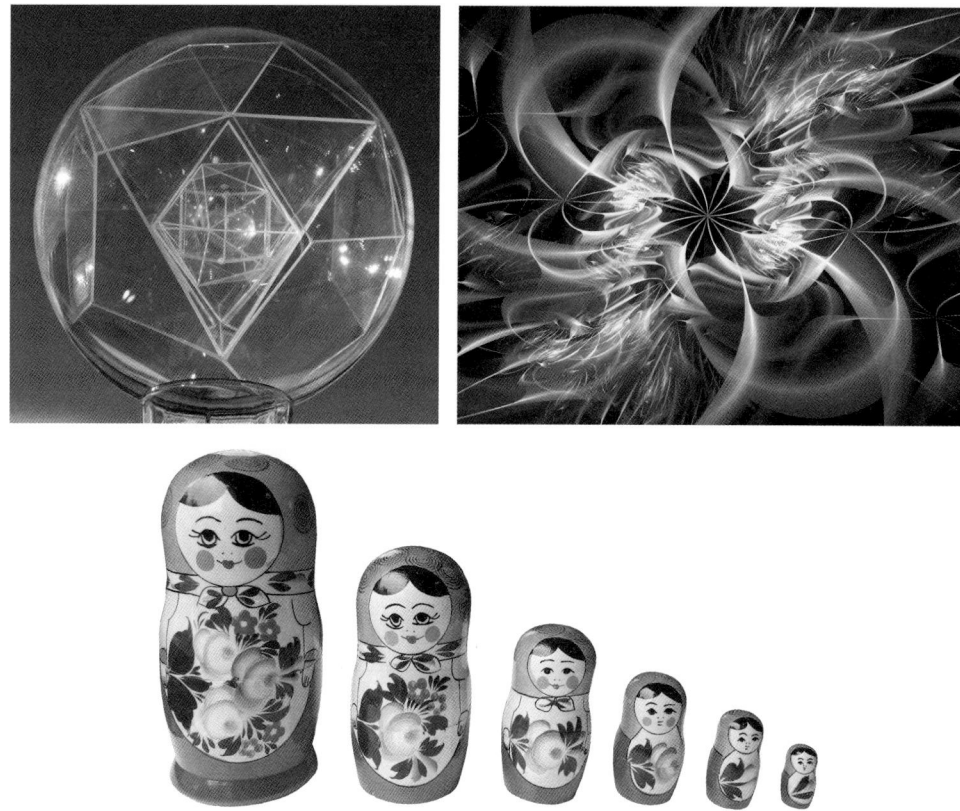

6.10 The Nesting of Forms a) Nesting Platonic Solids (courtesy Robert Armon) b) Fractal (courtesy "Shutterstock") c) Matryoshka Dolls

Fractal geometry provided a conceptual model for the integration of self-similar patterns occurring at different scales both near and far as seen in Figure 6.10b. The urban–rural transect provided a good horizontal spatial structure in which to organize sustainable scaling strategies, however, if taken too rigidly, could inhibit spontaneous development. In addition, nesting was a conceptual framework for addressing the trans-scaler integration of sustainable measures, much like the Matryoshka (Russian) dolls, pictured in Figure 6.10c, that fit together in decreasing size of typically with at least five "diminutive matrons." The sustainable recursions can move from window-to-room, room-to-building, building-to-site, site-to-block, block-to-neighborhood, and so on. Aldo van Eyck's tree-leaf metaphor (1968) suggested an inseparable reciprocity between city and house. A complicating characteristic of the connections among these various scales was the nature of dynamic flows of energy, resources, materials, and people, and the fragmented forms of 50 years of non-sustainable urbanization. While these examples represented abstract models of nesting, they do illustrate the integrative qualities and the notion of sustainable strategies appropriate at a particular scale.

Greater levels of *connectivity* were in part a response to this fragmentation, functional zoning and piecemeal development common to many urban and suburban environments. Connectivity was equally important to restoring the integrity of ecological zones spanning both urban and rural contexts. Connectivity also meant accessibility—joining nucleated places focused on gathering with multi-modal circulation corridors and ecological green zones focused on movement and exchange. Tissue architecture regulated the coherent patterns, supply, demands, and flows of goods, services, resources and people within a region. This included implementing smart grids that integrate and manage highly variable renewable, alternative energy sources. Great affinity occurs between connectivity and infrastructure architecture where object-focus is replaced with process interventions and integrative tissues. Network Urbanism supported the concept that technical networks paralleled urban development, citing the example of the pervasive use of the automobile and its territorial effects, but now suggested new technologies including virtual networking, e-commerce, social media, and cyber urbanism could influence new land use patterns and their consequent urban forms.[33]

Urban designs, buildings and sustainable systems that were more *integrative* provided opportunities for greater efficiency and synergy. This included spatial, programmatic and tectonic considerations for informing new paradigms of land use, development and mixed use building projects. Normally isolated non-residential land uses, such workplaces, commercial, agriculture, and energy production, could now be envisioned to be integrated into mixed use residential developments and place-defining infrastructural projects. US trip distances tripled since the 1960s, so focus was on automobile fuel efficiency, trip distances and trip frequency reductions with clean technology and encouragement of pedestrian connectivity. Urban design projects needed to address density, the appropriate uses that can greater contribute to life support, and to integrated agriculture. Urban and suburban infill projects would contribute to greater density and accessibility, and to support a more environmental structure of experience. Integration also suggested a more unified design language.

The ways in which *diversity* expressed through sustainability were in varying cultural, geographic and climatic responses, such as designs that modify climatic extremes in cold and hot or dry and humid weather, or with desert or mountainous terrains. Culturally sustainable designs were quite different reflecting differing historic and social conditions. As mentioned previously, sustainability approaches were contradistinctive from rural to urban contexts with varying building scales, typologies and uses. Existing and new contexts suggested possible differing approaches as well. Sustainable design evolved over time and therefore, expressed variant technologies and design strategies. For example, the sustainable architectural languages from the 1970s, 1980s and 1990s changed dramatically due in large measure to the evolving technologies, changing architectural styles, contemporaneous programs, and integrative practices.

Sustainability and the greening of architecture were evolving and proliferating *globally*. Obviously, where economies were stronger or the need most immediate, this process expressed more readily. Earlier demonstrations served as models for continued growth and development. However, in areas where there were strong environmental concerns and ethics, change also was likely to occur. The diverse cultural conditions and differing geographical contexts form the basis for tremendous variety of interpretation for sustainable strategies. Extreme expressions occurred from the carbon-free Belgian Antarctic Base to the sandstone living wall in the Sahara Desert. Differences were also seen from the greening of high-rise buildings in Kuala Lumpur to the design of low-rise desert cities in Abu Dhabi, and the infrastructure architecture of the informal settlements in Medellin, Columbia and Sao Paulo, Brazil to the urban high-rise informal settlements of Kota, Indonesia and the strange Ghost Cities of China. Commonplace expressions of photovoltaic electricity were found with everyday objects, such as calculators, wristwatches, signage lighting, security cameras, traffic lights, and even a solar powered scarecrow. They were also given to expression in large-scaled solar farms.

To better center the Indonesian cultural and political activities there was need for a more symbolic and functional relationship between the Kota, Jakarta and its neighboring informal settlements. The visionary work of Robert Gilson and Catherine Caldwell produced provocative images of a vertical informal settlement called the "Kampunkota Tower," as shown in Figure 6.11a where the adjacent informal settlement grows right up and into the high-rise form. The other images projected future possibilities for the greening of architecture included the focus on infrastructure architecture by Teddy Cruz and Alberto Brillemberg of Urban Think Tank as represented in Figure 6.11b for their urban cable car with five stations and 1.3 miles (2.1 km) of airborne cable lines in the Barrio of San Agustin, Venezuela (2010). The Green Urbanism expressed community-centered architecture of the in-between. And finally, green design was expressed in the NASA image of a Toroial Colony planned for outer space, Figure 6.11c. The new green became an interplay between sustainable placemaking and infrastructure—interaction with oppositional energies of agglomeration, concentration, diversity, object and in-place modes of pedestrian movement versus the interstitial, flow, transport, speed, between-place connections, with movement of goods, people and resources.

According to Pulitzer Prize-winning Donald Barlett and James Steele, the American Dream of last century was a lure that provided the workforce, the skills and the demand for the expanding middle class and promised prosperity and a better life. Historian James Truslow Adams spoke of this luring effect being not merely material plenty, but one offering freedom and an enabling process of self-actualization. Today however, with a complex global economy, where many jobs and manufacturing are outsourced and siphoned away, Barlett and Steele suggest, the American middle class has systematically been impoverished.[34] Just as the previous American Dream of centuries ago produced specific architectural and urban responses, it brings up the questions as to what form will the New American Dream take as we move forward in this Metamodern time, and does it manifest a truly Global Dream? More common concepts of prosperity will most likely need to include sustainability. The Center for a New American Dream focuses on connections among consumption, quality of life, and the environment. According to Richard Florida, the New American Dream is denser, smaller, closer to workplaces and amenities, but still private.[35] Florida suggests that long commutes by automobile are being seen as "taxing and enslaving." According to Walter Russell Mead, the evolving American Dream will be an urban dream—where physical proximity allows work life, home life, and social life to be more coherently integrated, and it will be an information technology dream.[36] Posited by journalist Fareed Zakaria, the American Dream is becoming a Global Dream with an accelerating "rise of the rest."[37]

Sustainable pluralism was an applicable concept and goal as it recognized the diverse needs and multifarious approaches to redefining the American Dream. It addressed our environmental issues, and attempted to promote simultaneous measures geographically and temporally. This was not a static process focused on a single outcome, but rather an evolving series of independent actions fine-tuning themselves to a more inclusive sustainable future. Pluralism was not diversity alone, but involved the energetic engagement among the diverse participants. The greening of architecture played a key role in this process, not only in response to needs of single users, but in the process of city-building and city re-building as well, especially in this Metamodern era. It was only 50 years ago that architecture was entering the height of modernism always seeking new terminologies, sources of inspiration and aesthetic effects.

2000s: SUSTAINABLE PLURALISM   151

6.11   A Future of Green Architecture a) Highrise Informal Settlement (Catherine Caldwell) b) Urban-Think Tank Metro Cable (eDesign Dynamics) c) NASA Space Colony (NASA Ames Research Center)

The technological expressions of green architecture evolved with great synthesis of form from the early modernist works of Le Corbusier, Frank Lloyd Wright and Alvar Aalto, the solar constructions of Steve Baer, Paolo Soleri and Michael Reynolds along with the solar principles of collection and storage, the postmodern forms of Glenn Murcutt, Brian MacKay-Lyons and Charles Moore, to the eco-tech designs of Sir Norman Foster, Renzo Piano, and Bernard Tschumi and the infrastructural insertions of Jerde Partnership, Populous Architects and James Corner. Further sustainable thinking is also needed with sustainable urbanism in existing city centers, reforms to suburbs, revitalizing of informal settlements, and re-invented infrastructure with new and hybrid sources of energy. This includes the metamodern concepts such as Thom Mayne's *"combinatory urbanism,"*[37] Nan Ellin's *"integral urbanism,"* Mohsen Mostafavi's *"ecological urbanism,"* Janine de la Salle and Mark Holland's *"agricultural urbanism,"* David Grahame Shane, *"recombinant urbanism,"* and Gabriel Dupuy's *"network urbanism."*

Throughout the global landscape, there should be continual model examples of green design that inspire and demonstrate sustainable solutions specific to varying regions. In addition, there is the need for further mainstreaming of sustainable architecture and urbanism with increments of change at all scales of human activity. In response to the Bundtland Commission Report, there should be greater focus on affordable solutions for sustainable interventions. Progressions of authentic examples of green architecture are far preferable to those, which are merely green for fashion purposes and marketing ploys. The next generation green should derive from real needs with a diversity of effective solutions, and as a living tradition, it should grow from the critical principles, climatic contexts, the science and advances performed in the past. A time-tested view of the greening of architecture provides a proven, as well as oscillating, menu of strategies and sustainable methods upon which to build. While the greening of architecture is a mutable evolving process, many universal principles and laws of physics remain present and applicable to future developments in the field.

A revolution in environmental sensibility and continued search for the elemental values embodied in the First Principles could contribute to a formal fusion of holistic, ecological, and sustainable intellectual capital with our evolving contemporary culture, styles of living, and the architectural and urban forms that they reflect. After all, it is the critical balance of the ecological footprint of our culture, the context of an expanding world population, and carrying capacity of our remaining finite resources that is ultimately in question. The value of the greening process to contemporary architectural discourse rests on developing a plurality of inclusive thinking, systemic processes, and effective concrete architectural actualizations, on all levels, in time to meet future circumstances, needs and challenges.

ENDNOTES

1   Melissa Leach, Ian Scoones and Andy Stirling, *Dynamic Sustainabilities: Technology, Environment Social Justice*. London, UK: Earthscan Publications, 2010.

2   John Roach, *2000–2010: A Decade of (Climate) Change*. National Geographic Daily News, December 11, 2009.

3   Source: http://www.treehugger.com/author/derek-markham/, accessed March 2013.

4   The increase of greenhouse gasses and consequent climate change are cause for considerable political debate over the science of global warming, its cause as to whether it is human-made or natural, and the possible responses to it. Lenny Bernstein, Peter Bosch et al., *Climate Change 2007: Synthesis Report*. Valencia, Spain: November 2007.

5   Charles Eames, *Powers of Ten*, website. Eames Office, 2010.

6   This book explained various scales of development from single building to regions, and the differing approaches to sustainable design at these different scales. Susan Owens, *Energy Planning and Urban Design*. London: Pion Press, 1985.

7   Thorburn observed in English villages an increase in density from the extremities to the center, but more importantly, there was a landscape shift from buffering along the road at the edge to walled-in gardens occurring in the rear of buildings near the center. Andrew Thorburn, *Planning Villages*. London, UK: Estates Gazette Limited, 1971.

8   Gunther Feuerstein, *Biomorphic Architecture: Human and Animal Forms in Architecture*. Berlin: Axel Menges Publisher, 2001.

9. Charles Waldheim (ed.), *The Landscape Urbanism Reader*. New York: Princeton Architectural Press, 2006.

10. Stan Allen and Marc McQuade, *Landform Building*. Baden, Switzerland: Lars Muller Publishers, 2011.

11. The interest in infrastructure is a shift away from building as object in the landscape and formal organizations to a new kind of architecture that is far more complex with disciplinary hybrids. Scott Lloyd and Katrina Stoll (eds), *Infrastructure as Architecture*. Berlin: Jovis Berlag Publisher, 2010.

12. Stephen Graham and Simon Marvin, *Splintering Urbanism: Network Infrastructures, Technological Mobilities and the Urban Condition*. London: Routledge, 2001.

13. Joshua Davie and Robert Hammond, *High Line: The Inside Story of New York City's Park in the Sky*. New York: Farrar, Straus and Giroux, 2011.

14. Michael Sorkin, *Wiggle*. New York: Monacelli Press, Inc., 1998.

15. Nan Ellin, *Integral Urbanism*. London: Routledge, 2006.

16. James Wines, *Green Architecture*. Köln: Taschen Press, 2000: 11–15.

17. Hans Monninghoff, *Hanover-Kronsberg: A Model for Sustainable Urban Development*. Hannover, Germany: Economic and Environmental Affairs, 2001.

18. Sergi Costa Duran and Julio Fajardo, *The Sourcebook of Contemporary Green Architecture*. New York: Collins Design, 2010.

19. Patrick M. Condon, *Seven Rules for Sustainable Communities: Design Strategies for the Post-Carbon World*. Washington DC: Island Press, 2010.

20. Douglas Farr, *Sustainable Urbanism: Urban Design with Nature*. New York: Wiley and Sons, 2008.

21. Janine de la Salle and Mark Holland, *Agricultural Urbanism: Handbook for Building Sustainable Food and Agricultural Systems in 21st-Century Cities*. Winnipeg, Canada: Green Frigate Books, 2010.

22. Andres Duany, *Theory and Practice of Agrarian Urbanism*. London: Prince's Foundation for the Built Environment, 2011.

23. This book is an account of the history and development of Serenbe Community over the past decade. Phillip Tabb, *Serenbe: and the Geometry of Place*. College Station, TX: Self-published, 2011. Initial visions meetings began in 2000 that were organized by the developers Steve and Marie Nygren and Rawson and Nan Haverty. The actual master plan was generated by Philip Tabb in 2001. The original design was planned for four hamlets totaling 850 dwelling units of varying type.

24. David Grahame Shane, *Recombinant Urbanism: Conceptual Modeling in Architecture, Urban Design, and City Theory*. London: John Wiley & Sons, 2005.

25. Source: http://www.guardian.co.uk/environment/2012/apr/12/windfarms-damage-bird-populations, accessed March 2013.

26. This study, conducted by SUNY Albany researchers, concluded that the slight temperature rise was likely caused by the turbulence in turbine wakes acting like fans pulling warmer air down to the surface. Source: http://www.tmdailypost.com/article/energy/do-wind-farms-cause-global-warming, accessed March 2013.

27. Living Building Challenge: https://ilbi.org/lbc/, accessed March 2013.

28. L. Wright, S. Kemp and I. Williams, "'Carbon Footprinting': Towards a Universally Accepted Definition," *Carbon Management*, 2 (1): 61–72. 2011.

29. Findhorn Community, *The Findhorn Garden: Pioneering a New Vision of Man and Nature in Cooperation*. New York: Harper and Row, 1975.

30. Nancy Jack Todd and John Todd, *From Eco-Cities to Living Machines: Principles of Ecological Design*. Boston: North Atlantic Books, 1994.

31. Melissa Leach, Ian Scoones and Andy Stirling, *Dynamic Sustainabilities: Technology, Environment, Social Justice*. London, UK: Earthscan Publications, 2010.

32. Ghost Cities. Source: http://www.youtube.com/watch?v=rPILhiTJv7E, accessed March 2013.

33. Gabriel Dupuy, *Urban Networks—Network Urbanism*. Amsterdam, NL: Techne Press, 2008.

34. Dopnals L. Barlett and James B. Steele, *The Betrayal of the American Dream*. New York: PublicAffairs, 2012.

35. Richard Florida, "The New American Dream: Denser, Smaller, Closer, But Still Private," *The Atlantic*. October 16, 2012.

36. Walter Russell Mead, "Growing Sideways," *Essays on the American Dream*. February 16, 2012.

37. Fareed Zaaria, *The Post-American World*. New York: W.W. Norton & Company, 2012.

38. Combinatory Urbanism is a concept that brings forward the idea finding a collective relationship and balance among the often, contradictory forces at work in urban growth especially between the disciplines of architecture and planning. Thom Mayne, *Combinatory Urbanism: The Complex Behavior of Collective Form*. Culver City, CA: Stray Dog Café Publishers, 2011.

Chapter 7
The Global Landscape of Green Architecture

A. Senem Deviren

We live in a world that increasingly tames difference. Built environments produced by global capital are the projection of global capitalism, expressing value systems that are often narrowly described as 'Western.' In the process, the local and the particular are lost, sacrificed to the global and general. As dominant power disseminates its preferred ways of thinking, such homogenization happens at all levels of our existence.[1]

As Lewis (1999) puts forward "There is no internationally-agreed definition for green architecture."[2] Green, or sustainable, or environmentally-friendly architecture is not simply an environmental benefit. It is place-sensitive; in a globalizing world it leads to location-specific architecture by responding to local climatic conditions and using local materials. It also offers better architectural quality with more natural and fewer artificial inputs; not only is less more, less is also beautiful.[3] However, the question remains: Is it really possible to give one global perspective of green architecture while there are social, economic, politic, demographic, climatic, ideological and cultural differences on earth? The question leaves the architects, who are going to genuinely deal with green architecture, with challenges and opportunities at the same time.

In regards to the circumstantial differences and in the light of regional "modifiers," this chapter is on contravening exemplifications of greening of architecture (Urban–Rural, High-Tech–Low-Tech, New–Existing, Extreme–Mainstream, X-Small–X-Large); regardless of their scale or context, giving a panorama of the landscape of greening architectural practices worldwide. Though, it may only be possible to just to give a glimpse of what potentials are laying in different parts of the world and the diverse ways in which green architecture is interpreted.

URBAN–RURAL

With increasing urban population on earth the importance of the presence of urban green buildings are also increasing. The importance and power of urban green buildings are sourced from their potentials to provide sustainable microclimatic environments within urban fabric. But not only that is important. On an urban scale the issues of conservation of fossil fuel and energy resources, and the need for more environmentally friendly energy sources are magnified.

7.1   Urban Projects a) Yusuhara Town Hall, Japan (Photograph: Takumi Ota Photography) b) Harmonia 57, Sao Paolo, Brazil (www.triptygue.com/Photograph Nelson Kon)

However, energy efficiency is not a goal in itself, but a part of an integrated search for sustainable development which recognizes the local, regional and global impact of cities on air, land, water, vegetation, wildlife and the human population.[4] The architects' responsibility becomes more significant at the scale of building site within the urban fabric. The design decisions taken at this level have great impact and consequences for future sustainability of the whole urban context and further. The following selected examples for urban projects have varying functionality from residential use to a public building. The common criteria for these projects here are to be newly built, bringing new understanding of design decisions for energy efficiency and urban sustainability while supporting place connectedness of people with local conditions, sources, community spirit and place memory.

The largest scaled wooden hall in Japan was built in the town of Yusuhara Kochi Prefecture, known for its urban development using "Japanese Cedar," by Kengo Kuma. The building is designed around a large atrium, for cold winters with snowing weather conditions, which serves as an indoor plaza for combining the two main functions of this complex: a market for local products and a small hotel (with 15 rooms). This atrium also functions as a cultural salon. While the architecture of building is capable of making people reconfirm the excellence of Japanese wooden structures it also helps to visualize how the local material of cedar sustain the structure. The traditional material is used in new forms to create the new characteristics for modern Yusuhara. The material serves as a connecter between the people, the land, the history and culture of their own place. With all its contributions to the effective integration of the buildings into their context and its respect for the environment the project won the Energy Performance and Architecture Award in 2007.

The ongoing efforts in Austria in the field of energy-efficient housing research, construction and design are creating a competitive environment for providing energy efficient housing. In 2009 the largest passive house project "Lodenareal" was completed in Innsbruck, the capital city of Tirol, Austria. The project is a development of local based firm Neue Heimat Tirol, a city and state-owned development company, well known with their new energy efficient and ecological low-income housing, elderly apartments and condo projects for the region. Lodenareal complex is designed by Architekturwerkstatt din a4 with Team K2. The whole housing is expected to save 680 tons of CO_2 per year and the cost of the whole project is not much more than code minimum buildings. The complex is designed in two L-shaped buildings, each forming a semi-open courtyard, which contributes to create both a shared common open space and microclimatic green areas. The whole façade of the buildings are surrounded by cantilevered balconies which minimize thermal bridging, roof-mounted solar collectors provide more than half of the domestic hot water needs and a pellet boiler is being used for space heating. The whole project has already proved that Passivhaus offers immediate and significant energy and CO_2 emission reductions.

Located in the west side of São Paulo, Brazil, Harmonia 57 is a residential project by Triptyque Architects. The project is offering an opportunity for bringing domestic green landscape design into architecture with the aim of creating a living organism. The building (studio) consists of two parts connected with a metal bridge, also used as an outside balcony. The façade is covered in small holes filled with vegetation. A special irrigation system is installed on the house to water the plants in the hot Brazilian climate. As the architects of the project indicate, "the water is the main feature in this project where the rain and soil water are drained, treated and reused, creating a complex ecosystem." The overall scheme and system of the studio is made around the simple idea of bringing landscape and architecture together in design of a living habitat.

Within the popular highly polished systems for effective climatic control we are all pleased to obtain our comfortable living conditions. However, in the long term, we are paying the price by high heating and cooling bills, increase of the CO_2 level in the atmosphere and global warming, which threatens every living organism on earth. Residential buildings have a high impact in urban areas as they cover the largest surface area within the urban fabrics. Therefore, housing projects designed according to energy efficiency and ecological living principles are becoming important for achieving the goals of sustainable ecological development. One of the most important aims for the architect is to reduce the ecological footprint while improving the quality of life both at the level of private and public living environments.

With their limited access to materials, skills and resources, provided by the urban systems, the projects in rural areas have situational necessities to obtain required materials and energy from renewable sources. The increasing awareness on the negative environmental impacts of high energy demanding luxurious buildings for these areas are now well known to green sensitive architects. The environmental suitability of local traditional building materials, lighting, ventilation and water saving strategies are being re-utilized for modern sustainable green buildings. The projects selected here for rural locations are demonstrating experimental yet big achievements in terms of highly efficient renewable energy use, climate and human comfort balance and promise for future sustainability of the single or groups of relatively new—not vernacular—buildings within the heart of less disturbed landscapes.

After a six-year study for the hut of the future at the architecture department of the Swiss Federal Technical University in Zurich (ETH) and the Swiss Alpine Club (SAC), the new Monte Rosa hut on Zermatt, Switzerland is opened in 2010. The building generates over 90 percent of its own energy and known as one of the most complex wooden structures in the country. It is covered with an aluminum shell with solar collectors mounted its southern façade. Warm air and hot water are provided with the help of this façade collectors and the ice melt is used for water needs. The program of the project includes accommodation for hikers and mountain climbers. The project was awarded with the bronze Holcim Awards Europe and will continue to serve as a research project in power and building service engineering. The building is also called "Mountain Crystal" as it resembles the Alpine ice-covered rural landscape.

7.2 Rural Projects a) Mountain Crystal, Zermatt, Switzerland (© Siemens AG, Munich/Berlin) b) Energy Lab, Preparatory Academy, Hawaii (courtesy of Flansburgh Architects, Photo: Matthew Millman) c) Hanil Visitors Center, South Korea (courtesy of BCHO Architects Associates)

Another science building dedicated to the study of renewable energy technologies is located in Hawaii and called the New Science Building at Hawaii Preparatory Academy, completed in January 2010. It is a zero-net-energy building generating all its power from photovoltaic and wind turbine sources, capturing and filtering all of its drinking and wastewater and generating hot water from solar thermal panels. It is totally naturally ventilated. The building has a LEED Platinum and Living Building Challenge certification. The program of the center is presenting a living energy laboratory for the educational purposes. The climatic comfort is provided just by the design and space configuration of the building itself, which links the interior study spaces with the outdoor experimentation and discovery areas.

A combination of research and accommodation program is applied for the Hanil Visitors Center and Guest House project in South Korea. The center has a high purpose of educating its visitors for the use of recycled concrete. Concrete is broken and recast in various materials creating both translucent and opaque tiles. The gabion wall and fabric formed concrete which constitute the main façades of the building, was erected first, and the concrete left over from it was recycled in the gabion cages, on the rooftop for insulation from sun, and as a landscape material at the street and around the factory. Thus, the building complex structure itself is also a showcase in how to reuse this material in different types of construction, casting formwork types as well as re-casting techniques. From its spatial form to its very surrounding landscape recycled concrete is used to show the evolving and changing potentials to the visitors.

Taking the local climatic conditions, materials and surrounding context as the root of their design, the architects of these rural projects struggle with providing comfort without using state of art technology and depletion of sources. Yet the results are worth to achieve with minimum footprint on land, increased living quality and ecological balance between man and nature.

HIGH-TECH–LOW-TECH

All big cities turning into metropolitan areas are now densely populated with high-tech, high-rise, multi-functional cutting edge towers. Yet reaching high and far, these towers are now also competing to fulfill their environmental task: to incorporate "green" features into their design to contribute to a sustainable future. The competition to become the "greenest" tower continues in different continents. Swiss Re Headquarters, also known as the Gherkin Tower, built by

Foster and Partners Ltd. in London, UK, is the city's first ecological tall building with its cleverly designed ventilations system that reduces the energy consumption by half of a similar type of regular high-rise building. Bahrain World Trade Center, in the city of Manama, rises 787 feet (240 meters) in height and has three 95-foot (29 meters) wind turbines, each supported by a 98.43-foot (30 meters) bridge spanning between two towers. It is the first building in the world to incorporate this sort of technology at this scale. Reaching from Arab peninsula to China, to Haizhu District of Guangzho (formerly known as Canton), the capital of Guangdong Province 2,001-foot (610 meters) tall Canton Tower (also known as the Guangzhou TV Tower) stands with one of the most complex building façade integrated photovoltaic systems in the world. By February 2011 the tower is the tallest building on earth. The LED technology applied for all lighting, as a result, the tower consumes only 15 percent of the allowed maximum for façade lighting. The tower is designed by Information Based Architecture (IBA), from The Netherlands in collaboration with Arup and Local Design Institute. The green features are not only building-integrated but also considered the master plan for the surrounding landscape with a 44-acre (17.9 hectares) park at the base level and a carefully planned 139-acre (56.6 hectares) multifunctional area with an elevated plaza, a pagoda park, retail facilities, offices, a TV center and a hotel.

Vietin Bank Tower, the first project of Forster and Partners in Vietnam, is a 322,917-foot squared (300,000 meters squared) mixed use development comprised by two connected towers, including conference facilities, luxury shops, cafes and restaurants and topped by roof top gardens, an energy-efficient new headquarters for Vietin Bank, a five star hotel, spa and serviced apartments. The scheme has a progressive environmental agenda and is designed to mitigate the effects of the area's high levels of humidity using a low-energy, desiccant wheel. The system draws in humidity, separating the water from the atmosphere and exhaling hot, dry air, which can then be cooled by ground water and released back into the buildings. This was the first time this technology has been applied in the region on such a large scale.

At a nearby geography, in the capital of Australia, Sydney, the Bligh 1 Office Tower also has earned the highest score in Australia's Green Star standard with its 28-story inner-atrium, allowing natural daylight to the extended office balconies and working as a natural cooling system, siphoning hot air and funneling it out the top of the building. With its double-skinned façade cooling inside, green roofs providing shared semi-open spaces for the users, onsite wastewater recycling system and bicycle parking contributes to Sydney city to become greener.

Not only the high-rise buildings are using cutting edge technologies to achieve the maximum levels in green architecture category, but also well-known industrial leaders are competing with each other to make their headquarter buildings more green. In 2003 BMW set out a design competition for a new building and distribution center located in Munich, Germany. The results were more than grand; not only is the new BMW Welt aesthetically pleasing with its sinuous curves and gleaming façade, but it was also consciously designed to save energy in its production of cars through efficient solar heating and natural ventilation systems.[5] The design of Coop Himmelb(l)au is centered around a multifunctional hall, which serves as a public–industry interface and the heart of all green features. The central multifunctional hall is designed as a solar-heated, naturally ventilated sub-climatic area, removing the normal requirements for building heating and ventilation.

Located at Atsugi, Kanagawa Prefecture, Japan, The Nissan Advanced Technology Center is designed around the central concept of promoting the creativity and imagination of engineers.

7.3 Low Tech Green Architecture a) A Yurt, Kyrgyzistan (courtesy stock.xchng) b) Quensel House, TR North Cyprus (© image courtesy A.Senem Deviren) c) Bali Green School, Indonesia (© Green School)

The features such as open balcony gardens, stepped workplaces facing green hills, central space all contribute to communication between people by creating an optimal and pleasant work environment in energy efficient and landscape blended complex. The building is awarded at the national and international levels promoting its overall positive influence both technical issues concerning high levels of energy efficiency and also promoting the quality of the life of users.

Although the technology dependent green buildings are contributing in raising awareness and stimulating debate about sustainable architecture, they have some limitations in achieving green dimensions. These buildings have higher initial investments than traditional constructions. On the other hand, using mainly natural, local materials and sources, low-tech green projects present the human nature engagement at a very basic yet most necessary level.

With building traditions developed by trial and error and handed to the following generations through local knowledge transfer systems, vernacular architecture is an undeniable base and will probably always serve as the main source of genuine sustainable habitat solutions. One of the earliest examples, the *yurts*, which are home to the nomads of Asia, are marvelous examples. A *yurt* completely intertwines and presents a whole life cycle of man and habitat under one simple shelter from birth, siting, construction, operation, maintenance, renovation, demolition, death and re-birth.

The modern interpretations of vernacular architecture, with the use of local materials, construction techniques and labor, are all well known to the Mediterranean building culture. The Mediterranean way of living close to earth, sun and all other natural sources is not only inspiring professional architects but also all who are looking for life quality enhancing conditions for sustainable living. The Quensel couple, who decided to settle down and live off-grid in Zeytinlik village, nearby Girne, TRNorth Cyprus, designed and constructed their own house with the help of local masons by using local materials. The house is located at the edge of a sloping hill with 1,205 feet squared (112 meters squared) indoor and 3,229 feet squared (300 meters squared) outdoor constructed space—including terraces, balconies, paths—700 feet squared (65 meters squared) garage and two workshops overlooking the Mediterranean sea at a distance.

The total size of the site is 25,618 feet squared (2,380 meters squared) where the remaining area—out of constructed spaces—is left to gardens and a small size vineyard. The rainwater is collected in underground water tanks with the total capacity of 2,472 feet cubed (70 meters cubed), which is even more than the need of both household and garden facilities. The electric power needed for the house and the water pumps in the garden is provided by solar PV panels—129 feet squared (12 meters squared) in total. Also, hot water needed for thermal floor heating and daily use is provided from solar thermal panels with vacuum tubes.[6] The plan is organized according to the sun, wind and view orientations to get the most beneficial and delightful atmosphere for living conditions.

Traditional building techniques and design strategies are not only providing information sources for houses but also some new green public projects particularly in remote locations where sources of materials and services are rare. The Green School in Bali, Indonesia, is constructed by using 99 percent natural local materials: mainly bamboo, grass and mud. The building is not using artificial cooling system; all spaces are naturally cooled down and ventilated. For the heating system, the methane produced from cow manure is used for fueling stoves and bamboo sawdust is used for hot water and cooking. Solar panels are also installed to support the system. The surrounding landscape is also integrated into the program of the school as the students practice organic permaculture exercises by growing rice, fruits and vegetables. The crops of all these gardens and fields are sold to support the school management. Students are also involved in producing coconut oil, chocolate, harvesting honey and breeding fish in campus aquaculture ponds. It is not a surprise that this green school has been named for the 2010 Aga Khan Awards for Architecture, which promotes local architectural excellence and improving the quality of life of the inhabitants. The school was also awarded "2012 Greenest School on Earth" by the USGBC Center for Green Schools.

NEW-EXISTING

Under the title of "new," the examples here present "new understanding of master planning" for green settlements and "new design approaches" to green working places in broad terms. Being one of the leading countries in the world with its traditional architectural schools, blending architecture well with landscape and creating its own design culture, Spain, is comfortably welcoming new experimental eco-settlements. The new 3,000 social homes are under construction for the Eco-City on the south facing slopes of hilly countryside in Logroño, Montecorvo. The project is designed by MVRDV in collaboration with GRAS and occupies only 10 percent of the site while leaving the rest of landscape to become an eco-park, both for green and for energy production. The total energy needed is generated onsite by solar panels on south facing hills and the windmills, which also become landmarks of the project. A greywater circuit and onsite natural water purification are parts of the plan that combines dense urban living with real ecological improvements. The aim is a totally CO_2 neutral footprint.

In 1990 Linz City (Austria) adopted a policy to develop a substantial stock of low energy social housing. At the end of 1991 Roland Rainer presented his master plan for the lakes district of Linz-Pichling. A functional, coherent concept that would open the entire area in terms of housing, work, public was commissioned to plan the "Linz-Pichling lakes district," a new urban district that would provide areas for housing, work, education and recreation. The scope of the planning was laid down in three plans, one each for development, transport and green spaces, organized into four planning phases.

7.4 New Green Settlements (Communities) a) Eco City Montecorvo, Spain (courtesy of GRAS Architects) b) Solar City, Linz, Austria (© image courtesy A. Senem Deviren) c) Sonnnenschiff, Freiburg, Germany (© image courtesy A. Senem Deviren)

These plans were: the "urban planning outline concept," the "urban planning measure concept," and the "design concept" for the new housing area, Pichling, including a design study for the areas at the tram stops Ebelsberg and Pichling.[7]

The concept planning stage for the development of this new urban district at the urban edge started in 1990s including well-known architects Foster + Partners, Richard Rogers Partnership, Herzog + Partner, Renzo Piano Building Workshop (presented by A. Giordano, worked with engineer Norbert Kaiser under the name READ) and local architects. The office of Latz and Partner designed the open spaces. The area was originally planned for 25,000 inhabitants. The Roland Rainer's master plan was modified during the development stages for the priorities given to buildings and open spaces for the extensive use of solar energy. A radial concentric plan is applied for the settlement layout and the entire development was restricted in height to prevent the need for the use of elevators. Comprehensive use of solar power and compact design mean the buildings largely face to the south, have intelligent façades, natural ventilation and large amounts of natural lighting as well as optimal heat storage and an overall heating requirement of less than 40kwh/meters squared per year. Different possible ways of utilizing solar energy were applied:

- Individual use to increase the feeling of well-being and comfort that relate to the quality of daylight, the view, and the integration of sunny areas.
- Technical use: the physical or biological utilization of sunlight to produce energy and to relieve strain on the environment.
- Social use: outdoor areas are created that receive plenty of sunlight, thus making them more pleasant to use and plant growth is stimulated.[8]

The main task of the planning of the Solar City is social housing with the goal of solar urban planning and the method was to build sustainable buildings that allow innovation. The main focus of the urban development project: low-energy construction, a future oriented approach to energy supply and waste disposal, the issues of building biology, local recreation and leisure time, the creation of a modern socio-cultural, family oriented infrastructure, as well as joint, group specific marketing campaign, all formulated in a project agreement. All construction was completed between 2001 and 2005. Each building in the settlement context has an urban planning concept, building design concept and energy concept.[9]

7.5 New Green Offices a) Vodafona Site Solution, Midrand, Africa (courtesy of GLH & Associate Architects) b) Solar Power Offices, Ljubliana, Slovenia (image courtesy OFIS Arhitekti)

The Sonnenschiff (Solar Ship) and Solarsiedlung (Solar Village), designed by Rolf Disch, was started out as a vision for a new community that can balance medium-density, size, accessibility, green space and solar exposure. The Solar Ship is a mixed use residential and commercial buildings whereas the rest of the village, with 52 homes, is connected together. The homes are designed to the Passivhaus standard and have great access to passive solar heating and daylight. There are rooftop gardens with rainwater recycling systems that irrigate the gardens while supplying the toilets with grey water. For heating a wood-chip boilers are being used. The overall impact of human footprint is decreased.

The number of new green working-places and offices are emerging all around the world. It is a common understanding of necessity of injecting green features into our daily lives. Since working places are more commonly used now than our apartments, they are becoming our new homes where we work, eat, meet and share a common life and spend most of the daytime. Therefore, some programming facilities by green features are also being tested with these new experimental work–live spaces.

One of the new greenest buildings in the southern hemisphere is the Vodafone Site Solution Innovation Center with the first six star Green Star SA accredited building in South Africa. The main idea was to create a harmonious and well integration between the building and its surrounding landscape. The building is surrounding and open air courtyard with a rainwater pond and wetland; use of daylight is maximized with using performance glass and motorized blinds; fresh air is cooled in the thermal rock store constructed below the building and distributed to the interior spaces; cooling and warming is also supported by water pumped through thermally activated slab; 292 PV panels are delivering 230 kWh of solar energy to the building which is twice the energy level required; water recycled in the wetland and reused and the structural elements of the building (bamboo carved from the site is mixed with steel) are excavated from the building site.[10] The overall idea of having well integration of the building and the landscape seems to be working well in this eco-sensitive work place.

The Solar Power Offices, designed by the architectural firm OFIS Architects, for Slovenian electricity company ELES, is a completely carbon neutral design. The design of the energy system gives priority to the exploitation of renewable energy sources such as solar and wind as well as sourcing locally to reduce energy consumption and reduce CO_2 emissions. Therefore, the concept takes into account local resources such as groundwater (for direct heating and cooling), wind to improve natural ventilation, sun for natural lighting and the use of solar energy, use of rainwater and wastewater recycling.

7.6 Green Regeneration of Existing Building Complexes a) Setagaya-ku Fukasawa, Symbiotic Housing, Japan (courtesy of Prof. Kazuo Iwamura) b) Vauban, Freiburg, Germany (© image courtesy A. Senem Deviren)

All ventilation systems are equipped with automatic regulation and control in the room depending on room occupancy and room monitoring air quality. Ventilation systems are linked to a central control system, which allows us to perform the ventilation system in order to optimize the system. The energy efficiency is also apparent from the exterior with the use of the solar roof element and also in the interior with the use of integrated greenery and atriums. The exterior solar membranes serve as the character of the building and the company, whilst also generating electricity. The facility is designed as modern, rational and with the use of organic materials. The workshops are designed as prefabricated concrete halls. The building is organized as a campus, or miniature "city" which clearly reflects the mission and activity of the company. It also creates a positive working environment.

While the excitement of new initiatives and experimental potentials are making "new" green buildings and eco-settlement exercises "hot," the main problem of how to turn our existing and decaying old building stock into green is a real challenge for every architect. But the architects are not alone in the process of urban regeneration; it requires public participation and support. Local authorities, constructors, NGOs and the representatives of the inhabitants are all becoming a part of the process of decision making and sometimes further a part of the initial master planning and design phases.

Japan is one of the most dense countries in the world where housing of people is a great challenge while preserving the natural sources and providing comfortable and healthy residential environments. In 1990, a group of professionals and private and public firms established the movement for environmentally symbiotic housing to encourage more sustainable housing practices. Symbiotic housing is a term used to describe housing developed in relation to the local and global environment. The Setagaya Ward in Tokyo decided to dismantle the 39 municipally owned wooden detached houses, built in 1952, and to replace them with a complex of five apartments of 70 dwelling units in total. The new housing is aimed to respect and preserve the historical elements of the place and the greenery surrounding the area, to enhance the quality of life, to decrease the environmental loads and to guarantee the increase of affordable housing capacity. The passive solutions of daylighting, heating and cooling integrated into the design are all a result of the deep consideration of local natural conditions. The program of the housing complex also offers possibilities for social mix with specially designed units for easy access of disabled people and elderly people with common ordinary built housing units. The complex is completed in

1997, awarded with World Habitat Awards in 2002, and is continuing to remain as a happy community settlement within the very dense city of Tokyo. The increase of communal and environmental sensitivity and awareness in the happy community life is proving the success of this governmental pilot project.

Located in the south of Freiburg, Germany, next to the French border, Vauban district used to be a French army base since 1930s until 1991. After the decision of the City of Freiburg, to turn the area into a new suburban residential area with the urban design objectives of low energy standards for all houses, shared and community designed green spaces, public access including a light-rail transportation and further public facilities such as kindergarten, primary school, offices, retail shops, a central market place and a community center, the area is developed for 5,000 inhabitants in a 93-acre (38 ha) area. The planning process started in 1993 and the project was completed in 2006. The primary success of the project has been to develop a very effective community participation body, Forum Vauban (now has an NGO status),[11] which allowed all citizens to participate with their ideas and commitment to create their own neighborhood. Also, from the local authorities Project Group Vauban, an interdisciplinary group for the coordination of the project, has been formed to work with both City Council Vauban Committee and the Forum Vauban. The concepts applied in the creation of Freiburg Vauban district show the project's achievement in creating minimum footprint: within the frame of ecological traffic and mobility concept about 40 percent of the inhabitants agreed to live without their own car; a car sharing system has been created and public transport and bicycle lanes has been provided; sustainable water management with onsite filtration; green roof applications with rainwater collection facilities; building waste management; preservation of existing landscape features like old trees and water creeks; creation of civic meeting places, kindergarten, youth facilities; two big garage buildings with solar panels on their rooftops for auto-parking and energy production for the neighborhood; more than 100 housing units with passive house standards (15kWh/meters squared) or plus energy houses (which produce more energy than they need) and all other houses are built with low energy standards (65kWh/meters squared) were all realized.

Another challenging task for architects in renewal of the existing structures is the problem of converting historically or culturally important but decaying old buildings into new green and sustainable living spaces. The first example here is a research center within the suburban campus of Kanto-Gakuin University located in Kanazawa-ku, Yokohama, Japan. The Frontier Center for Environmental Symbiosis Technology building is facing a small plaza in front of lively university cafeteria. The idea here was to transfer the wall-like dead façade into a new, lively, extended space with a bright glass surface and a green-wall with rose plants. The renovation was designed to retain as much of the existing structure as possible; the new skins cloaking the particularly decrepit external walls were made up of elements of environmental symbiosis. These relate to each other both internally and externally in their air, heat and water environments, giving the facility new life as a single new building with integration of design ideas, structure and equipment.[12] This green renovation project was completed in 1995 and rated with four star A CASBEE—as stated in the Japanese Sustainable Building database—and awarded by the Institute for Building Environment and Energy, Association of Building Engineering and Equipment in 2007, The Society of Heating, Air-Conditioning and Sanitary Engineers of Japan in 2008.

7.7 Green Renovation of Existing Buildings a) Frontier Center for Environmental Symbiosis Technology, Japan (Photographed by Toshiharu Kitajima) b) Paineiras Hotel, Rio de Janeiro, Brazil (image courtesy Hiperstudio + Arkiz)

In the heart of one of the densest places on earth, Manhattan, New York, the New Hearst Tower, standing on its 1928 Hearst International Magazine Building as its pedestal, has been designed by Foster + Partners. The building starts its energy and source savings from the cleverly designed structural system. The diagonal grid structural system, with no vertical steel beams at all, saves 2,000 tons of steel, a 20 percent savings over a comparable conventional office building. Ninety percent of the Tower's structural steel contains recycled materials. Twenty-six percent less energy is used than in a building constructed to standard building code. The annual carbon dioxide reduction associated with the decreased energy usage is 869 tons, equating to 174 cars being taken off the road. The roof collects rainwater, reducing the amount of water dumped into the city's sewer system during rainfall by 25 percent. Light sensors inside control the amount of artificial light on each floor, based on the amount of natural light available at any time.[13] The tower holds a gold certificate under the LEED rating system by the US Green Building Council, and was the first skyscraper in Manhattan to be awarded with that certificate.

With the World Cup scheduled to take place in Brazil in 2014 and the Summer Olympic games following in 2016, officials in Rio de Janeiro thought it was high time to revitalize the abandoned Paineiras Hotel and turn it into a model for sustainable tourism. The original Hotel Paineiras was built in 1884 by the Pedro II, Emperor of Portugal as a luxurious rest stop for wealthy travelers on their way to the Corcovado statue, the symbol of Rio de Janeiro. At Paineiras, visitors to Corcovado would board a train to continue the rest of the way up to the famous monument. Over time the hotel has since fallen into disrepair and for the last 30 or so years, has been left abandoned. This renewed design for the Hotel Paineiras Complex received an honorable mention in the Aliah Project national contest. The complex sits in the middle of the Tijuca National Park, approximately 0.6 miles (1 km) from the famous monument of Christ The Redeemer. The old hotel, which is unfortunately in a state of total disrepair, must be torn down in order to renovate the site. In its stead, a new complex will be built, consisting of tourism center for the memorial and national park and an eco-hotel and convention center.[14] The architects of the project chose to place the hotel complex near the higher ground in a longitudinal axis along the land's ridge, accommodating itself on the natural topography and providing beautiful views towards the landscape. The sensitive analysis of this region is reflected in the way in which the building interacts with the ground, establishing a dialectical relationship in which architecture acts as a physical support for contemplation. In the design process the main concern was to avoid large movements of earth and disturbances in the site configuration, elevating the parking floors and revealing them in a creative way, using the natural morphology of the site to accommodate them. To integrate them with the surrounding landscape, green layers were designed to involve the parking floors and the public boulevard, merging the constructed mass into a powerful green pavilion that emerges from the forest. The concerning here was to develop a scenario of consistent ambience and healthy coexistence between the built and the natural landscape, not trying to deny the new intervention.

The eco-renovations of existing structures and buildings in the landscape, when compared to totally new structures, are struggling with a highly critical mission of keeping the environmental impact minimum while preserving the historical character of the place and also responding to the needs of contemporary massive movements of people and consumption systems.

EXTREME–MAINSTREAM

Why not go ahead and carry the notion of green architectural projects to a futuristic level? The ideas and forms behind extreme green projects that are selected here may not have new inspiration sources in roots—unlikely, they are sourced from local building typologies or natural characteristics and landscape features of their very location on earth—although they may seem like high-tech constructions creating sci-fi environments. While some of the extreme projects here are under construction as experimental projects, the rest remains as un-built, conceptual and promising intellectual exercises for our common green future.

The Ziggurat, designed by Dubai based design firm Timelinks, is offering a gigantic eco-pyramid, which will cover 568 acres squared (2.3 kilometers squared) area and will be inhabited by one million people. The sustainable community life foreseen is supporting super-efficient public transportation system, public and private green spaces with leisure and agricultural facilities. The extreme point is that the whole settlement is aiming to be totally off-grid by utilizing only renewable energy sources. Yet the project remains as a brilliant envision and a futuristic sustainable city for now.

The Cloud, two connected luxury residential and mixed use towers, are going to be standing right up at the Yongsan Business District of Seoul, Korea in 2015. The project is designed by MVRDV as a residential development for the extending business district. The southern tower reaches a height of 260 meters with 54 floors, the northern tower 984 feet (300 meters) with 60 floors. The total surface are of the towers is 1,377,780 feet squared (128,000 meters squared). Halfway, at the level of the 27th floor, the cloud is positioned, a 10-floor tall pixelated volume, connecting the two towers.[15] The public program of this mainly residential complex is offering a large ground floor level, with gardens designed by Martha Schwartz, and a sky lounge with a large connecting atrium, a wellness center, conference center, pools, restaurants, cafes, decks and gardens. It is not only the cross ventilation and the fine daylight conditions that are being offered to the users of this complex, but also the well-integrated public program into the tower, starting from the ground level and rising among the floors, is a promise for sustainable future community life, yet in extreme scale.

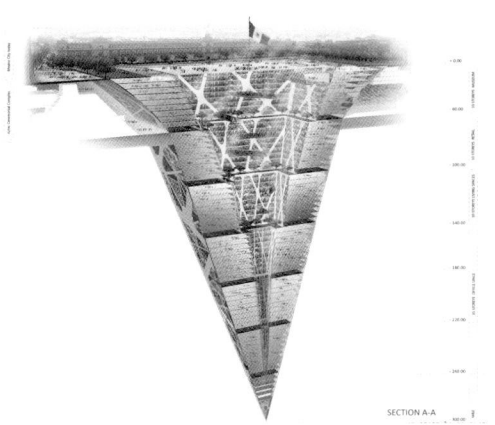 

7.8   Extreme Green Projects From Macro to Micro Scales a) The Earthscraper, Mexico City (© image courtesy BNKR) b) Marine Research Center, Bali (courtesy of Architectural Design: solus4. Visualization: Tangram3DS)

The Earthscraper project of Mexico-based architects BNKR Arquitectura is pushing the structural, topographical density limits of common well-known green architectural projects in urban contexts. In the heart of the city center, with increasing population, mass of traffic and other networks, old historic context and strict building regulations limiting building heights, the site of the project is located. The idea of the Earthscraper comes from historical Aztec pyramids, inserted upside down deep into the earth while allowing an open multifunctional urban plaza for public use for gatherings, concerts, exhibitions, cultural celebrations and other public events. With its huge scale 8,342,030 feet squared (775,000 meters squared) floor space in total, the Earthscraper also has attractions in the first 10 floors of the pyramid, the following 10 floors are given to retail shops while the deeper 35 stories offer office facilities. The glass roof covering allows natural light access down into the earth to all the floors. As the architects of the project emphasize, "it respects the value of both empty space and high densification. It becomes a new species of landmark building: both invisible and monumental." The urban plaza on the top of this mammoth scale complex in the very heart of this historical city remains as a delicate touch, preventing the high impact of the footprint of such a huge structure, and moreover, brings a clever idea for the densification of the city center.

The scale and the program of the Marine Research Center competition winner project for Bali, Indonesia cannot be compared to the macro scales and complexity of functions of the Earthscraper for Mexico City, the Cloud for Korea or the Ziggurat for Dubai. But with floating structure in the ocean, located 492 feet (150 meters) offshore from the Kuta beach, the inspiration of its form and spaces from the tsunami waves and its well respond both to the programmatic needs for a marine research center and energy-saving design principles, make the project extremely sensitively designed. The 26,909 feet squared (2,500 meters squared) research center is housing research labs, accommodation for researchers, a seawater pool, aquatic garden library and an auditorium, all located under the sea-level. The project is intended to be totally energy efficient with rainwater collection and seawater conversion system for domestic water needs, PV embedded glass panels on the façades and tidal/current generators for power supply, deeper seawater circulation over the façades for cooling the mass.

7.9   Mainstream Green Buildings a) Pixel building, rendering of the west façade b) Pixel building, in real context, Australia (both images courtesy of Studio 505)

The overall design and form of the building seems like so well integrated with its surrounding water context while preventing source consumption and being self-sufficient.

Beside the extravagant programs and arrogant square feet areas of giant green structures for housing the masses of people, public and private facilities, working places, services and all, there are also more modest and experimental projects started up to appear in our everyday urban contexts—at least in the countries, where the building regulations are being updated or changed by more green alternative rules. With upcoming mainstream green projects, these initiatives are keen on decreasing the impact of our footprint on this planet.

Grocon's new Pixel building, the first carbon neutral office building in Australia, has achieved the highest Green Star score ever awarded by the Green Building Council of Australia. The building is designed by Studio 505 architects and engineered by Umow Lai and VDM Consulting; all local firms. The project's five main aims are carbon neutrality, a vacuum toilet system, the anaerobic digestion system and reduced car parking.[16] The building is particularly striking with its uniquely designed sun shade system on the exterior of the building. That provides the maximum amount of daylight while preventing the effects of direct sunlight and heat with automatically opening windows during nights to cool down and refresh the inside air. Other unique designs include "Pixelcrete" (a kind of concrete cutting the carbon level in the mix in half), wind turbines invented in Bendigo, the living roof covered with local grassland species and tracking photovoltaic roof panels.

Another mainstream green building, the Office Center in Obvodny, St Petersburg, designed by Tsytsin Architectural Studio, is awarded with a gold LEED certificate. It is the first Russian housing–office project awarded with a LEED international standard. The building's heat and power saving achievement is exceeding 40 percent when compared to a common building of same type. The building is designed with the motto of the architectural studio team: achieving efficiency, solidity and harmony in building design. They see the building design as creation of the sites in harmony with ecological systems and cultural surroundings, which is promising for green architecture in a country with rich natural and cultural sources.

X-LARGE–X-SMALL

The structures and form of the x-large projects presented here are mainly designed with a holistic understanding and design conceptualization of ecology and architectonics. The expected result is the great equilibrium between men and nature through design with imitation of the working principles of natural systems and forms. As long as the same holistic attitude will be applied into the production of materials and the construction techniques of these large scale projects it is inevitable that the next generation extreme green and sustainable architecture will promote a real eco-friendly footprint on earth.

At the site of the existing Lansdowne Road Stadium, which is the oldest international rugby ground in the world, a new international stadium with 50,000 sitting capacity was created. The giant stadium is designed by Scott Tallon Walker Architects and Populous (formerly HOK SVE). Keeping the height and form of the structure in harmony with the adjacent two-story houses was a major challenge for the architects. Other challenges were to arrange the public transportation and access to the site during event times and to provide all the facilities expected from a new modern stadium within the existing restricted footprint.

Aeon Mall Kusatsu, built in an exceptional location right by the Kusatsu side of the Omi Ohashi Bridge and across from Otsu on Lake Biwa, was designed as an "eco shopping mall coexisting with local communities and blending in with the surrounding nature." The exterior of the building was designed to fit the landscape of Lake Biwa and rustic scenery of the surrounding area and energy efficiency was incorporated into design features such as an environmental-friendly lighting system. Furthermore, a variety of environmental technologies including natural energy and greenery utilization were introduced. The mall also promotes the importance of environmental efforts among visitors by offering information on its initiatives through eco-info terminals and panel displays. The sustainable design of the building followed the 2008 CASBEE guidelines for new construction, earning the CASBEE-S ranking (BEE = 3.8), multiple use building, retail and auto-parking, based on a comprehensive evaluation by an independent institution (IBEC).[17]

The world's largest solar-powered building, a 807,293 feet squared (75,000 meters squared) office facility, is built in Dezhou, Shangdong Province in northwest China. The mixed used office complex program of the Sun Moon Mansion includes exhibition centers, scientific research facilities, meeting and training facilities and a sustainable hotel. The building has a circular geometry and is all surrounded by solar panels continuously generating energy.

7.10   X-Large Green Buildings a) Aviva Stadium, Ireland (courtesy of Scott Tallon Walker Architects) b) Sun Moon Mansion, Dezhou, China (courtesy of Himin Solar Co. Ltd.)

The roof and the wall insulation systems reduce 30 percent more energy than the national energy saving standard.[18] The office center is located in the Solar Valley, which is aimed to be the biggest solar energy production base in the whole world. The plan is being developed by Himin Solar Energy firm, which is also located at the offices in the Sun Moon Mansion. Beside its energy-efficient and intelligent design this giant structure also symbolically resembles the Chinese characters for sun and moon with the white exterior symbolizing clean energy. However, the rural farmers are being relocated to make way for this ambitious development.

The idea of a great green wall came as response to a major concern: tackling the combined effects of drought and natural resources degradation in rural environments. Building on the experiences of green belts and barriers in circum-Saharan countries, the present note sheds light on the concept of the Great Green Wall Initiative, and suggests practical modalities of implementation. The "Great Green Wall" initiative saw the light of day when efforts made in the implementation of the Convention to Combat Desertification proved well below the objectives sought, both in terms of natural resource conservation and poverty alleviation. This made it essential to consolidate, accelerate and strengthen the National Action Programs to Combat Desertification. This initiative, which is linked to sustainable development, reflects a strong political will to conduct in well delineated regions of the Sahelian and Saharan countries a set of concerted and coherent interventions with the aim of achieving simultaneously the three following goals: natural resource conservation, development and management; strengthening infrastructure; improving the living conditions of the resident communities.[19]

A 3,728 mile (6,000 kilometers) long stretch of solidified sand dunes is proposed, which will architecturally support the Green Wall Sahara initiative: 24 African countries coming together to plant a shelterbelt of trees right across the continent, from Mauritania in the west to Djibouti in the east, in order to mitigate against the encroaching desert. In 2008, DUNE—Arenaceous Anti-Desertification Architecture won first prize ($15,000) in the Holcim Awards' "Next Generation" category for Africa/Middle East.[20]

Although their small scale, when compared to enormous square feet multifunctional green complexes, the following projects are offering various opportunities for developing green architectural design concepts and technologies. With their high experimental potential they provide micro-scale exemplar basis for sustainable design.

At 7,382 feet (2,250 meters) height in the Eastern Alps at Reisseck, South East Austria, the Viennese architects, Zechner and Zechner, won an international project competition for a new railway station. Following the contours of the land the building form resembles a hooded snake with a curved roof covering the top of the restaurant protecting it from the snow and sheltering the extended observation deck towards the steep cliff. The terminal will be equipped with solar thermal collectors for self-sustaining energy production and an adjacent grid of solar panels will provide most of the power for the complex's heating and hot water systems. While the ground floor will be constructed by stone, the sloping roof and deck will be made from sustainable wood, and provide protection from wind and snow, while being unobtrusive to the view. The installation of large banks of reflective glass on the exterior of the building will further highlight and reflect the views. The unique form designed for this particular site also helps to present the sensitive approach of the client (Verbund, the Austrian hydro power firm) to the ecology and use of renewable energy.

7.11 X-Small Green Buildings a) Reisseck Terminal, Austria (courtesy of Zechner & Zechner ZT GmbH) b) Hardanger Retreat, Norway (courtesy of Saunders Architecture) c) The Sled House, New Zealand (courtesy of Crosson Clarke Carnachan Architects / photo by Jackie Meiring)

The Hardanger retreat, designed and built by two young Norwegian architects, Todd Saunders and Tommie Wilhelmsen, is a self-initiated and self-financed project. As emerging young architects in the field of sustainable design they went quite experimental with this minimalistic off-grid retreat: finding and buying the plot of land in Hardinger, on the edge of one of Norway's most dramatic fjords; using the felled wood from their land for the construction (with the help of carpenter Mats Odin Rustøy); using recycled newspapers for the insulation of the structure. The small retreat uses no electricity and is not connected to the grid. Instead, natural gas is used for cooking and heating. As the retreat will be used mostly during the summer months, when there is only around four hours of darkness, no lights were installed and if lighting is needed, candles are used. The total floor area of the retreat is only 215 feet squared (20 meters squared) with the open deck around the room that provides a comfortable observation platform for the surrounding landscape.

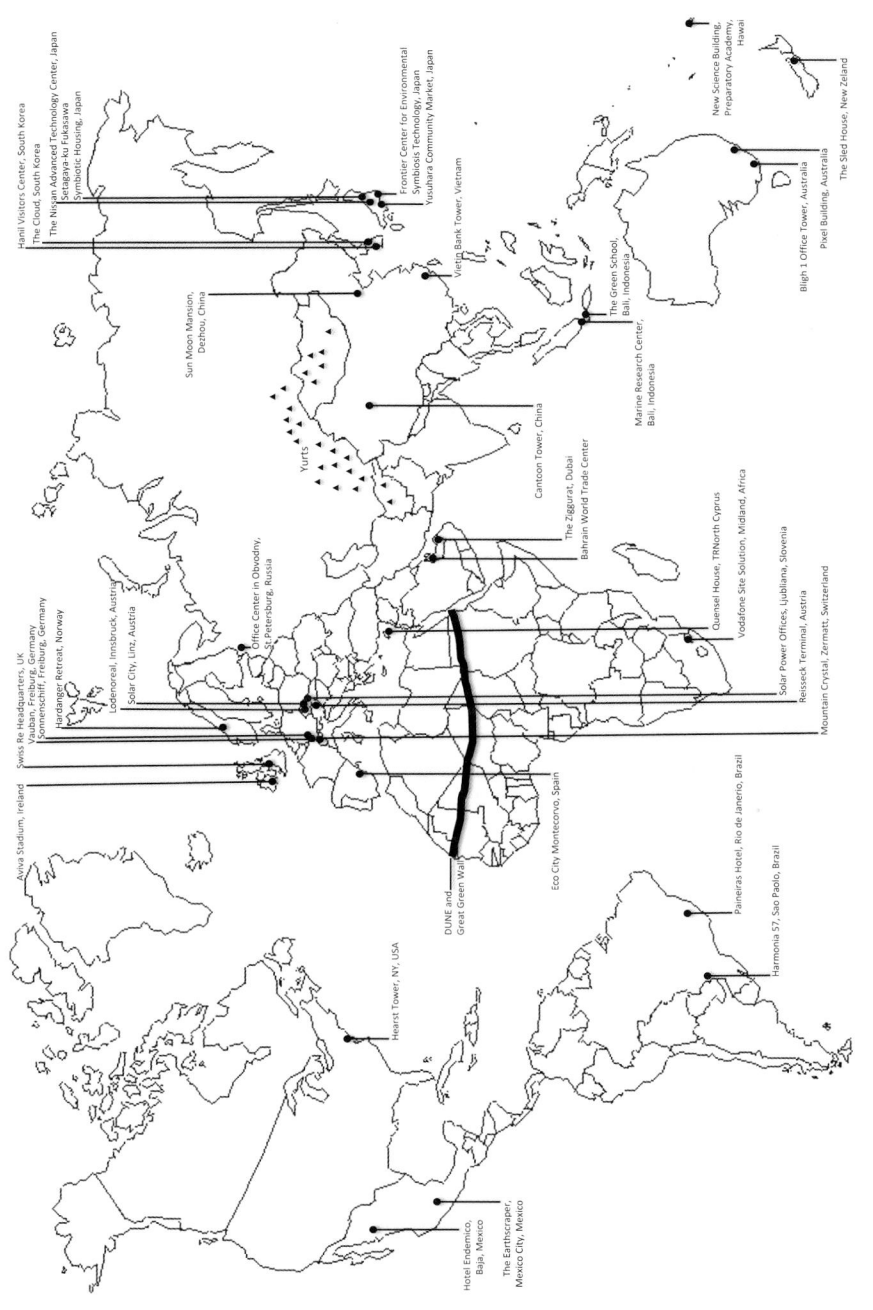

7.12 Locations of Selected Green Projects © courtesy of A. Senem Deviren

The Sled House is built as a beach holiday hut in Whangapoua beach, Coromandel peninsula, New Zealand in May 2012. Yet, it is not a common holiday home. The site is located in a coastal erosion zone where the building rules are preventing any permanent structure to be built on the waterfront due to movements of the sand dunes; only re-locatable or temporary structures are allowed to be built. Therefore the house is built on two thick wooden sleds so it can be portable and moved around depending on owners' needs or when required by local planning authorities due to shifting sand dunes. Besides its sensitive approach to the fragile beach ecosystem the building is also applying green technologies through its construction with natural materials, sustainable water-saving waste treatment system. A worm tank system treats the family's waste while two tanks hold grey water that can be recycled. One of the shutters doubles as an awning that protects against the harsh summer sun while also allowing winter sun to permeate the interior, and a small wood-fired stove keeps the tiny space nice and warm.[21] The total floor are is 430 feet squared (40 meters squared) including dining, kitchen, living and bathroom space along with two bedrooms. The double-height wooden shutter can be opened, by folding, for shading, letting the sun and light in and closed when protection is needed. The tiny beach hut has been nominated for a number of awards like Residential Architecture Excellence and Sustainability Design Award in Timber Design Awards 2012, New Zealand.

> *Perhaps there should be no special category called 'sustainable design.' It might be simpler to assume that all designers will try to reshape their values and their work, so that all design is based on humility, combines objective aspects of climate and the ecological use of materials with subjective intuitive processes, and relies on cultural and bio-regional factors for its forms.*[22]

PROLIFERATING GREEN ARCHITECTURE

In the last century, our efforts to make highly climate controlled and comfort assured environments with the use of artificial—and extensively energy consuming—sources for lighting, cooling, heating and ventilation, has separated us from outdoors and the natural environment. As a result of the artificial microclimatic conditions created throughout the past century, we are now mostly spending our time and life indoors and in well-sealed environments that are assuring our comfort. Our location on the earth, seasons, outdoor climatic factors like temperature, wind or humidity have little relevance to our daily routines and living patterns, at least on the northern hemisphere.[23] Men, landscape and the architecture became separated in broad terms, not only physically but also ecologically. The contravening green architecture examples (Urban–Rural, High-Tech–Low-Tech, New–Existing, Extreme–Mainstream, X-Large–X-Small) here present only a small exemplar percent of the recent projects on the search for reuniting human and nature continuum through experimental architectural practices for future sustainability of our living environment.

Urban green projects have the potential of supporting place connectedness of people with their local natural and cultural conditions and sources while the new rural green projects have to struggle with the problem of using state of the art technology yet trying not to be out of local context. Reaching high and up or around and welcoming the surrounding landscape for the comfort of their users the high-tech green buildings show similar tendencies in different geographies, while low-tech vernacular architecture proves to be the source of genuine green thinking in creating livable human habitats. New eco or green settlements do not seem to have only architectural agendas for going greener but also tend to carry the responsibilities of social and economic sustainability issues; our daily working spaces such as offices, factories etc. are also turning greener. But the challenging task of transforming existing building stock into healthy green environments requires a more participatory process of urban regeneration including local authorities, constructors, NGOs and the representatives of the inhabitants into the design process. While extreme ideas and projects push the limits of our imagination with images of an ideal or utopian green future, the task of the mainstream green projects is to keep us on earth with fusing latest green technological innovations into our daily lives through architecture. The extra-large size green buildings, regardless of their location on earth, tend to blend into landscape with the holistic idea of combining ecology and architecture, while extra-small size green buildings are offering experimental playgrounds for our everyday pleasure in sustainable living. With opportunities and challenges, shown here by the contravening examples, the experimental green architecture is blooming up, yet not sprawling all around the world.

At the same time in our contemporary world, which is facing an expanding financial and social disparity between people, the loss of public goods such as a clean environment and social welfare and destruction of historical urban fabric, issues like sustainability and ecological balance are becoming serious concerns to maintain healthy and livable environments. While the selected projects here are presenting the ongoing greening of architecture in varying scales and locations on earth, it is crucial to see how our greening activities are changing and converting our known landscapes into *new territories* of *green technologies* and *architectural landscapes*.

The scale of these *new landscapes* are varying in size and form from buildings' surficial properties to volumetric organization of building groups and to the master plans for new eco-cities and regions. Within the context of the *new landscapes,* architecture and landscape are coming back together for urban and rural green design, both conceptually and physically, as *site invaders* for habitat creation and its sustainability; the physical and the digital worlds are becoming more intertwined that is opening new ways for developing ecological research, contributing to the production of sustainable tools and materials for greener constructions. In parallel, the increasing level of communications and transportation of materials is causing homogenization in architectural space creations globally. While the free-circulation of goods and materials seems like supporting the global industry by bringing rivalry in providing more economic conditions for construction and energy production, and opportunities for proliferation of green architecture, the share of the benefits are not the same everywhere, nor the architecture is going totally greener. At the extremes, new highly insulated and materialized constructions labeled as eco-architecture examples are appearing on sites as "stand alone" structures with no ecological integration even to their very surroundings. The homogenization at the material, spatial and architectural levels are presenting a major threat against one of the most important mottos of green architecture: the making of "location-specific architecture by responding to local climatic conditions and using local materials."

Thinking on proliferation and considering the increasingly globalizing circumstances, two consecutive critical questions emerge primarily: Are there chances for creating genuinely green architectural landscapes with great localization? And accordingly, are there possibilities for proliferating these *new landscapes* without causing global spatial homogenization?

The "medialized" and isolated form of eco-architecture is a clear danger for living places and it has disabilities in creating living relations with the surrounding ecology.[24] Rapid population growth, modernization and urbanization have directly impacted the environment, and now, the architects' responsibility of thinking in context and networks goes way beyond solving the problem of isolated "stand-alone" structures. Architecture is not freed from landscape, culture and nature, nor is its understanding and practice separable from ecological understanding. New landscapes are inclusive and require network thinking; in broad terms, it is architecture, landscape, engineering, culture, nature, ecology with network thinking together make the buildings a part of the living environment. That brings a higher ethical responsibility to the architects, along with the need of co-working contexts and networks with all other disciplines, for meditating on and making architecture greener.

> *What is happening to the once-beautiful landscape is an enormous catastrophe for which the future will curse us. If there is a future. Most contemporary architecture has forgotten the age-old lessons of design which took nature, climate and the elements into consideration.*[25]

ENDNOTES

1   Darko Radovic, "Eco-Urbanity, The Framework of an Idea," *Eco-Urbanity: Towards Well-Mannered Built Environments*, edited by D. Radovic. New York: Routledge, 2009: 9–18.

2   J. Owen Lewis, *A Green Vitruvius: Principles and Practice of Sustainable Architectural Design*. London: James and James, 2009.

3   Ibid.

4   Source: http://www.buildup.eu/cases/6892, accessed April 2012.

5   Source: http://www.inhabitat.com/bmws-stunning-energy-efficient-production-plant, accessed April 2012.

6   A. Senem Deviren, "An Eco-House: On Design and Living with Ecological Design Parameters," (in Turkish), *XXI-Architecture-Design-Space Magazine*, 47: 84–6. July–August 2006.

7   J. Rainer, "Roland Rainer's 1992 Masterplan for Linz-Pichling," *Solar City Linz Pichling, Sustainable Urban Development*, edited by M. Treberspurg. Stadt Linz, Wien, New York: Springer, 2008: 24–6.

8   N. Kaiser, "Comfort, Energy, Environment," *Solar City Linz Pichling, Sustainable Urban Development*, edited by M. Treberspurg. Stadt Linz, Wien, New York: Springer, 2008: 36–42.

9   A. Senem Deviren, "Tackling Eco-Urbanity: Housing and Placemaking at the Urban Edge," *AIZ ITU Journal of the Faculty of Architecture*, 7(2): 163–84. Autumn, 2010.

10 Source: http://www.witnessthis.wordpress.com/tag/vodafone-site-solution-innovation-centre/, accessed April 2012.

11 Source: http://www.vauban.de/info/abstract.html, accessed April 2012.

12 Source: http://www.ibec.or.jp/jsbd/AF/index.htm, accessed April 2012.

13 Source: http://www.hearst.com, accessed April 2012.

14 Source: http://inhabitat.com/rios-paineiras-hotel-to-receive-eco-renovation/, accessed April 2012.

15 Source: http://www.morfae.com/1196-mvrdv/, accessed April 2012.

16 Source: http://www.wow.sg/#/projects/tanjung-benoa-resort, accessed April 2012.

17 Source: http://www.ibec.or.jp/jsbd/AG/index.htm#, accessed April 2012.

18 Source: http://www.ecofriend.com/entry/eco-architecture-world-s-largest-solar-powered-office-building-unveiled-in-china/, accessed April 2012.

19 *The Great Green Wall Initiative for the Sahara and the Sahel*, OSS; CEN-SAD, Introductory Note Number 3. Sahara and Sahel Observatory, Tunis, 2008: 44.

20 Source: www.magnuslarsson.com/architecture/dune.asp, accessed April 2012.

21 Source: http://inhabitat.com/amazing-whanapoua-sled-house-can-be-slid-around-the-beach-in-new-zealand/, accessed April 2012.

22 Victor Papanek, *The Green Imperative: Ecology and Ethics in Design and Architecture*. Singapore: Thames and Hudson, 2005: 10.

23 A. Senem Deviren, "Can Energy Efficient Architecture Create Eco Urbanity: Rethinking the Role of the Landscapes In-between," *Yearbook 2010 of the Institute of Advanced Studies on Science, Technology and Society*, edited by A. Bamme, G. Getzinger and B. Wieser. Profil Verlag, Munich/Vienna 2011: 111–24 (IFZ).

24 Ibid.

25 Victor Papanek, *The Green Imperative: Ecology and Ethics in Design and Architecture*. Singapore: Thames and Hudson, 2005: 10.

Chapter 8
Conclusion

When an offshore oil rig explodes, the seemingly sound pretext for a way of life is also called into question.[1]

The greening of architecture is both a concept and practice of the ongoing process and continual refinement toward greater architectural and urban responses to the environment. This process has many dimensions that cover both space and time as well as different intensities from remedies of unsustainability, to maintaining sustainable balances, and finally to creating benevolent abundances. The patterns of change through the past five decades give an indication to the areas of unsustainability and correspondence between the evolving greening methods and the changes in contemporary architecture—both of which have been moving targets. The global disposition of green architectural and urban works is a prelude to the potential pervasiveness of this phenomenon. Signature architects still play an important role in this maturation process by providing exciting, innovative and inspiring models. Yet, it is the architecture of the everyday that is still in most need of attention. James Wines concludes in his book *Green Architecture* (2000) that "architecture still has one of the most important conservation and communication roles to play in any new ecologically responsible vision of the future."[2] Design education, too, will play a critical role in the future greening of architecture.

The First Principles in architecture contain an unwavering set of concepts that inherently address sustainability. It might be better served to focus less upon mutable sustainable and technological determinism and the ways in which they influence building design, but rather focus more directly on the architecture process and reinforce its essential nature and purpose, which is to weave into manifest form the unity, generative, formative, corporeal and regenerative principles. It is unfortunate that the word "architecture" needs to be modified with the term "green" in order to render it with sustainably responsible meaning. It should naturally include green intentions and practices, however it is not surprising, with present economic pressures and generally low development standards, that mainstream architecture is generally unsustainable. In many ways, the greening process should start at home with more climate-responsive designs and the purchase of efficient products and equipment, energy-efficient lighting, and a recycling center in the kitchen for organic, paper, glass, plastic and aluminum waste. This includes expanding to the garden, the site, neighborhood and the urban environments as well. It is the dynamic interactions within a particular context that extend architectural singularity of focus to more systemic considerations.[3] Infrastructure architecture, too, is an interesting green idea and frontier about both ecological and urban connections. The relational and in-between realms are a challenging landscape for sustainable planning to occur. Concepts of plurality, hybridity, resilience and biometrics are informing a new generation of green environments.

The greening of contemporary architecture has been illustrated over more than five decades from the early examples of Le Corbusier and Alvar Aalto to the more recent works of Bill Dunster and James Corner. This slice of time establishes patterns of innovation and re-direction in building and city making through modern, postmodern and metamodern periods. The intent was to demystify the various approaches to sustainable design, to weave together better working and more inclusive definitions, and to create clear and model demonstrations that might contribute to an ongoing greening process.[4] The greening of architecture is linked to external events whether they are natural disasters, vacillating economic conditions, new knowledge concerning the environment, changes in regulatory policies, political turnovers, creation of new technologies, or development of extraordinary designs. The greenest building in the world is still an elusive target. Is it Bullitt Center in Seattle, BedZED in London, Findhorn Eco-Community in Scotland, Clinton Presidential Library in Little Rock, BMW Welt in Munich, CH2 in Melbourne, COR in Miami, IUCN Building in Geneva or Bank of America in New York?

A comprehensive and effective way to articulate the diversifying effects of globalizing green architecture was to divide and contrast representative works into the various dualities: urban–rural, high-tech–low-tech, new–existing, small–large, and extreme–mainstream. This gives a broad spectrum of the differing approaches to sustainable design through quite varying contexts and extreme conditions. It seems clear that there is no consistent architectural language to these exemplifications; however, certain sustainable approaches are common among most of the projects. Residential projects, which were inherently skin-dominated, typically employed passive solar heating, natural ventilation, daylighting, higher insulating values, and energy efficient appliances. In warmer climates, they incorporated a number of different sunshading, solar control devices, evaporative cooling, and natural ventilation. Non-residential projects, which were load-dominated, typically incorporated daylighting, solar control devices, green roofs, atriums, photovoltaic electricity production, and high efficiency HVAC systems. Urban projects tended to focus on density of built form, mixes of use and cross programming, and encouraging pedestrian places and movement with connections to public transport. The demonstrations of sustainable practices were expressed through differing architectural forms that generally included vernacular revivals, high-tech, modernist, and biomorphic languages. Regional and cultural differences also informed many of the designs.

John Ehrenfeld posits that true sustainability "lives in a world distinct from the present: one with a new vocabulary and cultural habits."[4] The challenge is to find the pathway that connects these two places. This is why he observed that most of our efforts now were aimed at reducing unsustainability.[5] Hopefully, in future the building and re-building of the habitable environment will be closer to pure renewable sustainability with attendant abundances. In some ways this addresses the degree of severity of our perceived unsustainable environments and the magnitude of the standards we set for creating a more sustainable future. The greening process both now and in the future is formed by the inextricable relationship among our societal and personal needs for energy and resources, the availability of existing and renewable resources, and the nature of the built environment in terms of configuration, density, mixes of use, methods of connectivity, and the quality of the sustainable measures. The goal is to achieve a healthy balance and climax ecological relationship with the environment as a whole.

The human environment comprises the transect from the most urban with intense cultural activity and density of built form to the most rural with dispersed habitation, direct connections to nature and larger areas of agricultural production. Implementing sustainable planning and design measures for these varying territories takes great skill especially in the face of current development practices, land ownership, and the spatial structure of the existing built environment. A challenge for forth coming decades is the creation of smooth and seamless connections, cascading modes of transport and recombinant urban forms between these extremes employing complementary visions and incremental processes of change. Heroic green architecture still plays an inspiring role, but more importantly, mainstream everyday architecture and urbanism will remain the domain and foil for the greatest areas of need and impact. This underscores the importance of sustainable measures within interstitial and infrastructural space and continued efforts to create more pedestrian, livable and mix use places of dwelling.

The physical characteristics of green urbanism follow Michel Foucault's systems of organization as they function as both place and network architectures. They share complicit roles in creating a sustainable future focused on the urban design scale. The energies of placemaking focus inwardly on being, rest, stasis, agglomeration, concentration, saturation, safety, dwelling, stewardship, pedestrian scale and experience. This means *being there* and being in place having supportive architecture and urban forms that contribute to nodes of sustainable living patterns. Connective tissue on the other hand is characterized by flow; it is moving, fluid, linear, interstitial, infrastructural and dynamic focusing on interchange, accessibility and systemic connectedness. It is the *go-between* where resources, nature, goods, energy, and people move and respond to differing kinds of speed-scale environments and between-place processes and modes of transport. Previously fragmented, this sprawling territory offers great opportunities for a new kind of reformed green architecture and eco-urbanism. The interface between urban dwelling place and infrastructure network suggest an ecological power-geometry and progressive sense of place. Constellating urbanism is a notion that unites urban agglomerations into a more comprehensive whole as illustrated with Serenbe Community's interconnected hamlets. Place becomes coherent and identifiable.

Each decade added to the continuing DNA of the greening of architecture in distinctive ways. They were radical and visionary in the 1960s, phototropic and solar oriented in the 1970s, historic and formalist vernacular in the 1980s, eco-technological in the 1990s, and eco-pluralistic in the decade after the millennium. The Terreform image in Figure 8.1a illustrates the integration of many accumulative strategies, including vertical urban farming, mass transit, urban agriculture, agro-high-rises, green walls, water harvesting and intense pedestrian activity. Far from a single object of sustainability, it is an environment of interrelated activities. More importantly, it shows the total environmental design affording multiple greening processes. The BedZED photovoltaic array and wind cowls, in Figure 8.1b, suggest a different green aesthetic and architectural language with celebration of the tectonic elements of the design. Critically important is the regeneration of informal settlements, where a billion people presently live, with focus on the architecture of the in-between and infrastructure as shown in Medellin, Colombia as pictured in Figure 8.1c.[6] This extraordinary work included the Metro Cable, which was a gondola lift system providing complementary transportation services.

8.1 Contrast in Green Architectural Languages a) Amsterdam Avenue New York City b) BedZED PV and Wind Cowls c) Informal Settlement in Medellin, Colombia

Myriads of images and thousands of built works are now being produced, largely enabled by the growth in environmental awareness, the need to reduce greenhouse gasses, and the desire for more healthy places to live and work. The challenge is to continue these advances into more integrated applications on all scales and with all new development. The First Principles of architecture remain a timeless guide, which are continually interpreted and positively contributing to an alignment with the mutable processes of the greening of architecture.[7] Not to be taken alone, they form a consummatory integration of processes.

- The *Unity Principle* integrates part and whole, nodes and networks, and coherent enclaves with efficient connective tissues and infrastructure across transects of multiple scales of consideration. It guides growth into harmonious integrative designs of complementary divisions and conflicting opposites. It interconnects and synthesizes varying scales of development with a fusion and balance of individuality and community.
- The *Generative Principle* connects context, culture and land to evolving expressions of place multiplicity and proliferation in geographic space over time. It promotes morphological and incremental urban growth and contextual diversity. It generates sustainable technologies in response to multiple needs, situations and the availability of differing natural resources. It celebrates diversity and place-oriented exemplifications.
- The *Formative Principle* guides sustainable architecture and planning practice into appropriate climatic, contextual, ecological, and tectonic spatial orders, urban forms and green technologies. This includes the formal integrative design processes that seek to translate needs into functions into appropriated forms. It encompasses the tectonic and high organizational qualities of sustainability.

- The *Corporeal Principle* grounds sustainable intentions into pragmatic physical realities, concrete strategies, practical technologies, achievable project delivery systems, affordability, and eventual occupation and effective use. It is substantive, quantitative, tangible, differentiated and material expression of green measures, architectural and urban designs. It is the process of realistic manifestation.
- The *Regenerative Principle* responds to both dynamic ecological and human cycles that reuse, recycle, and recreate. It regenerates unproductive land, brownfields and abandon or obsolete buildings that create new beginnings. It promotes processes that restore, renew and revitalize in an ecology of responsive environmental design. Rather than an object of sustainability, it promotes an ongoing process of evolutionary change.

Architecture, in response to evolving human activity and concerns about the environment, becomes more effectively green with improving technology, model examples, and globalizing effects. If "architecture" is the weaving into manifestation the First Principles, then the greening of architecture has been a process that combines these informing principles with sustainable practices. Taken all together this multilayered approach enables designers to make catalytic leaps toward ever-increasing levels of morphogenic sustainability and balance with the environment. The exploration of the greening of architecture has been a process of defining, unfolding, explaining, illustrating and analyzing measures that transform architecture and urban design practice into more sustainable forms. This process is one that affects these works in both space and time.

The Brundtland Commission Report of 1987 has particular application to this conclusion on sustainable architecture and urban design.[8] For sustainability to truly be effective both now and in the future; it must incorporate new visions and narratives of engagement. The greening of architecture will be informed by incremental changes, dynamic interactions with immediate surrounding environments, social equity and response to the diversity of needs, affordable applications, connectivity at all scales of human activity, and proliferation throughout the varying contexts on a planetary scale. And finally, there hopefully will no longer be the need for this greening process in the future; as architecture will naturally embody and fully actualize effective green principles.

ENDNOTES

1   Katherine Stoll and Scott Lloyd, *Infrastructure as Architecture: Designing Composite Networks*. Berlin: Jovis Berlag Publisher, 2010: 11.

2   James Wines, *Green Architecture*. Köln: Taschen Press, 2000: 233.

3   "Pathways" is a dynamic temporal value-based approach to sustainability that proposes alternative participant frames of determinant action. Melissa Leach, Ian Scoones and Andy Stirling, *Dynamic Sustainability: Technology, Environment, Social Justice*. London, UK: Earthscan Publications, 2010: 155–7.

4   Ken Yeang and Authur Spector, *Green Design: From Theory to Practice*. London: Black Dog Publishing, 2011.

5   John R. Ehrenfeld, *Sustainability by Design: A Subversive Strategy for Transforming Our Consumer Culture*. New Haven, CN: Yale University Press, 2008: 215.

6 In an article by David Mohoney (2011), the public architecture in South America is promoting viable, scalable and transformable neighborhood projects. Improvements at Medellin, Columbia include permanent housing, utilities and sewers, and a pedestrian walkway, all accomplished without displacing the former population. Source: http://www.cooperhewitt.org/conversations?page=4, accessed April 2012.

7 T.H. Irwin, *Aristotle's First Principles*. Oxford, UK: Oxford University Press, 1988.

8 The Brundtland Commission Report titled, *Our Common Future* (1987) delineated three pillars of sustainable development, which were economic growth, environmental protection and social equality. Since that time, it is clear that efforts to accomplish the Commission's mandate have grown through the greening of architecture.

Index

Numbers in **bold** refer to figures.

Aalto, Alvar 1, 7, 8, **9**, 89, 151, 178
abstraction 1, 9, 11, 78–79
Academic Building Cooper Union 118–**19**
ACROS International Hall **112**–13
active living 20, 116
Aeon Mall, Kusatsu 170
Aga Khan Awards 161
agglomeration 2, 95, 126, 150, 179, 181
agricultural urbanism 16, 88, 127, 137–**9**, 40, 151
agrophelia 129
Alamillo Bridge 100, **102**
Alexander, Christopher 71
algorithmic urbanism 103
alternative technology 65
Ambasz, Emilio 95, **112**–13
ambiguity 1, 11, 43, 77, 79, 146
American dream 25–**7**, 29, 32, 150
Amsterdam Avenue **180**
Ando, Tadao 114
Andrews, John 45
Ant Farm 25, 41–**2**
Antarctica xx
Anthroposophy 40, 115
archê xvii
archetype xvii, 5, 84
Archigram 25, **37**, 40, 42, 69, 106
architecture defined xvii–xx, 1, 5, 7
arcology 37
Arcosanti 37, 40, **42**
Arctic City **35**, 45
artificial lighting 14, 29, 68, 100, 107, 115
Arts and Craft Movement 40
Arup, Ove 19, 69, 95, 106, 159
Asmussen, Erik **39**–40, **115**, 122
AT&T Building 76–**7**
atmosphere 31, 57, 78, 87, 93, 117–18, 139, 157, 159, 161
atrium 56, 68, 71, 101, 106–7, 113, 115, 118, 156, 159, 164, 167, 180

authenticity 8, 11, 15, 20, 36, 75, 80, 134
avant-garde 13, 80, 89, 110

Bacon, Edmund 4
Babcock Ranch 14, 135
Bachelard, Gaston 39
Baer, Steve **37**, 41, 151
Bahrain World Trade Center 159
Baker House 8–**9**, 45
Balcomb, Douglas **58**–9
Banham, Reyner 45, 100
Barragan, Luis 95
BCHO Architects Associates x, **158**
BedZED 141, **143**, 178–**80**
between place 93, 131, 144, 150, 179, 181
bio-climatic 13, 18, **35**, 61, 146, 162
biology 103, 120, 128, 130, 141, 146, 162
biometrics vi, ix, 10, 127–30, 145, 178, 180
Black Rhino **ii**, 123
Bligh 1 Office Tower 159
BMW Welt 159
BNKR x, **168**
Böer, Karl 53
Bosch House 139, 142–**3**
Botta, Mario 94
Bramwell House **58**–9
Brand, Stewart 1, 18, 42
Braungart, Michael 114
breezes 5, 7, 34, 82, 93, 101, 105
Breisach House 91–**3**
Brill, Michael 93
Brion Tomb **90**
brises-soleil 7
British Pavilion 106–**7**, 108
Bronx Grand Concourse 137
brownfield 106, 131, 181, 183
Brundtland Commission xvii, 13, 181
Butti, Ken and John Perlin 2, 21, 52

Calatrava, Santiago 19, 100–**102**, 101, 106–7, 128
Caledonia Pavilions 101–**2**, 105
California Academy of Sciences 113, 129–**30**, 131
Calthorpe, Peter 65, 68, 86, **88**
Canton Tower 159
Cape Cod Ark 64
carbon footprint 141, 143–4
carrying capacity 21, 29, 152
Carson, Rachel 1, 18, 25, 28, 31
cascading energy 105, 125, 179
Casey, Edward S. 94
Castello di Gargonza **17**
Castiglion Fiorentino, Italy **17**
Central Place Theory 86
Centre for Alternative Technology 65
Centre Georges Pompidou 37, 69–**70**, 100
Chandigarth High Courts 7–**8**
CIAM 11, 18, 36, 47
Citicorp Center **70**
city 8, 18, 120, 156, 159, 164–8, 180
    Arctic viii, **35**, 45
    capital 156
    center 131, 133, 135, 147, 151, 168
    council 165
    Drop viii, 37, 41–**2**, 46
    eco- 161–2
    Freiburg 165
    Hannover 119, 134, **136**
    Incheon **130**
    Island 14
    Linz 161
    Masdar 20, 135–6
    Mexico x,168
    Moscow 135–**6**
    New York x, i, 11, 17, 33, 41, 118, 133, 180, 182
    Seville **129**
    solar x,134, 162, 176
    sustainable 167
    Sydney 159
    Tokyo 165
    Vegetal **130**, 137
Clark, Wilson 50
climate xix–xx, 1–2, 4, 7–8, **35**, 72, 82–4, 86, 88–9, 157, 174, 176, 180
    change 21, 30, 72, 120, 123–4, 143–4
    cold 5, 39, 52–3, 90
    hot 5, 35, 91
    local 89
    micro 18, 105
    -responsive 179
    zone 4

Coates, Gary 115
cogeneration 101–2, 118, 125, 134, 146
cohousing 65–**7**, 68
Collage City (Rowe & Koetter) 76
collector 52–4, 65, 68, 118
    array 54, 58, 66, 106, 108
    concentrating 50, **54**–5
    hot-water 58–9, 118
    photovoltaic 15, 62, 64, 92
    solar 19, 52–3, 57, 70, 106, 157, 171
    tilt 19, 60–**61**
combinatory urbanism 151, 154
community xx, 14–15, 20, 39, 41, 84–6, 133, 156, 163, 165, 182
    climax 20, 105, 179
    destination 87, 131, 133
    Eco- 180
    intentional 66, 115, 138
    pioneering 105, 163
    satellite xiii, 69, 86, 131, 138
    solar 14, 65–6, 76, 135
    sustainable xiii, 33, 40, 68, 71, 115, 134, 167
complexity 1, 6, 10, 15, 18, 34, 36, 40, 43, 60, 76, 78, 168
compost 40, 71, 109
computer-aided-design 99–100, 103–**4**
Condon, Patrick 15. 137
connectivity 15, 64, 93, 118, 131–**2**, 134, 148, 181
conservation vi, 13, 17, 36, 79–**81**, 144–6, 155, 171, 179
constellating urbanism 40, 106, 109, **139**, 179
contaminants 30–32, 114
contemporary 1, 113, 118, 128, 133, 142–6, 152, 167, 175–6, 179–80
contextualism 78–9
contradiction 11, 43, 76–**7**, 97, 139
Cook, Jeffrey 61
Cook, Peter 37
Coop Himmelb(l)au 91, 128–**9**, 159
Corner, James **132**
Corporeal Principle xix, 181
cosmology 38, **93**
Critchlow, Keith xiii, xv, 39–40, 56
critical regionalism 19, 76, 89–**90**
Crosson Clarke Carnachan Architects xi, **172**
Crowther, Richard 53, 55, 57, 73
Crystal Cathedral 68, **70**–71
Crystal Island 135–**6**
Curtis, William 7, 11, 69, 75, 78, 92, 100, 103
Cutter, James 84

Daniels, Farrington 73, 103

Daniels, Klaus 103, 109
daylighting 36, 69, 82, 90, 100–101, 103, **107**, 125
deconstruction 75, 79, 91, **93**
deep ecology 40
deforestation 31, 49, 93, 123
density xix, 16, 37, 46, 125–6, 129, 168, 180–81
    densification 20, 88, 131, 168
    high 22, 60, 127
    low 12, 26, 60, 94, 127, 129
    medium 134–5, 163
design build 41, 84
Despommier, Dickson **112**–13, 121
determinism 4, 95, 177
development 115–16, 119, 125–6, 129, 133, 156, 161–2, 171, 180–82
    agricultural 137
    amenity-driven 135
    ecological 157
    housing 12, 135, 141
    mix use 159
    residential 167
    scales 15, 17, 36, 125, 180
    solar 66, 120
    sustainable xvii, xx, 142, 144, 156–7, 171, 184
    urban 156, 162, 176
Deviren, A. Senem xiii, 155, 160, 162, 173, 176–7
Disch, Rolf 163
dog-trot 34
double coding 75, 78–9, 92
Doxiadis, Constantinos vii, 1, **10**–11, 17
DPZ 87
Drop City 37, 41–**2**, 46
Duany, Andres **88**, 126, 138
DUNE 171
Dunster, Bill 141, **143**, 178, **180**
Durack, Ruth 88, 97
dynamic sustainability 146

Eames, Charles 124, 152
earth sheltering 59, 106, 111
Earthships 62–**3**, 64, 74, 142
Eberhard, John 52, 72
Echenique, Marcail 12
Ectypal 103, 115
ecology xix, 29, 37, 86–7, 115, 119, 124, 126, 129, 170–71, 175–7, 183
    cyclical 2
    Deep 40
ecological footprint vi, 141–**3**, 152, 157
Eco City Montecorvo x, **162**
eco-technology 37, 69, 71, 99, 105, 107–8
Eden Project 106–**7**, 108

EDITT Tower **112**–13
Eisenman, Peter 43, 91
Ekistics **10**, 11, 17
electromobility 145
electronic medium 103
elemental 7, 18, 30, 35, 39, 93, 114, 116, 145, 152
Ellin, Nan 15, 17, 76, 85, 94–5, 134, 137, 151
embodied energy xix, 14, 19–20, 78, 80, 82, 114, 126
energy conservation 19, 36, 51, 72, 90
Enlightenment 11, 75
Erskine, Ralph xvii, 1, 25, **35**, 45
eurhythmy xviii,
evidence-based design 116
experimental 42, 46, 48, 53, 57, 86, 142, 157, 161, 163–4, 167, 169, 171–2, 174–5
Eyck, Aldo van 36, 43, 79, 148

fabric 60, 125–6, 129, 131, 133–5, 147, 158
    urban 155–7, 175
Farr, Douglas 137
Fathy, Hassan xviii, 7, **8**, 25, 35, 91
fenestrations 8–9, 103, 146
Feng Shui 26, 38
Findhorn Garden **39**–40, 46, 115, 142–**3**, 178
First Principles xviii, xix, 152, 177, 180–81
Fisk, Pliny 65
Fitch, James Marston 14, 34, 36, 146
Flansburgh Architects x, **158**
Flying Elephant 142–**3**
flywheel 5
Form-Based Code 87, 127
Foster + Partners xvii, 69, 100–**102**, 135–**6**, 151, 159, 162, 166
Fuller, Buckminster 1, 18, 25, 37, 40–42, **44**, 106
fractal geometry 148
Frampton, Kenneth 19, 89, 92, 95, 130
functional zoning 12, 26, 86, 140, 145, 148

GAP Headquarters Building 114–**15**
Gateway Arch **44**
Geddes, Patrick 20
Gehry, Frank 91, **96**, 103–**4**, 110, 117, 128
General Systems Theory 29
Generative Principle xix, 4, 16, 98, 180
genius loci 38, 93
geology 18, 129–30
geomancy 26, 38
Gherkin Tower 159
Ghost Cities 147, 149, 154
glass 5–7, 12, 70, 82, 101, 165, 179
    glazing systems 6, 52, 99, 108, 163
    Low-E 6, 18, 82, 102

panel 168
performance 163
reflective 171
roofs 68, 77, 168
types 6, 43, 55, 59, 163
GLH & Associate Architects x, **163**
globalization 76, 89, 95, 103
global warming 30, 32, 49, 72, 120, 123–4, 143, 157
Gordon, Alastair 40, 46, 48
Gore, Al 29, 47
GRASS Architects x, **162**
Graves, Michael 76–**7**, 78, 95
Great Green Wall 171, 177
Greene, Herb 128–**9**, 145
green architecture 155, 159–60, 169, 174–5, 179–81, 183
green roof 19, 59, 109, 111, 113, 115, 118, 130, 159, 165, 178, 180
greening 134, 141, 143, 145, 149–55, 174, 177–8, 180–81, 183
greenhouse effect 6, 30, 55, 123
Green School, Bali x, 160–61, 163
green walls 19, 112–13
grey water 163, 173–4, 179
Grimshaw, Nicholas 19, 71, 95, 100, 106–**7**
Gruen, Victor **12**
Guangzhou TV Tower 159
Guggenheim Museum Bilbao 103–**4**, 129
Gurdjieff, George Ivanovich 26, 39

habitat 32, 72, 94, 111–12, 126, 160, 165
  living 157
  preservation 125
  sustainable 160
  wetlands 128
Habitat '67 **44**, 45
Hadid, Zaha xviii, 91,
hamlet 115, 135, 138–**9**, 147, 153, 179
Hanging Gardens 111–**12**
Hanil Visitors Center x,158
Hannover World Fair 119, 134, **136**, 153
Hardanger Retreat xi, 172
Hardy Hugh 43, 69
Harmonia 57, x, 156–7
Hawken, Paul 20, 23, 119
Hawkes, Dean 60
Hay, Harold 57
hazards mitigation 116
healing environments 115–16, 122
healthy buildings **115**, 116–18, 125, 164, 174, 180
Heat Mirror Glass 6, 59

Herb Greene 128–**9**, 145
heroic architecture xviii, 7, 16, 69, 93, 100, 135, 143, 179
Herzog, Thomas 95, 100, 106, 134, 145, 162
High Line Park **132**–3
high-tech vi, 37, 99–100, **102**–3, 105, 107–8, 110, 113, 117, 134, 142–3, 145, 155, 158, 167, 174, 180
Hiperstudio x, **166**
historicism 79–80, 120
Holl, Steven 92–**3**, 95, 130
Holloway, Denis **58**–9, **67**–8
Holtz, Michael 52
Hopkins, Michael 106
Hot-water 52–3, 58–60, 62, 108, 118, 157–8, 161, 171
hybridity 15, 75, 78–9, 84, **93**–4, 125, 134, 146, 178
Hyderabad, Pakistan **4**

IBM Tower **112**–13
in-between xvi, 36, 106, 118, 131, 134, 147, 150, 177–81
indoor air pollution **31**–2, 119
Incheon Stadium 131–**2**
infrastructure vi, xx, 15–16, 29, 33, 62, 78, 125, **132**–4, 137, 144–5, 147, 149–51, 153, 171, 178–80
Inland Steel Building **12**
integral urbanism 15, 134, 151
integrative xix, 16, 53, 64, 71, 138, 145, 148–9, 180
interiority 70, 93
internal gains 14, 57, 68, 100
irony 69, 79

Jacal 109–**10**
Jacobs, Jane 29, 47, 134
Jarna Community **39**–40, 46, **115**
Jencks, Charles 7, 49, 75, 94–5
Johnson, Philip 7, 68, **70**, 76–**7**
Joint Venture Architects 53–**4**, 73
Jones, Fay **70**, 145
JVC New Entertainment Center 128–**9**

Kappe, Ray 109–**10**, 118
Katz, Peter 87, 97
Kaufman House **10**
Kaufmann, Michelle **110**–11
Knowles, Ralph 19, 60–**61**
Kreider, Jan 52–3
Krier, Leon 12, 86, **88**, 94, 97, 126
Kronsberg District 20, 108, 119, 134, **136**–7

Kroon Hall 106
Kuma, Kenga 156
Kunstler, James 43, 48

Laguna West **88**
Lake Flato Architects 19, **83**–4, 109–**10**, 111, 138
Lambeth, James 19, 59
landfill 32, 65
landform architecture 129–**30**, 145
landscape 155, 157–61, 163, 165, 167, 170, 174–6, 180
    architectural 175
    global 155
    new 175
    rural 157
    surrounding 159, 161, 163, 172, 174
landcape design 157
landscape urbanism 10, 129–**30**, 131, 145
Las Vegas Library 92–**3**
Late Modern 68–**70**, 71
LAVA 135–**6**, **104**
Le Corbusier xviii, 1, 7–**8**, 11, 25, 151, 178
LEED 109, 111, 117–**19**, 130, 135, 141, 158, 166, 169
Lever House 11
Levittown **12**
Lewis, J. Owen 13, 21, 155, 176
Lieb House 43–**4**, 45
light mass building 56–7, 99
light pipes 107
light shelves 107, 109
Limits to Growth 29, 47
liquid architecture 103
Living Building Challenge 141, 153, 158
Living Homes 109–**10**, 111, 118
living in place 116
living machine 64, 142
Lloyds of London 69, 96, 100
load-dominated 17, 71, 99, 143, 178
Lodenareal 156
Löf, George 53
London City Hall 101–**2**
Lovins, Amory 55, 73
low carbon emissions 142
low-tech vi, ix–xx, 95, 108–9, **110**, 120, 140, 142, 144–5, 155, 158, 160, 174, 180

MacKay-Lyons, Brian 19, 82–**3**, 151
Mackintosh, Charles Rennie xviii, 25
Marcus, Clare Cooper 116, 122
Marine Research Center, Bali x, 168
Masdar City 20, 135–**6**
Mass walls 5, 59

materiality xix, 9, 93, 113
Matryoshka dolls **96**, **148**
Mazria, Edward 56, 73, 144
McDonough, William 19, 22, 114–**15**, 119
McHarg, Ian 1, 25, 34–6, 47
Medellin, Columbia **180**
megastructure 18, 37, 45–6
Mesa Verde **4**–5
Meta-modern 150–51, 178
Metropol Parasol Building **129**, 139–40
Mexcaltitan, Mexico 14–**15**
Michel Trombe wall 59
Miller Hull Architects 84
Millican Reserve xiii, 138–40
Miralles, Enric 91, 100, 106
Mississauga Civic Center **90**–91
mix use 86, 88, 92, 113, 116, 129–30, 134, 138, 146, 159, 163, 167, 170, 179, 181
Mockbee, Samuel 19, 84
modern movement 2, 6–7, 11, 14, 25
Monier Residence 109
Moore, Charles 43, **77**–8, 95, 151
Moore, Steven 76, 89, 97
Morphosis Architects 118–**19**
Mountain Crystal x, 157–**8**
multiplication 86–7
Murcutt, Glen **85**
MVRDV 134, 161, 167, 176

Nader, Ralph 28, 47
Namba Park **xxi**, **132**–3
nanoscopic 145
nature 119–20, 123, 128–31, 135, 141, 144–5, 158, 160, 170–74
Nesbit, Kate 11, 17, 77
nesting 124, 147–**8**
net-positive 142
network vii, 10, 15, 17, 29, 40, 64, 88, 125, 131, 133, 135, 139, 147, 149, 168, 176, 182–3
    architectures 181
    cellular 104
    circulation 131
    information 103
    infrastructure 181
    intelligent 145
    mesh- 99
    native-IP 104
    thinking 176
    utility 102
Network Urbanism 149, 151, 154
New Alchemists 64, 74
New Gourna Village **8**
New Hearst Tower 166

New Urbanism 19–20, 71, 97, 126–7, 131
  principles 86, 88
  town plans 16, 76, 95
non-toxic 46, 125–6, 144
Norberg-Schulz, Christian 93, 98
Northland Shopping Center **12**
Nouvel, Jean 111
Novac, Marcos 99, 103
Nuttgens, Patrick 101

Odeillo Furnace 53–**4**
Odum, Howard and Eugene 25, 29
off-grid vi, viii, xx, 62–**3**, 64, 104, 108–9, 160, 167, 172
OFIS Arhitekti, x, **163**
Oia, Santorini **3**, 4
Oil Embargo 19, 29–30, 49–**51**, 71
Olgyay, Victor 25, 34–**5**, 36, 47
Oliver, Paul 4, 92, 98
Olympic Sculpture Park **130**–31
Omega Center 141, **143**
on-site resources 19, 34, 36–7, 46, 62, 64, 78–9
orientation 3, 8, 18–19, 34, 38–40, 53, 60–**61**, 82, 84, 101, 125, 143, 161
out-gassing 32
Owens, Susan 15, 22, 36, 125, 152
ozone 32

Paineiras Hotel x, **166**, 176
Pantheon **39**
passive solar 6, 55–**8**, 62, 64–5, 68, 70, 72–3, 82–4, 94, 108, 120, 125, 141, 163, 178, 180
pattern language 71, 74
Pawlyn, Michael 128
Pelli, Cesar 101, 135
performance-based design 59, 72, 75, 95, 141
Petronas Towers 101–**2**
phenomenology 93, 98
photovoltaics 55, 82, 109, 118, 137, **140**–42, 146, 150
Piano, Renzo xvii, 19, 37, 69, 71, 95, 100–**102**, 105–6, **130**, 151, 162
Piazza del Compo Siena **17**, 90
Piazza d'Italia **77**
place viii, xiii, xvi, xix, 2, 13–15, 17, 20, 27, 30, 33, 36, 38–40, 45–6, 70, 72–4, 76, 79, 82, 84–95, 97–8, 101, 105, 116, 125–6, 134–5, 137–9, 142, 145–6, 156, 161, 164, 167, 180–82
  -adapted 8
  between-131, 144, 150, 181
  connectedness 156, 174
  -defining 149
  design xiv

ecology of 129
-enhancing 92
healing 115
in- 150
living 38, 176
-marking 17, 92, 129
memory 156
-oriented 1, 19, 93, 133, 182
-sensitive 155
-specific 139
spirit of 38
Pixel Building x, 169
placelessness 19, 76, 85, 89, 93, 95
placemaking xiii, xx, 11, 16–**17**, 22, 38, 46, 69, 89, 92–5, 131, 150, 179
Plato xix, 26, 39–40, 100, 147–**8**
pluralism 78, 94, 123, 150
pollution 29–30, 116, 120,
  air **31**–3, 119
  energy **31**
  land **31**–2,
  water **31**, 50
Pompidou Centre 37, 69–**70**, 100
Portland Building 76–**7**
Portman, John 68, 71
Portmeirion, Wales **81**
Postmodern 68–9, 71, 75, 78–9, 94, 101, 178
  Architecture 61, 72, 75–6, **77**, **85**, 91–**3**, 95, 151
  Theory 19, 45, 76, 85
  urban design 19, 76, 86, 94
Poundbury, Dorchester 86, **88**
Powers of Ten 124, 152
Predock, Antoine 92–**3**, 95
Preparatory Academy Hawai x, **157**–8
preservation 13, 17–19, 35, 49, 79–**81**, 125, 138, 165
Prickly Mountain 40–**42**
Priene, Turkey **3**–4
Prius Hybrid 120, **127**
Pruitt-Igoe 43

Quadracci Pavilion 105, **107**–8
Quantrill, Malcolm 9, 83, 97

radical architecture 19, 25, 40, **42**, 46, 104, 179
radon gas 32, 114
Rainer Roland 161–2, 176
rainwater viii, 62, **81**–3, 92, 105, 108–9, 111, 113, 118, 130, 161, 163, 165–6, 168
Rapoport, Amos 34, 36, 47
Rasin Building **96**
recombinant urbanism 15, 17, 151, 153

reconstruction **3**, 79–80, 129
recycling 34, 72, 80–**81**, 104, 125, 133, 147, 159, 163, 177, 179
Regenerative Principle xix, 177, 181
regionalism 8, 78, 89, 92, 95
   critical 19, 76, 89–**90**, 97
   postmodern 79, 92
repurposing 17, 80, 109, 125, 147
resilience 33, 145–6, 178, 180
restoration 80, 147
Reynolds, Michael 62–**3**, 74, 142, 151
Robie House 9–**10**
Rogers, Richard xviii, 69, 96, **70**, 100, 162
roof ponds 57
Rossi, Aldo 94
Rowe, Colin 86
Rural Studio 84–**5**
Ryker, Lori 109

Saarinen, Eero **44**–5, 100, 128
sacred sites 38–**9**, 48
Sailes, David 38, 40
San Gimignano 45
Saunders Architecture xi, **172**
scaler xix, 40, 124, 145, 148
Scarpa, Carlo 90
Scott Tallon Walker Architects 170
Schumacher, E.F. 1, 10, 18, 25, 29, 47
Seaside, Florida 16, 86–**8**, 92
Seagram Building 12, 100
Selborne, England **6**
Selborne, Georgia 138–**9**
Sellers, David 40, **42**
Serenbe Community xx, 20, 115, 138–**9**, 140, 142–**3**, 153, 179
Setagaya-ku Fukasawa Symbiotic Housing x, **164**
Shane David Grahame 15, 17, 137, 151, 153
sick building syndrome 32, 114
Siena, Italy **17**, 90
Sierra Club 49, 72, 80
site xiii, xx, 3, 9, 18–19, 30, 36, 38, 41, 57, 60, 66, 78, 84, 89, 105, 117, 128, 131, 134, 140, 148, 156, 161, 163, 166–71, 174–5, 179
   development xx, 135
   disposal 32, 65, 106
   invader 175
   on- 2, 125, 131, 139, 141–2, 144, 159, 161, 165
   resources 62, 64, 79, 82, 100, 125, 131, 144
SITE 25, 41
Skidmore, Owings and Merrill 11, 45
skin 19, 14, 68–9, 83, 90, 101, 106, 108, 118, 135, 144, 165,
skin-dominated 17, 68, 71, 90, 108, 146, 178, 180

Sled House, Whangapoua **172**, 174
Slessor, Catherine 99, 101, 117, 121
Smedt, de Julien 1, 13
Sofdie, Moshe **44**–5, 68
soft energy 55, 73
Solar Decathlon **124**
solar energy 5, 19, 38, 49, 51–2, 69, 105, 162–3, 171
   active systems 162–3
   communities 65, **67**–8, 86, 88
   direct gain 56–7, 59
   electricity 135, 171
   hot-water 52, 60, 108, 118
   passive systems 36–7, 55, 57–**8**, 73, 83, 142
   section **61**, 68, 83
   shading 5, 59, **102**, 135
   society 50, 72
   sunspace 56–9, 62, 141,
   tempering 10, 56, 83
solar envelope 60, **61**
   access 3, 6, 53–4, 60–**61**, 65, 125–7
solar furnace 53–**4**
Solar Power Offices, Ljubliana x, **163**
Solarsiedlung 163
Soleri, Paolo 25, **37**, 46, 151
Solus4 x, 168
Sonnenschiff, Freiburg x, **162**–3
Sorkin, Michael 42, 46, **132**–3, 153, **180**
space xvi, xx, 3, 8–10, 17, 27, 43, 53, 62, 70, 93, 103, 106, 129, 137, 157, 159, 161, 163, 168, 174–6, 179–83
   atrium 71, 101
   buffer 94
   central 160
   ceremonial 38–40
   configuration 158
   constructed 160–61
   green 161, 163, 165, 167
   in-between 54, 57, 115, 118, 145, 147
   interior 163
   open 162
   outer 30, 33, 37, 40, 55, 150–**51**
   public 86–7, 125–6, 139, 146
   temporal 36
spatial organization 8, 45, 57, 138
Spiegelhalter, Thomas 91, **93**
SPIN farming 140
spirit of place 38
splintering urbanism 15, 153
sprawl 29, 65, 74, 78, 85–6, 117, 174, 179
Stein, Carl 11, 14, 97
Steiner, Rudolf 26, 39–40, 115, 128
Stern, Robert A.M. 95

Stirling, Raymond 121
Studio 505 x, 169
suburbs **12**, **27**, 19–20, 26, 29, 60, 68, 84, 87–8, **119**, 151
Summit Village 139
sunpath diagram 34–**5**, **61**, 92
Sun–Moon Mansion **127**, **170**
Sunraycer 96
sunspace 56–**8**, 59, 62, 141
super-insulation 109
Superstudio 25, 37, 40, **42**
sustainability xvii, 1–2, 11, 13, 18, 40, 107, 156–7, 174–5, 177–81
   architectural xix, 14, 68, 78, 83, 90, 119
   environmental 33, 108, 141–2
   social 32–6
   unsustainability 99, 120, 140, 142–4, 147
   urban 14, 16, 97, 124, 134–7
Swiss Re Headquarters 158
Sydney Opera House **90**, 128
synergy 40, 125, 145, 149

Tabb, Phillip xvi, **15**, 21–2, 59, 73–4, 138, 153
Team Ten 18, 36, 45, 47
tectonics 94, 113, 117, 120, 124, 146, 170
technology xviii, 1, 7, 11, 68, 96, 134, 144, 158–60, 166, 174, 181
   digital 69, 103–**4**
   eco-technology 37, 69, 99–100, 105–**7**, 108, 114
   fabrication technology 12, 37, 110, 130
   high-technology xx, 8, 20, 50, 70–71, 95, 100–**102**
   information 20, 103–4, 121, 150, 159
   low-technology 20, 95, 108–**10**, 140
   photovoltaic 55, 62, 108
   renewable **15**, 52, 64, 102, 112
   solar 52, 54, 68, 71, 75
   survival technology 37
techne xviii
techno-romanticism 100
temporality xix, 11, 18, 20, 36, 60, 79–80, 94, 150, 181
Terry House (David Wright) **58**–9
The Cloud, South Korea 167–8
The Cost of Sprawl 65, 74
The Earthscraper x, 168
The Frontier Center for Environmental Symbiosis Technology x, 165–**6**
The Nissan Advanced Technology Center 159
The Solar City Linz x, 162, 176
The Ziggurat, Dubai 167–8
thermal mass 56–9, 68, 110

thermosyphon **63**
Thorburn, Andrew 126, 152
Thorncrown Chapel **70**–71
tilt angle 19, 53, 55, 57, 60–**61**, 108
Tinggarden Cohousing 66–**7**
tissue 30, 68, 147, 149, 179–80
Tjibaou Cultural Center 101, **103**, 105
TOD 86, **88**, 146, 150
Todd, John and Nancy 64, 74, 153
Transbay Transit Center 135
transect 35, 87–8, 124, 126–7, 148, 179–80
transportation xx, 13, 16, 26, 65, 86, 125, 140, 175
   automobile 2, 11, 87, 123, 135
   bicycle 101, 116–17, 138, 159, 165
   material 11, 70, 125, 147, 175
   pedestrian **15**, 16–17, 66, 86, 133, 137–8, 149–50, 178–9
   public 71, 88, 120, 124–5, 127, 165, 167, 170, 179
Trombe Wall 56, **58**–9
Tschumi, Bernard 91, 151
Tuan, Yi-Fu 93–4, 98
twin phenomena 14, 36, 43, 79, 144, 146
typology 10, 20, 26, 43, 46, 65, 78, 91–2, 135
Tzonis, Alexander and Liane Lefaivre 89

underground architecture **4**, 7, 41, 59, 133, 129
Unity Church 9
Unity Principle xviii, xix, 9, 15, 177, 180
urban 16, 20, 37, 49, 71, 85, 113, 179–81, 183
   design 17–18, 20, 60, 72, 85–7, 95, 116, 125
   eco-urbanism 181
   growth 30, 60, 86, 182
   integral 15, 17, 134, 151, 153
   splintering 15, 153
urbanism 15–17, 19, 36–7, 40, 60, 75, 86, 181
Urban-Think Tank 150–**51**
Usonian houses 9–10
utopia **37**–8, 41–2, 46, 100, 174
Utzon, Jorn 91, 94, 128
u-value 59, 64

van der Rohe, Mies 12, 43, 100
Van der Ryn, Sim 68, 74, 119
van Eyck, Aldo 36, 43, 47, 79, 148
Vanke Center 130
Vanna Venturi House 76–**7**
Vauban, Freiburg x, **164**–5, 176
Vegetal City **130**, 137
ventilation 53, 69, 81–82, 100–101, 106, 109, 114–15, 118, 125, 135, 142, 144, 146, 157, 159, 162–4, 167, 174, 180
Venturi, Robert 43, 45, 48, 76–**7**, 86, **44**

vernacular architecture 2–3, 6, 8, 13, 19, 40, 71, 75–9, 81–3, 90–94, 101, 142, 160, 174, 178–9
vertical farming 113
Vidar Clinic **115**
Vietin Bank Tower 159
village **4**, **8**, 20, 38, 65–**7**, 86, 135, 138–**9**, 160
    eco-village 142–**3**
    English xx, 2, **6**, 81, 126, 152
    solar 21, 66–**7**, 163
Village Homes 20, 65–**7**
virtual architecture **104**
Vitruvius xviii, 5, 26, 39, 100
Vodafona Site Solution x, **163**

Waldheim, Charles 153
waste xx, 11, 13, 28, 30–**31**, 32–4, 84, 91, 104–5, 111, 114, 118–19, 125, 128, 143–5, 147, 162, 165, 174, 179
    -water 157–9, 163
water 2, 9, 52–53, 56–60, 62, 64, 69, 72, **81**, 92, 94, 101, 105–6, 109–11, 113–14, 117–18, 125, 128, 130–31, 137, 144, 147, 156–9, 161–3, 165–6, 169, 171, 174
    -front 174
    grey- 161
    ground- 163
    rain 161, 163, 165–6
    -saving 174
    sea- 168
water harvesting 62, 64, 69, 81–82, 108–9, 118, 179
water wall 106
Watson, Donald 75
weather 2, 4, 16, **35**, 39, 112, 135, 145, 147, 149, 156

Wells, Malcolm 19, 59, 111, 145
Whole Earth Catalog 42, 48
Why Factory **127**
wind 161, 163, 171, 181–2
wind catchers **4**
wind turbines 62, 135, **140**, 142, 159, 169
windmills 161
windows 3, 5–6, 34, 41, 53–6, 58, 70, 78, 82, 94, 115, 146, 169
Wines, James 20, 23, 119, 134, 177
World Trade Center 45, 159
Wright, David **58**–9
Wright, Frank Lloyd xviii, 1, 7, 9–**10**, 25, 151

X-urban 76

Yamasaki, Minoru 43, 45
Yanqing Guyaju, China **4**
Yeang, Kenneth 16, 19, **112**–13
Yergin, Daniel 29, 47, 50
Yestermorrow 84–**5**
Yurt x, 160
Yusuhara Town Hall, x, 156

Zechner and ZechnerZT GMBH 171–**2**
zero carbon 142
zero-detailed roof **83**
Zoka Zola 142–**3**
Zomeworks **37**, 41–**2**
zone coupling 57
zoning 88, 127
    functional 12, 26, 86, 140, 145, 148
    integrated 86–7
    solar 60